To:

_____

From:

_____

Date:

_____

Message:

_____

_____

_____

My Own Keepsake Bible

Copyright © 2016 by Christian Art Kids,
an imprint of Christian Art Publishers,
PO Box 1599, Vereeniging, 1930, RSA

359 Longview Drive, Bloomingdale, IL, 60108, USA

First edition 2016

Text previously published by Christian Publishing Company

Edited by Carolyn Larsen
Cover designed by Christian Art Kids
Images used under license from Shutterstock.com

Scripture quotations are taken from the *Holy Bible,* New Living Translation®,
copyright © 1996, 2004, 2007, 2013, 2015 by Tyndale House Foundation. Used by permission
of Tyndale House Publishers, Inc., Carol Stream, Illinois 60188. All rights reserved.

Printed in China

ISBN 978-1-4321-1581-4

22 23 24 25 26 27 28 29 30 31 – 23 22 21 20 19 18 17 16 15 14

Printed in Shenzhen, China
JULY 2022
Print Run: PUR402530

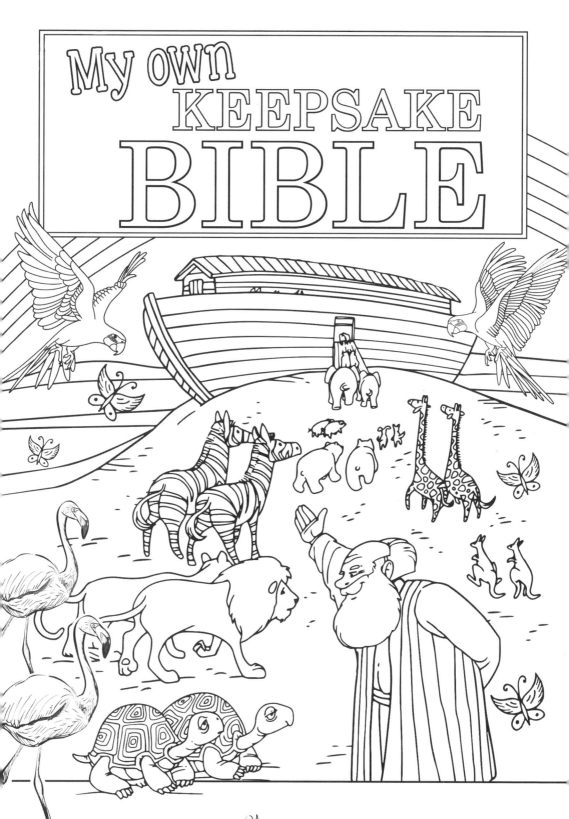

My own KEEPSAKE BIBLE

christian art kids

Contents

Old Testament

New Testament

OLD TESTAMENT

In the Beginning

Genesis 1–2

This world is a lovely place, but it didn't start out that way. Before God made the world and everything in it, everything was dark. There were no living things. There were no flowers. There were no birds. There were no animals. There were no people.

Then God said four simple words, "Let there be light." For the first time light appeared to divide the darkness and make day and night. This happened on the first day of Creation. Heavy wet clouds hung everywhere so God spoke and the clouds separated. Now there was a clear division between the sky above and the waters on the earth. The second day of Creation came to an end.

There was still no place for living things so God moved the waters that covered the earth to make rivers and oceans. Dry land rose up out of the water. On the same day God made the first grass and bushes and trees. Each kind had its own seeds, which spread plants over all the earth. All this happened on the third day.

The next day God made the sun and moon and stars. God made the sun to rule in the daytime and the moon to rule at night with the stars to help light the dark night sky. At the end of this fourth day, God looked at what He had made and He was pleased.

There were still no birds or fish. They were made on the fifth day. On that day birds filled the sky, and everything that lives in the waters was made. God was pleased with all these creations.

On the sixth day God made all the creatures that live on the ground – from the smallest insect to the largest animal. On the same day God made His greatest creation: man. He used the dust of the earth to form the first man, and then breathed the breath of life into him. Man became a living person. The first

God creates heaven and earth. (Genesis 1:1)

man was called Adam, which means "one made from dust."

God gave Adam a lovely place to live called the Garden of Eden. The garden was planted where four great rivers came together. We know only one of them now: the Euphrates River. So that the garden would grow and remain beautiful, God made springs come up from the ground to water the earth.

There were two special trees in that garden: the Tree of Life and the Tree of Knowledge of Good and Evil. God told Adam that he could eat the fruit of all the trees in the garden except the Tree of Knowledge of Good and Evil. God told Adam he would die if he ate the fruit from that tree.

God gave Adam the job of naming all the animals. Then God saw that Adam was lonely. So He put Adam into a deep sleep, took out one of his ribs and closed up the skin. Then God used that rib to make the first woman and brought her to Adam. When Adam saw her, he was filled with happiness. He said, "She is bone of my bones, and flesh of my flesh. Because she was taken out of man, she will be called woman." Adam named her Eve.

God was pleased. He looked at everything He had made. It was all very good. So on the seventh day He rested.

In the beginning God created the heavens and the earth.

Genesis 1:1

God creates Adam and Eve. (Genesis 1:27)

The Beginning of Sin

Genesis 3

Adam and Eve lived happily in the Garden of Eden ... for a while. Yes, for a while they obeyed what God had commanded. Every day He came to the garden and talked with Adam and Eve. They were happy and remembered that God had said they should not eat the fruit from the Tree of Knowledge of Good and Evil.

Then one day a serpent spoke to Eve when she was near the forbidden tree. The serpent was really Satan. He said, "Eve, it won't do any harm for you to taste the fruit from the Tree of Knowledge of Good and Evil."

"No," Eve said. "God said not to touch it." But that didn't stop the serpent. He said that God was trying to keep the best things away from them. He said that it was because God didn't want them to be able to know good and evil like He did.

The serpent convinced Eve that God didn't really mean what He said. So she took a bite of the fruit. Then she gave some to Adam who ate it too. Right away they both knew they had done something very bad. They had disobeyed God. That was the first sin. From then on all humans would be sinners.

God was very sad when He found out Adam and Eve had disobeyed Him. He said to the serpent, "Because you lied to Adam and Eve, you will never be able to walk like other animals, but you will slither in the dirt. Humans will be your enemy. One will come who will totally defeat you, because you are the devil."

God told Adam and Eve to leave the garden. From then on they would have to work hard to make a living and to grow the food they needed. From dust they had been made, and when they died, their bodies would go back to dust.

The LORD God banished them from the Garden of Eden.

Genesis 3:23

Eve eats fruit from the forbidden tree. (Genesis 3:6)

Jealousy and Murder

Genesis 4:1–16

When God sent Adam and Eve out of the Garden of Eden, they found another place to live. After a little while their first son was born. His name was Cain, and later they had a second son called Abel. When the boys grew up, Abel was a shepherd and Cain was a farmer.

One day Cain and Abel each built an altar to offer gifts to God. Abel brought gifts from his flock. God was pleased with his offering. But God was not pleased with Cain's offering. Cain did not have the right attitude about giving his offering.

When God refused his offering, Cain was angry. One day when he and Abel were out in a lonely field together, Cain killed his brother! Later God asked him, "Where is your brother Abel?" Cain was terrified, so he answered, "I don't know. Am I my brother's keeper?" God knew Cain was lying. He knew that Cain had killed Abel. He said, "Cain, your brother's blood cries out to Me from the ground where you spilled it. From now on My curse will be on you. I will make you a wanderer, always running from men, and you will have to work hard to grow food."

"This punishment is too much for me," Cain said. "You've driven me away from my family, and anyone who sees me will do his best to kill me." God had pity on Cain. He marked him with a special mark so that everyone would know that he was under God's protection.

Cain and his wife moved to the land of Nod, sometimes called the Land of Wandering.

"Why are you so angry?" the LORD asked Cain. "Why do you look so dejected? You will be accepted if you do what is right. But if you refuse to do what is right, then watch out! Sin is crouching at the door, eager to control you. But you must subdue it and be its master."

Genesis 4:6-7

The Big Storm and a Rainbow

Genesis 6–9

After Cain killed his brother Abel, Adam and Eve had another son. His name was Seth.

Years passed and soon there were many people in the world, living in many villages and towns. But people had stopped obeying God. They didn't even think about Him much. God tried to get people to start obeying Him again, but they didn't pay any attention. Finally, He decided that He needed to wipe out humankind and start over. But there was a man named Noah who was different from everyone else. Noah tried to always obey God.

God told Noah that He was going to destroy all living things by sending a great flood on the earth. He promised to protect Noah and his family because they did their best to obey Him.

To take care of his family, God had Noah build a great ship, called the ark. In that ark there would be room for Noah and his three sons, Shem, Ham and Japheth, and their families. The ark was also like a giant stable. God sent a pair of every unclean animal to go into the ark. Those are animals that people don't eat. He also sent seven pairs of every animal that could be eaten so that there would be enough food to last them a whole year.

When the animals and Noah's family were inside, God closed the great door of the ark. Then it began to rain. It rained for 40 days and nights without stopping. The water rose higher and higher until all the land was covered. Not even a mountaintop showed. Not a green bush or tree could be seen. No one outside the ark survived the great flood.

Then the rain stopped. But for another 150 days water still covered the land. As the water went down, the ark came to rest on the mountains of Ararat. Noah sent birds out from the ark to see if there was dry

Noah, his family and two of each animal enter the ark. (Genesis 7:1-3)

land. First he sent out a raven. Then he sent a dove. When the dove came back with an olive leaf in its beak, Noah knew that the trees were beginning to show again. A week later the dove did not come back at all. Then Noah knew that there was dry land at last.

The first thing Noah did when he came out of the ark was to say thank You to God. Noah built an altar and gave an offering to God to show that he and his family would continue to live as God's people, serving Him every day.

God gave a wonderful promise to Noah that He would never again destroy the world with a flood. As a sign of His promise, God put a rainbow in the sky and said, "This will be the sign of My promise for all the time to come. I will put My rainbow in the clouds. When I bring the clouds over the earth and you see the rainbow, I will be looking at it, and I will remember My promise."

God told Noah and his sons to have children so that the world would be filled with people again.

"I have placed My rainbow in the clouds. It is the sign of My covenant with you and with all the earth."

Genesis 9:13

The Tower That Was Never Finished

Genesis 10:1–11:9

When Noah and his family came out of the ark they all moved to different places. Before long they had children and grandchildren. The families grew bigger and bigger. The families grew so large they were called tribes.

All the tribes spoke the same language and were really all from the same family, but they didn't all think the same way. Some of the people began to disobey God again. Since they knew how to make bricks, they decided to build a great tower that would reach all the way to heaven. They would build a huge city around the tower. They felt this would make them the greatest people who ever lived!

So they baked their bricks and started building. The tower rose higher and higher. But God was watching. He knew if they did what they planned to do, they would decide they didn't need Him at all. So God mixed up their languages. Soon everyone was speaking a different language! What trouble that brought! The brick makers couldn't understand the builders, and the builders couldn't understand the brick makers, so all the building stopped. The people who spoke the same language moved off together, each group in a different direction.

The great tower was never finished. The place where they tried to build it was given the name of "Babel," which means "confusion," because that was where God changed their languages and caused confusion.

That is why the city was called Babel, because that is where the LORD confused the people with different languages. In this way He scattered them all over the world.

Genesis 11:9

God confuses people's speech at the tower of Babel. (Genesis 11:7)

Going Where God Leads

Genesis 11:27–13:18

Not far from Babel, or Babylon as it was later called, was the town of Ur. Terah lived there with his three sons. One of the sons, Abram, became a very great man of God. Terah decided to move and he took Abram and his wife, Sarai, and their nephew, Lot, with him. They traveled through the desert until they came to a place called Haran. They lived there until Terah died.

God told Abram to move again. So Abram and Lot took their families and their sheep and cattle, and headed south. They crossed rivers and mountains. Finally they reached the land of Canaan. God wanted them to stay there. He promised Abram He would give that land to Abram and his children and his children's children. Abram was thankful to God so he built an altar and gave an offering of thanksgiving to God. Abram was a rich man and owned a big herd of cattle. Lot also had a large herd of cattle. A lot of pastureland was needed.

So Abram gave Lot the choice of where he wanted to live with his flocks. Lot chose the plain of Jordan with its fertile lands. He settled near the cities of Sodom and Gomorrah where the people cared nothing at all about God. After a while Lot moved right into Sodom.

God remembered His promise to Abram. He said, "Stand still and look around you, to the north and the south and the west and the east. All the land you can see I will give to you and all your children and their children forever. And I will give you as many descendants as the grains of sand on the earth." Abram believed God's promise even though he and Sarai did not have any children at all.

The Lord said to Abram, "Look as far as you can see in every direction. I am giving all this land, as far as you can see, to you and your descendants as a permanent possession."

Genesis 13:14-15

Abram says thank You to God. (Genesis 13:18)

A Boy Named Laughter

Genesis 16–17

God had promised Abram and Sarai a big family, but now they were old. So Sarai took matters into her own hands. She suggested that Abram marry her servant, Hagar. He did and before long Hagar was expecting a baby. Hagar made fun of Sarai because Sarai had no children. That made Sarai angry and she treated Hagar unkindly. Sarai was so mean that Hagar finally ran away.

Hagar traveled for a long time before she stopped near a small lake to rest. Suddenly an angel from God appeared. "Hagar, where are you going?" the angel asked. "I'm running away from my mistress, Sarai," Hagar replied. "Don't worry, Hagar," the angel said, "your baby will be a boy, and God wants you to call him Ishmael. He will be the leader of a great nation. God will take care of you, so do not be afraid. Go back to Sarai, because God will be your helper." So Hagar went back to Abram and Sarai. When it was time, she had her baby and called him Ishmael, just as the angel had said. Ishmael means "God shall hear." Every time Hagar looked at her son she remembered the promise God's angel gave her.

God again promised Abram that he would become the father of many nations. Abram believed God, even though he was 99 years old and Sarai was 90. God changed Abram's name to Abraham, which means "the father of many people." God changed Sarai's name to Sarah. God told Abraham and Sarah that they would have a son and they should name him Isaac, which means "laughter." God gave Isaac that name because when He told Abraham that Sarah was going to have a baby, Abraham laughed to himself.

"Sarah, your wife, will give birth to a son for you. You will name him Isaac, and I will confirm My covenant with him and his descendants as an everlasting covenant."

Genesis 17:19

God keeps His promise and gives Abraham a son. (Genesis 21:2-3)

Abraham's Visitors

Genesis 18–19

Abraham set up camp in the plains of Mamre with Sarah, his family and all his servants and animals.

One day he was sitting outside his tent when he saw three men nearby. He went to them and invited them to stay and eat with him. Then he told Sarah to cook a special meal for them.

While Sarah was cooking, one of the men said, "I will come back about this time next year. By then Sarah will have a son."

Sarah heard him say that she would have a baby and she laughed to herself. "As old as I am, how could I possibly have a baby?" she wondered.

The man, who was actually God Himself, said to Abraham, "Why did Sarah laugh? Is anything too hard for the Lord? I will certainly give her a son as I have promised." Sarah was afraid so she lied and said that she hadn't laughed. But the Lord said: "No, you *did* laugh."

As the three men started to leave, the Lord said, "There is terrible evil in the cities of Sodom and Gomorrah. I'm going to see whether things are really as bad as they seem. If they are, I will punish the people." The other two men left, but Abraham stayed and pleaded with the Lord not to be too hard on the cities, because Abraham's nephew, Lot, and his family lived in Sodom.

"Are You going to destroy the good people along with the bad?" Abraham asked. "What if there are fifty good people in the city. Won't You spare it for their sakes?" God said He would. Abraham kept asking until God promised that even if there were only ten good people in the city, He would not destroy it.

Two of the angels who came with God to visit Abraham went to Sodom that evening and found Lot sitting at the city gate.

Lot invited the strangers to eat at his house and spend the night. But the men of the city found out there were two strangers in Lot's house. They pounded on the door and tried to break it down. They wanted to hurt the strangers. But the angels made the townspeople blind so they couldn't even find the door of the house.

The angels told Lot to get his family and to leave the city because God was going to destroy it. Since Lot was the only good man in the city, he and his family would be saved.

But Lot's sons-in-law would not go. In the early hours of the morning the angels dragged Lot and his wife and his two daughters out of the city to safety. When they got out of the city, the angels said, "Now run as fast as you can. Don't look back, and don't stop until you reach the mountain, otherwise you too will die when the city is destroyed."

God poured out fire on the cities of Sodom and Gomorrah. The cities were burned up by the terrible fire. Lot and his two daughters escaped, but Lot's wife turned to look back at the city and she was immediately changed into a pillar of salt.

"Is anything too hard for the LORD?"

Genesis 18:14

The Most Difficult Test

Genesis 21:1–7; 22:1–19

The Lord had promised a son to Abraham and Sarah. When Abraham was 100 years old and Sarah was 90, the boy was born. They named him Isaac as God had told them to do. When Isaac was about 15 years old, God asked Abraham to do something very difficult. He told Abraham to go to a mountain in the land of Moriah and offer Isaac as a sacrifice to Him. Abraham was very sad to receive this command from God. But he obeyed, because he trusted God.

Abraham took Isaac to the place God had said and they built an altar and put wood on it. Then Abraham tied Isaac's hands and feet and laid him on the wood. He slowly took a knife and prepared to kill his only son, Isaac.

But at that very moment a voice cried out to him from heaven, saying, "Abraham, Abraham!"

"Here I am," Abraham said. Then an angel of the Lord called out, "Don't hurt the boy. Now I know that you fear God and want to serve Him more than anything. You have not kept back your only son from Him."

Then Abraham saw a ram caught by its horns in a thorn bush. Abraham and Isaac caught the ram and offered it as a sacrifice to God. They thanked God for His provision and worshiped Him.

"This is what the Lord says: Because you have obeyed Me and have not withheld even your son, your only son, I swear by My own name that I will certainly bless you. I will multiply your descendants beyond number, like the stars in the sky and the sand on the seashore. Your descendants will conquer the cities of their enemies."

Genesis 22:16-17

God stops Abraham from sacrificing his son. (Genesis 22:11-12)

A Bride for Isaac

Genesis 24

When Sarah died, Abraham knew that he wouldn't live much longer either. In those days the parents found wives for their sons. Abraham called his oldest, most trusted servant and told him how to find a wife for Isaac. The servant went back to Abraham's homeland, Haran, to find a wife for Isaac. Abraham's brother Nahor still lived in Haran. Abraham hoped that his servant would be able to find a wife for Isaac from Nahor's tribe.

When the servant arrived, he stopped near a well outside Haran. The women of the town would be coming soon to get water. The servant prayed that when he spoke to the women, God would make the one who should be Isaac's wife answer him in a special way. If he asked one of them to give him a drink of water, then the right one would not only give water to him, but to his camels as well. Rebekah, the daughter of Bethuel, did just that. After the servant explained why he was there, Rebekah ran home to tell her family what had happened. The servant came to Rebekah's house and explained to her family why he had come. He explained who Abraham was and gave them the presents Abraham had sent. The servant told how he had prayed for God to show him the woman who should become Isaac's wife. He said he was sure that Rebekah was the right one. Her father, Bethuel, and her brother, Laban, agreed.

When Rebekah and the servant arrived, Isaac was out in the field. He saw them coming and went out to meet them. When he and Rebekah saw each other, they fell in love right away. Soon they were married. For the first time since his mother had died, Isaac was not lonely.

"Praise the LORD" he said. "The LORD has shown unfailing love and faithfulness to my master, for He has led me straight to my master's relatives."

Genesis 24:27

"Give Me Your Birthright"

Genesis 25, 27-30

Abraham died when he was 175 years old. His sons Isaac and Ishmael buried him alongside Sarah in the cave of Machpelah. Isaac was now the head of the family. He and Rebekah had two sons, twin boys named Esau and Jacob. Esau was a hunter who liked to be outside. Jacob liked to stay home and enjoyed cooking.

It was the custom in those days that when a father died, the eldest son received twice as much of his father's wealth and property as the rest of the sons. This was called the birthright. Esau was just a few minutes older than Jacob so the birthright was his. But he was too interested in hunting to worry about his birthright.

One day Jacob cooked a pot of delicious stew. When Esau came home from hunting, the smell of the stew made him hungry. He asked Jacob to give him some, but Jacob was very clever. He quickly came up with a plan. "Give me your birthright and I will give you some stew," he said.

Esau said, "You can have it. What good is a birthright when I'm dying of hunger?"

Isaac was an old man and he was going blind. He knew that he wouldn't live much longer so one day he said to Esau, "My son, I am very old now, and I know I will die soon. Go out with your bow and arrow and shoot some wild game; then roast the meat in the way I like it and bring it to me. After I eat I will give you my blessing, before the end of my life comes."

Rebekah heard what Isaac said and she told Jacob. She sent him to kill two young goats so she could cook them for Isaac. Jacob could take the meat to his father and receive Isaac's blessing before his brother came back from hunting.

Jacob did what his mother said. When he took the meat to Isaac, his father asked him who he was. Jacob lied and said he was Esau. After Isaac ate, he placed his hands on Jacob's head and blessed him, thinking all the time that he was blessing Esau.

When Esau heard what Jacob had done, he was very angry. He decided that after Isaac died, he would kill Jacob. Rebekah was afraid that Esau might actually kill Jacob, so she told Jacob to go away and stay with his Uncle Laban, far away in Haran.

It was a long journey to Haran. When he got there, Jacob stopped to rest near a well. He was talking with some men when he saw a beautiful girl. The girl was Rachel, the daughter of Laban.

Jacob fell in love with Rachel and promised to work for seven years for Laban so that he could have Rachel as his wife.

In those times the brides wore heavy veils over their faces until after the wedding was over. On his wedding day, when Jacob lifted the veil from the face of his wife, he found he had been tricked! He had married Leah, Rachel's sister. Laban promised Jacob that he could marry Rachel if he worked for another seven years to pay for her. He did, and before long Jacob's two wives gave him twelve sons.

Isaac said, "Your brother was here, and he tricked me. He has taken away your blessing."
Genesis 27:35

A Life-Changing Wrestling Match
Genesis 32:1–33:15

After 20 years in Haran, Jacob was a very rich man. Part of his wages for the work he did for Laban was paid to him in sheep and cattle. So, just as God had promised, his herds grew bigger and bigger. Then God told Jacob it was time to go back to his own homeland. God promised to take care of him on the long way back.

Jacob had left his home because his brother Esau wanted to kill him. He was afraid that Esau still wanted him dead. On the way back home he decided to send messengers ahead to find out if Esau was still angry.

When the messengers returned they brought frightening news. Esau was on his way out to meet them and he had 400 men with him!

That night, after setting up the camp, Jacob sent Esau 550 goats, sheep, camels, cattle and donkeys. Then he took his wives and children across the brook of Jabbok where they would be safe. He went back to the camp alone to pray.

As he was praying, Jacob felt a Man grab him and the two of them began to wrestle. The wrestling match went on all night until sunrise. It was a powerful fight. Finally the Man realized that He wasn't going to win so He struck Jacob's hip and dislocated it. The Man cried out, "Let Me go, because the sun will soon be rising."

Then Jacob knew that the Man was actually God. He would not let Him go until the Man blessed him. The Man asked his name and Jacob told Him, "My name is Jacob."

The Man said, "Your name will no longer be Jacob. It is now Israel, because you have wrestled with God and won."

The next morning when Jacob crossed the river, there was Esau and his men right in front of him. Jacob bowed down to Esau. Esau ran to meet him and kissed him.

The two brothers wept with joy to be together again after so many years apart. Esau forgave Jacob for the way he had treated him many years ago.

"Your name will no longer be Jacob," the Man told him. "From now on you will be called Israel, because you have fought with God and with men and have won."

Genesis 32:28

Dreams Turn into Nightmares

Genesis 37

Jacob, Rachel and Leah had 11 sons. The boys were named Reuben, Simeon, Levi, Judah, Issachar, Zebulun, Joseph, Dan, Naphtali, Gad and Asher. Soon after they returned to Canaan, Rachel and Jacob had another son, Benjamin. Rachel died while Benjamin was still a baby.

Jacob cared more for Joseph than any of his other sons. When Joseph was 17 years old, Jacob gave him a coat with long sleeves, made of bright colors. Joseph's brothers were already jealous of how much Jacob favored Joseph. Now they really hated him.

One night Joseph had a dream that all the brothers were cutting wheat in the fields and each one tied what he had cut into a bundle. Then Joseph's bundle of wheat stood up and all the other bundles bowed down to it. Joseph told his brothers about his dream and they hated him even more.

A few nights later Joseph had another dream. This time he saw the sun, moon and 11 stars bowing down to him. Once more he told his brothers about his dream. This time his father heard about it and it made him angry. "What is this?" he asked. "Am I and your mother and your brothers all to kneel before you?"

A while later all the brothers except Joseph and Benjamin went to care for their father's sheep in a faraway field. Several days later Jacob sent Joseph to find out how they were getting along.

When he was still a long way off, Joseph's brothers saw him coming. They were filled with hatred and came up with a plan to kill him.

The brothers took Joseph's coat off him and threw him into a deep hole. Then they noticed a caravan of Ishmaelite camels on their way to Egypt with all kinds of spices to sell there. Judah came up with a plan. "Why should we kill Joseph? We can sell him to the Ishmaelites to be sold as a slave in Egypt. We'll tell our father that a wild animal killed him."

So they tore Joseph's coat and dipped it in the blood of a goat they had killed. Then they sent this blood-stained coat back to Jacob. When Jacob saw it he was very sad because he believed that a wild animal had killed his favorite son.

His brothers hated Joseph because their father loved him more than the rest of them. They couldn't say a kind word to him.

Genesis 37:4

From a Prison to a Palace!

Genesis 39–40

When the Ishmaelite traders arrived in Egypt, they sold Joseph to Potiphar who was captain of the guard of the Egyptian pharaoh. Joseph worked hard and the Lord blessed him. Potiphar was impressed with Joseph and before long he put him in charge of all the other slaves in his household.

But then Potiphar's wife tried to make Joseph do something that was wrong. Joseph wouldn't do it and she got angry with him. She lied to Potiphar and told him that Joseph had tried to hurt her. She said Joseph ran away when she shouted for help.

Potiphar was angry and immediately had Joseph thrown into prison.

Joseph met two other men in the prison. One was Pharaoh's chief butler. The other was his chief baker.

One night each of them had a dream. The butler saw a vine that had three branches. The branches grew bunches of ripe grapes. He took those grapes and squeezed their juice into Pharaoh's cup. Then he gave the cup to Pharaoh. Joseph explained that the three branches were three days. In three days' time, Pharaoh would release him from prison and give him back his job as butler. Joseph asked the butler to remember him and to ask Pharaoh to free Joseph from prison, because he had done nothing wrong.

Then came the baker's turn. In his dream he saw himself carrying three baskets on his head, one on top of the other. In the top basket there were all kinds of cakes and baked food,

but the birds flew down and ate everything. The meaning of this dream was not so good. It meant that in three days, the baker would be hanged from a tree and the birds of the air would eat his flesh.

The LORD was with Joseph, so he succeeded in everything he did as he served in the home of his Egyptian master.

Genesis 39:2

Joseph's Rise to Power

Genesis 41:1–57

When the butler got out of prison he forgot all about Joseph. He did not tell Pharaoh about him as Joseph had asked him to do. Joseph was in prison two more long years. Then Pharaoh himself had a dream. He dreamed that he stood by a river where seven cows were drinking. They were fat and healthy and they went to a meadow to eat. Then seven thin cows came from the river and ate the seven fat ones!

Pharaoh had another dream. He saw seven fat heads of wheat

on a stalk. Then seven thin and withered heads came up. The seven thin heads swallowed up the seven plump heads. Pharaoh wanted to know what the dreams meant. He called for all the wise men and magicians in Egypt. None of them could explain the meaning of his dreams.

The butler remembered Joseph and how he had known the meanings of the dreams he and the baker had had two years before. So Joseph was brought to Pharaoh. With God's help he ex-

Joseph interprets Pharaoh's dream. (Genesis 41:25-27)

plained the dreams to Pharaoh. Both dreams meant the same thing. The seven fat cows and the seven plump wheat heads were seven good years. The seven skinny cows and the seven thin wheat heads were seven bad years. The seven good years would be years of plenty with wonderful crops and plenty of food in Egypt. But then would come seven years of drought and famine. The crops would be poor and there would be so little food and so much hunger that the seven good years would be forgotten.

Joseph suggested that someone should be appointed to put away a fifth of the crops during the good years so that there would be enough food for the famine years.

Pharaoh was very amazed at Joseph's wisdom so he put Joseph in charge of all the food supplies in the land. He made Joseph the second greatest ruler in all of Egypt, second only to himself in importance.

Joseph put his plan into action to save food during the seven years of good crops. Just as Pharaoh's dream had shown, the seven years of good crops passed, and the years of drought and famine arrived.

Only Egypt had put away enough food for the bad years. Because Joseph listened to what God said, Egypt had enough food that they could sell some to other countries.

Back in Canaan Joseph's family was starving. His father, Jacob, heard that there was food in Egypt that they could buy. Jacob had plenty of money so he sent 10 of Joseph's brothers to Egypt to buy wheat. Only Benjamin, the youngest, was kept at home. Jacob was afraid that something might happen to him, as it had to Joseph. They were both the sons of Rachel and he loved them very much.

Pharaoh said to Joseph, "Since God has revealed the meaning of the dreams to you, clearly no one else is as intelligent or wise as you are. You will be in charge of my court, and all my people will take orders from you. Only I, sitting on my throne, will have a rank higher than yours."

Genesis 41:39-40

Joseph sells food during the seven years of famine. (Genesis 41:56)

Jacob's Sons in Egypt

Genesis 42:1-38

Joseph's brothers arrived in Egypt and went straight to the governor in charge of the wheat. They didn't know that he was their brother. They bowed down to him – exactly as Joseph's dream had predicted.

They didn't recognize Joseph, but Joseph knew who they were. He didn't let them know who he was; he treated them as if they were strangers.

"Where do you come from?" he asked.

"From Canaan to buy food," they answered.

"I don't believe you. I think you are spies," he said. "I think you've come to see how you can conquer our land."

"No," they said, "we just want to buy food. We're all brothers. Our youngest brother is still at home with our father and another brother disappeared years ago. We only want to buy food. We're not spies."

But Joseph wouldn't listen to them. "I'm going to give you a test. I'll keep all but one of you in prison. The one brother must go home and get your youngest brother. If that boy doesn't come here, then all of you will be treated like spies."

The brothers were put in prison for three days to think about Joseph's plan. Then Joseph changed the plan. Now only one of them would stay in prison, while the rest went to get the youngest brother. Simeon was chosen to stay in prison. The rest of the brothers were sent home.

The brothers stopped for the night, and one brother opened his sack to give some grain to his donkey. He was amazed to find the money he had paid for his wheat in the bag! Even more amazing was that there was money in the sacks of the other brothers as well!

When they got home they told their father what had happened. Jacob was very upset because now two of his sons had been taken from him. Joseph had disappeared a long time ago. Now Simeon was gone and his other sons wanted to take little Benjamin to Egypt, too. Jacob wouldn't allow it. He couldn't stand the thought of losing Benjamin, too!

Since Joseph was governor of all Egypt and in charge of selling grain to all the people, it was to him that his brothers came. Although Joseph recognized his brothers, they didn't recognize him.

Genesis 42:6, 8

"I Am Your Brother"

Genesis 43

Soon the food that Jacob's sons brought from Egypt was gone. So Jacob told his boys to go back to Egypt and buy more food.

But Judah said, "The man who sold us the food said we must bring Benjamin to Egypt. Will you let him go with us? If you don't, we can't go back. He will put us all in prison." Jacob had no choice but to let his youngest boy go with his brothers.

When the brothers arrived in Egypt, Joseph paid no attention to them. Instead, he sent his servant to take all 11 brothers to his home. He had his servants prepare a fancy feast.

The brothers didn't know what was going on. They still didn't know that Joseph was their brother.

When Joseph came home, they gave him presents they had brought. Joseph was friendly, but he still didn't tell them that he was their brother. He just asked how they were and how their father was. Then he looked at Benjamin and asked if this was the youngest brother they had told him about. They told him that the boy was Benjamin. Then Joseph was overcome by his feelings. He hurried to his room and cried. Then he washed his face and went back to his brothers. He gave orders that the meal should begin. Since the Egyptians would not allow the Hebrews to eat with them, Joseph sat at a different table from his brothers. The brothers were surprised to see that they were seated at the table according to their ages. They didn't understand how the Egyptians knew who was older and who was younger. Another strange thing happened: Joseph ordered that Benjamin be given five times as much food as the others.

Joseph filled their plates with food from his own table, giving Benjamin five times as much as he gave the others.

Genesis 43:34

The Silver Cup

Genesis 44–45

When the meal was over Joseph called his servant. He told him to fill the brothers' sacks with wheat and, just as he had done the last time, to secretly put their money back in the bags, too. Then he told him to do one more thing. "Put my own silver cup in the bag of the youngest brother," he said.

The next morning the brothers started home. They weren't far from the city when Joseph sent his servant after them. When he caught up with the brothers, the servant asked them how they could have stolen Joseph's cup after he had been so kind to them. Of course, they said they hadn't stolen anything. They didn't know what was in their bags.

The servant opened Benjamin's bag and found the cup. The brothers were taken back with the servant to face Joseph's anger.

When they arrived, the brothers threw themselves on the ground in front of Joseph and promised to become his slaves. Joseph told them to go home to their father. However, the one who stole the cup had to stay in Egypt. That was Benjamin, the

Joseph's silver cup is found hidden in Benjamin's bag. (Genesis 44:12)

favorite son of their elderly father, Jacob. The brothers didn't dare go home without him. Judah begged Joseph to let him stay in Benjamin's place.

Joseph couldn't stand it any longer. He sent all the Egyptians out of the room. When they had gone, he told his brothers who he was.

The brothers were terrified. They knew what they had done to Joseph all those years earlier and they were afraid he would punish them. But he said, "Don't be afraid because of what you did to me. You meant it for evil, but God meant it for good. He wanted me here. It is because God helped me and showed me what to do that there is food in Egypt, and that you didn't die of starvation. I came here as a slave, but God has made me a great man in Egypt. God told me that there would be seven years of famine. Two years have passed, but there are still five years to come. I still have work to do. Since there is also famine back in your land, you must go home and get our father and your families and your flocks and herds. Come to the land of Goshen, on the eastern side of Egypt. I will see to it that Pharaoh gives you a place to stay and you can live in peace. I will also see to it that you always have enough to eat."

Joseph hugged and kissed all his brothers.

"But don't be upset, and don't be angry with yourselves for selling me to this place. It was God who sent me here ahead of you to preserve your lives."

Genesis 45:5

Together Again!

Genesis 45:16–49:28

Joseph's brothers went back to their father in Canaan. They were happy to tell him the wonderful news about their "lost" brother. They told him about Joseph's position in Egypt and his invitation for them to live in Goshen. Jacob told them to prepare for the journey.

Jacob's large family and their hundreds of animals began the long trip to Egypt. When they reached Beer-sheba, where Abraham and Isaac had stopped many years before, they also stopped for a very important reason. Jacob owed great thanks to God for giving Joseph back to him. He built an altar of stones and gave an offering of thanksgiving to God.

That night, God spoke to Jacob in a dream: "Jacob, I am the God of your father. Don't be afraid of going down into Egypt. I will be with you. You will see your son Joseph. I will make you a great nation, and when the right time comes I will bring that nation out of Egypt again." When they arrived in Egypt, Joseph rode out to meet his father. Pharaoh gave them permission to live in the land of Goshen, the fertile land east of the Nile River.

When Jacob was 147 years old, he knew that his death was near. Joseph took his two sons, Ephraim and Manasseh, and went to see his father so he could bless them. Jacob blessed all his own sons and Joseph's two sons as well. But Joseph was surprised when Jacob gave a greater blessing to his younger son, Ephraim, than to the eldest, Manasseh. Manasseh would become a great man and the father of a great tribe, but Ephraim's greatness and power would be greater than Manasseh's. A few years later, that is exactly what happened.

"Manasseh will also become a great people, but his younger brother will become even greater. And his descendants will become a multitude of nations."

Genesis 48:19

A Brave Mother

Exodus 1:1–2:10

When Jacob brought his family to Egypt, there were only 70 of them, including Joseph and his sons. But by the time Joseph died, the children of Israel filled the land of Goshen. They lived in all the cities of Egypt. They were rich and powerful. A new pharaoh ruled in Egypt now and he didn't know anything about Joseph and the wonderful work he had done for Egypt. The Egyptians became jealous of the wealth of the Israelites and they feared them because they were so many. Pharaoh ordered that the Israelites be made slaves of the Egyptians.

Then he made an awful decision. He ordered that all the Israelite baby boys be killed as soon as they were born. But one Hebrew mother did her very best to see that her little boy was not killed by the cruel Egyptians. For three whole months she hid her baby. When he was too big to hide, she made a basket from the tall grass. She coated it with tar so that the water couldn't get in. She put her little boy inside and set the basket in the river. The baby's sister, Miriam, watched to see what would happen.

After a while one of Pharaoh's daughters came down to wash in the river. She saw the little basket and when she opened it, the little baby cried. Miriam ran to the princess and offered to find an Israelite woman who could look after him. Miriam brought the baby's own mother! When he was old enough, the princess took the baby to live in the palace and treated him like her own son. She called him Moses, which means "drawn out," because she had taken him out of the river. So a little Israelite baby became an Egyptian prince.

When the boy was older, his mother brought him back to Pharaoh's daughter, who adopted him as her own son. The princess named him Moses, for she explained, "I lifted him out of the water."

Exodus 2:10

46

Moses Runs Away

Exodus 2:11–24

Moses lived in the palace as an Egyptian prince and grew to be a young man. One day he was watching his own people, the Israelites, as they worked at their hard slave jobs. They were treated badly by the Egyptians.

On this day he saw an Egyptian beating an Israelite worker. Moses got angry at the way his people were treated. He attacked the Egyptian and killed him for beating the Israelite. Then he buried the body in the sand. The next day Moses saw two Israelites fighting. He asked one of them, "Why do you hit your brother?"

The Israelite responded, "Who made you a prince and a judge over us? Do you plan to kill me like you killed the Egyptian?"

Moses was scared because someone knew he had killed a man. He ran away to a land called Midian. When he got there he was invited by Reuel, a priest of Midian, to come and live with his family.

Many years later, when Moses had grown up, he went out to visit his own people, the Hebrews, and he saw how hard they were forced to work. During his visit, he saw an Egyptian beating one of his fellow Hebrews.

Exodus 2:11

The Bush That Didn't Burn Up

Exodus 3:1–15

Moses stayed in Midian and became a shepherd. One day he was with the sheep near Mount Horeb when he saw a bush that was on fire. He went over to look at this strange sight. He was amazed to see that the fire burned and burned, but the bush did not burn up.

Suddenly, a voice called to him out of the bush, "Moses! Moses!"

Moses answered, "Here I am."

The voice was coming straight from the burning bush. "Do not come near, Moses. Take off your shoes because the ground where you are standing is holy ground." Moses was afraid, but he did as he was told.

Then the voice spoke again, "I am the God of your father, the God of Abraham, the God of Isaac, and the God of Jacob." Immediately Moses hid his face.

He was afraid to look even at the fire that spoke of God's presence. The Lord spoke again, "I have seen the terrible trouble of My people in Egypt. I am going to free them from the slavery of the cruel Egyptians. I am going to bring them to a land that is so fertile it flows with milk and honey. I mean the land of Canaan, which I promised to their forefathers long ago. Moses, I want you to go to Pharaoh and ask him to let My people leave Egypt."

God promised to be with Moses and give him all the strength he needed for this big job. God told Moses that when the people came out of Egypt, they must travel to Mount Horeb and worship God there.

But Moses was scared of this big job. He asked, "When I go to the children of Israel and tell them that the God of their fathers has sent me to them, they will ask me, 'What is His name?' What should I tell them?"

God's answer was, "I AM WHO I AM. This is what you must say to the children of Israel, I AM has sent me to you."

God replied to Moses, "I AM WHO I AM. Say this to the people of Israel: I AM has sent me to you."

Exodus 3:14

God speaks to Moses through the burning bush. (Exodus 3:2-4)

Moses Is Sent to Egypt

Exodus 3:16–4:31

The first thing Moses had to do was to call together the elders or leaders of each family to explain why God had sent him. Then he had to take the elders with him to ask Pharaoh's permission to take the Israelites into the wilderness to worship God. But strangely, God told Moses that Pharaoh would not let them go. God would then punish Egypt by sending terrible plagues on them. In the end, Pharaoh would let the people of Israel leave Egypt.

Moses was still afraid. He was sure the Israelites would not listen to him. So God gave him a sign that His power and presence was with Moses. Moses carried a shepherd's staff, a walking stick which he used when watching the sheep. God told him to throw it on the ground. Moses did and immediately it turned into a snake. Moses jumped back in fright. God told him not to be afraid, but to take hold of it by the tail. Moses did and the snake turned back into a staff.

Then God gave Moses a second sign. He told Moses to put his hand inside his coat. Moses did and when he pulled his hand out it was white with the terrible sickness of leprosy. When he put his hand back inside his coat and pulled it out again, the leprosy had disappeared. Then God said to Moses, "Go to the people of Israel and, if they refuse to listen to you, show them these two signs. If they still refuse to listen, dip some water out of the river and pour it on the ground. It will turn into blood."

Moses was still afraid. He argued that he was not a good speaker. By now God was impatient with Moses. He said, "Am I not the Lord who made man's mouth? Do I not make all men? Aaron the Levite is your brother. When you get to Egypt, he will come out to meet you. He will go with you and he will be your spokesman. But do not forget your staff. You will use it to show great signs."

So Moses took his wife and sons and returned to Egypt. Aaron came out to meet him just as God had said. Moses told Aaron all that God had told him. Then they gathered all the elders of Israel and gave them God's message.

"I will be with both of you as you speak, and I will instruct you both in what to do. Aaron will be your spokesman to the people. He will be your mouth-piece."

Exodus 4:15-16

Moses Goes to Pharaoh

Exodus 5:1–7:13

Moses and Aaron spoke to the elders of Israel and told them that God planned to free them from slavery. Then they went to Pharaoh and asked him to allow the Israelites to travel out into the desert so they could worship God there. Pharaoh's response was, "Who is the Lord that I should listen to Him? I do not know the Lord and I will not let the Israelites go." Then he told the workers in charge of the slaves to make the Israelites work even harder.

Moses was discouraged. But God spoke to Moses again. He promised that Pharaoh would let the people of Israel go and that Moses would lead them to the Promised Land.

The next morning Moses and Aaron went to Pharaoh again. This time they showed him the miraculous powers God had given them. When Moses told him to, Aaron threw down his staff in front of Pharaoh and it turned into a snake! But Pharaoh was not impressed. He called his own magicians and they turned their staffs into snakes, too. But there was one big difference. Aaron's snake ate up all the magicians' snakes. But Pharaoh still would not listen to God's servants.

"Say to the people of Israel: 'I am the LORD. I will free you from your oppression and will rescue you from your slavery in Egypt.'"

Exodus 6:6

God Sends Plagues on Egypt

Exodus 7:14–10:29

The next morning God sent Moses and Aaron to the Nile River to meet Pharaoh. They asked him again to let the Israelite people leave so they could worship God in the wilderness. God had Aaron stretch out his staff over the river. When he did, the water turned to blood. In fact, all the water in Egypt turned to blood. But Pharaoh still would not let the people go.

A week later, God sent Moses and Aaron to Pharaoh once more. Again they asked him to free the Israelites. They said that God would send a plague of frogs on the land if he didn't agree. Pharaoh refused again.

So, again Aaron stretched out his staff and the land became a hopping, squirming mass of frogs. This time Pharaoh was a little afraid and he begged Moses to have God take the plague away. He said he would let the Israelites go if God took the frogs away. So Moses asked God to take away the frogs and He did. But the next day Pharaoh changed his mind and wouldn't let the Israelites leave.

Again God sent Moses and Aaron to Pharaoh. He had another plague to convince Pharaoh. This time Aaron took the staff and hit the ground. The dust flew up and became horrible bugs that bit the people and animals. But Pharaoh still wouldn't let the people go.

Next God sent a plague of flies all through the land, except in Goshen where the Israelites lived. God was taking care of His people.

When the flies had covered the land, Pharaoh said, "Go and sacrifice to your God, but do not leave the land." Moses explained that they had to leave the land, because the Israelites worshiped differently than the Egyptians. So Pharaoh said they could make a three-day journey into the wilderness.

God sends a plague of frogs. (Exodus 8:5-6)

God took away the flies. Of course Pharaoh changed his mind again and refused to let the Israelites leave.

Moses and Aaron went to Pharaoh again and warned of a fifth plague if he didn't let the Israelites leave. God said He would send an awful sickness that would kill the animals in the land. The cattle and sheep and even the camels would die. But Pharaoh still would not listen. So thousands of animals belonging to the Egyptians died, but God protected the animals where the Israelites lived.

God tried again to convince Pharaoh to listen. He told Moses and Aaron to throw handfuls of ash into the air. As the ash was spread by the wind and fell on people and the animals that were left, painful boils and blisters broke out on their skin. Still Pharaoh would not let the Israelites go.

There were still more terrible plagues to come as God tried to convince Pharaoh to release His people. Next, a powerful hailstorm blew across the land. Once again the Israelites were protected. Not a single hailstone fell where they lived. Pharaoh was terrified, but as soon as the storm went away, he broke his promise to release the Israelites.

Moses stretched out his staff. This time a powerful wind from the east blew for a whole day and night. The next morning, huge swarms of locusts came sweeping in on the wind. There were so many of them that they stripped every green leaf still left on the bushes and trees after the great hailstorm.

Right away Pharaoh called Moses and Aaron. He asked them to pray for the locusts to go away. But as usual, once God had taken the locusts away, Pharaoh forgot all about his promises to the people of Israel. Then God sent another plague. Darkness covered the land for three days. It was so dark the people could not even see enough to walk. Again Pharaoh was quick to promise to free the Israelites. That is until the plague was taken away.

This time Pharaoh was angry. He told Moses and Aaron to leave Egypt immediately. If he saw them again, he would have them put to death right away.

And Moses answered, "You have spoken the truth. I will not see you, nor plead with you again."

But the LORD hardened Pharaoh's heart once more, and he would not let them go.

Exodus 10:27

The Plague to End All Plagues

Exodus 11:1–12:42

The Egyptian people suffered through nine terrible plagues, but Pharaoh still refused to let God's people leave. Now there was one plague left and it was the worst of them all. Pharaoh had broken all his promises before, but this time he would simply have to let the people of Israel go.

Moses explained the last plague to the Israelites. He warned them that they must carefully do what they were told or else the plague would hurt them, too.

He said, "At midnight tonight God will send His angel to every house in Egypt and in each of them the eldest son will die.

Every Israelite family must protect itself in a special way. The head of each family must select a year-old lamb. The lamb must be perfect in every way. Then the lamb must be killed and its blood smeared on each of the doorposts and across the top of the door of each home. Then the meat of the lamb must be roasted with bitter herbs and eaten with bread made without yeast, which is unleavened bread. If any of the meat is left over, it must be burned in the fire. No meat must remain until the morning. When you eat it, you must not be sitting down. You are to stand around the table, dressed, and ready to leave with your sandals on. You should even have your

The Israelites smear animal blood on their doorframes to protect them from the last plague. (Exodus 12:7, 12-13)

walking stick in your hand. This way you will be ready to leave Egypt."

The people did everything Moses told them to do and that night the angel of death passed over all the homes with doors marked with blood. God had promised, "When I see the blood, I will pass over you and the plague shall not be upon you. And in the future, every year you and your children after you must keep the Feast of the Passover to remind you of how I turned death away from you."

That night was the most horrible night Egypt had ever seen. Every single home lost its eldest son – even Pharaoh's palace did not escape it.

Pharaoh was upset when his eldest son died. He sent a message to the Israelites to get out of Egypt and not leave anything behind. He even begged them to pray that God would be merciful and not punish Egypt any more. So in the morning, all the people of Israel began the journey out of Egypt. They were very orga-

nized. They walked tribe by tribe, and family by family. About 600,000 grownups and many children started the long, long journey. They didn't take any food with them, just the dough left over from the unleavened bread prepared on the Passover night. They baked the bread at their first stopping place, which was Succoth.

The Israelites were walking into the desert. There were no marked roads and it would be very dangerous to get lost, so the Lord Himself became their guide. He went before them in a pillar made of clouds in the daytime. At night He led them in a pillar of fire. They knew they were never alone.

"The blood on your doorposts will serve as a sign, marking the houses where you are staying. When I see the blood, I will pass over you. This plague of death will not touch you when I strike the land of Egypt. This is a day to remember. Each year, from generation to generation, you must celebrate it as a special festival to the LORD. This is a law for all time."

Exodus 12:13-14

Red Sea Protection

Exodus 14:1–15:21

Pharaoh let the Israelites leave Egypt after the 10 terrible plagues on his people and his land. They headed southeast, in the direction of Mount Horeb. The Red Sea was just ahead of the Israelites. Suddenly behind them were the chariots of Egypt.

It didn't take Pharaoh long to realize that he had let all of his slaves leave. He called 600 chariot captains to lead the army of Egypt against the Israelites. Pharaoh wanted them back.

The Israelites were caught between Pharaoh's army and the waters of the Red Sea. The people were scared! Then God commanded Moses to raise his shepherd's staff over the sea. When he did, the waters began to divide so the Israelites could walk through on dry land. The pillar of cloud moved between the Israelites and the Egyptians.

That night the pillar of cloud looked different on the two sides. On the Israelite side it was light, but on the Egyptian side it was very dark. The Israelites were hidden from the Egyptians. Early the next morning the Israelites picked up all their possessions and marched between the two parts of the sea, which were like walls of water on either side.

The Egyptians tried to follow them into the Red Sea, but God made the wheels come off their chariots so that they got stuck in the desert sand. Then, as they came between the two parts of the sea, God told Moses once more to stretch out his staff over the sea. This time the water came rushing back, covering the chariots and drowning every horse and every Egyptian soldier.

Moses told the people, "Don't be afraid. Just stand still and watch the LORD rescue you today. The Egyptians you see today will never be seen again. The LORD Himself will fight for you. Just stay calm."

Exodus 14:13-14

**The sea parts and the Israelites walk
through on dry land. (Exodus 14:16)**

The Journey through the Wilderness Begins

Exodus 15:22–16:36

When the Israelites lived in Egypt they always had plenty of food even though they had been slaves and the Egyptians had been hard on them. In the desert it was different. There was sand as far as they could see. There were big mountains shimmering in the heat. They could only find water once in a while. Sometimes, when they did find some, it was too bitter to drink.

One place where the water was like that, God told Moses to throw a tree into the water. Right away the water became sweet enough to drink.

The Israelites traveled on and on. Finally they got angry with Moses. They wanted to go back to Egypt where they had food and water. They remembered the food in Egypt and blamed Moses for bringing them to the desert to starve. Moses cried out to God for help and He had an answer. He told Moses what He planned to do and Moses and Aaron told the people, "You will soon know that it's not Moses, but God, who has brought you out of Egypt. Each evening He will give you meat to eat and each morning there will be bread, too."

That night, just as it got dark, a great swarm of small birds, called quail, settled in the camp. All the people had to do was to catch them and cook them. In the morning when they woke up, the ground was covered with something that looked like frost. They didn't know what it was. They gave it a strange name: manna.

That evening vast numbers of quail flew in and covered the camp. And the next morning the area around the camp was wet with dew. When the dew evaporated, a flaky substance as fine as frost blanketed the ground.

Exodus 16:13-14

Moses leads the people to the mountain to meet God. (Exodus 19:16-17)

God Gives Instructions to the People

Exodus 17, 19–20

From the day the people of Israel left Egypt, they grumbled and complained about how hard the journey was and how they didn't have enough food or water. They quickly forgot the wonderful ways God had helped and protected them.

When they came to Rephidim, there was once again no water. The people got angry with Moses again. "Why did you bring us out of Egypt?" they asked. "We had water there; we're going to die of thirst out here. All our animals will die of thirst." They were so angry that Moses was afraid they would attack him. He cried out to God to help him and God told him what to do. Moses took some of the elders to a rock on the slopes of Mount Horeb. Then he raised his staff and struck the rock. Immediately a stream of water burst out from it. There was enough water for all the people and their animals. Once again God showed them that He was with them.

Three months after the Israelites had left Egypt, they came to the place where God would give His Law to His people. It would help them know how He wanted them to live together. God told Moses that none of the people could come near the mountain and the cattle couldn't graze there. The mountain was a holy place and from it God would speak to His people. When they heard the sound of trumpets blowing, the people should come to the mountain and listen to the voice of the Lord.

On the third morning after they had arrived there, a thick cloud like smoke formed around the top of the mountain. In the cloud the thunder rumbled and lightning flashed. Suddenly the people heard the sound of a great trumpet. They were terrified, but Moses led them out to stand at the foot of the mountain as God had directed.

As the mountain smoked, fire flashed and the earth shook, a

God gives Moses the Ten Commandments. (Exodus 20:1-17)

voice spoke to Moses out of the cloud. God had come down to meet His people. Now God called Moses to come up into the mountain to receive His message for the people.

Moses climbed the mountain and disappeared into the cloud. On that mountain, God told Moses many things He wanted His people to do. Moses received God's message for the people. God Himself wrote the Law on two tablets of stone, so that the people would never forget it.

God said, "I am the Lord your God, who has brought you out of the land of slavery.

1. You shall have no other gods except Me.
2. You shall not have any carved likeness of anything in heaven or earth, or in the sea, to kneel before it or worship it.
3. You shall not use the name of the Lord your God in vain. (That means do not use His name as a swear word, or without reverence.)
4. Remember to keep holy the Sabbath day.
5. Honor and respect your father and your mother.
6. You must not murder.
7. You must not commit adultery. (That means a husband and a wife must be true to one another.)
8. You must not steal.
9. You must not bring false witness against your neighbor. (That means you must not tell lies.)
10. You must not covet." (That means you must not be greedy for what belongs to someone else.)

"I am the LORD your God, who rescued you from the land of Egypt, the place of your slavery."
Exodus 20:2

The Golden Calf

Exodus 32–34

While Moses was with God up on the mountain, there was something bad happening down in the Israelite camp. The people went to Aaron and said, "We don't know what has happened to Moses. Maybe he isn't coming back. Maybe God left with him. We need gods to lead us now. Make gods for us like the ones we saw in Egypt."

Then Aaron did a terrible thing. He told the Israelites to bring to him all the golden ornaments and jewelry they had. He melted the gold and shaped it into a golden calf. He built an altar in front of the calf and told the Israelites they could make sacrifices and worship the Lord there.

Up on the mountain, God knew what was happening with the Israelites and He was very angry. He told Moses that the nation must be destroyed. But Moses begged God not to treat them so harshly. God agreed not to destroy them, but to punish only those who did wrong.

Moses went down the mountain with the two tablets of the Law in his hands. From a long way off he could hear the singing and celebrations. When he saw what was going on, he was so angry that he threw down the tablets of stone and they broke into pieces.

Then Moses took the golden calf and burned it. He then ground it into powder and threw the powder into water, which he made the people drink.

Then Moses called out to them, "Who is on the Lord's side? Let him come to me." All the children of Levi came to him. Moses told them to take their swords and go through the camp and kill everyone who had worshiped the golden calf. About 3,000 people were killed that day.

Then Moses told the rest of the people to beg God to forgive them. He himself would go back up the mountain and pray for them.

This time Moses was gone for 40 days, but the Israelites did not misbehave while he was away. God told Moses to get two pieces of stone and He would write the Law once more on those slabs. When Moses went back to the people, his face shone like the sun. They were afraid to go near him. He had to cover his face with a veil while he spoke to them.

"Yahweh! The LORD! The God of compassion and mercy! I am slow to anger and filled with unfailing love and faithfulness."

Exodus 34:6

God's Special House

Exodus 35–40

God told the Israelites to build a special place where they could worship Him, bring their offerings and ask forgiveness for their sins. God gave them the exact plans for building the place of worship. It was called a Tabernacle or tent.

The altar for burnt offerings was inside the Tabernacle. It was made of wood covered with a thick layer of brass, and was shaped like a box with a grate on top. It had rings at the sides that made it easier to carry when the Tabernacle was moved to a different place. The altar was big. It was about seven and a half feet square and around four and a half feet high. Every evening and every morning a special offering was made on the altar for the sins of the people.

There was a room inside the Tabernacle called the Holy of Holies. The Ark of the Covenant was in this room. It was a large wooden box covered with gold. The two stone tablets on which God had written the Law were inside it. On the top of the box were two golden statues of angels, called cherubs. The cherubs' wings stretched out and met above the Ark.

God made Aaron the high priest and he was in charge

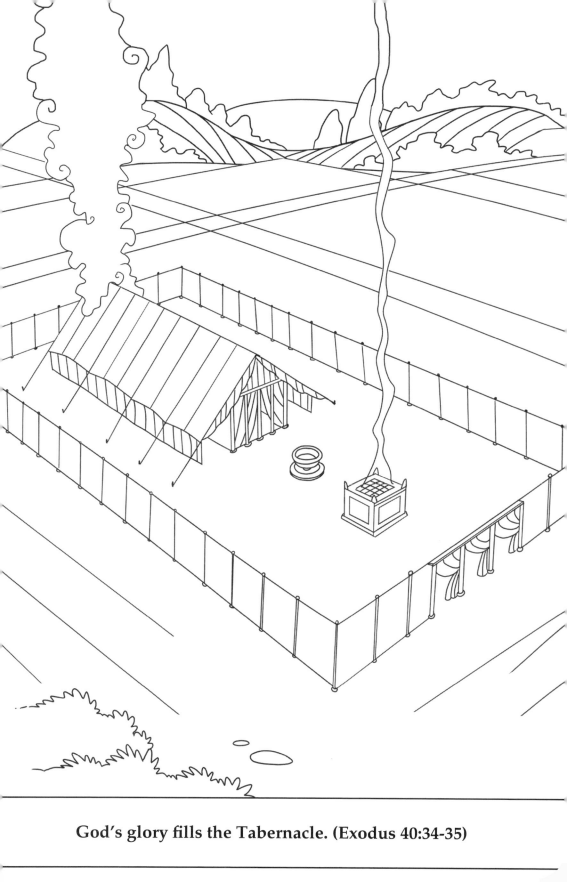

God's glory fills the Tabernacle. (Exodus 40:34-35)

of everything that happened in the Tabernacle. His sons helped him. He led the Israelites in their worship.

What happened each day in the Tabernacle? Every morning when the sun came up a fire was made on the great brass altar. That fire was never allowed to die out completely.

At about nine o'clock in the morning the first burnt offering was given. Either an ox or a lamb was killed in the courtyard. Its blood was caught in a big bowl. The meat was put on the altar and the blood was sprinkled over it. Then the altar fire was fanned to make it very hot so it burned away the whole sacrifice. The sacrifice helped God's people remember to give their lives to Him completely. At three o'clock in the afternoon another sacrifice was made in the same way.

Then the cloud covered the Tabernacle, and the glory of the LORD filled the Tabernacle.

Exodus 40:34

God Means Business

Leviticus 10

Aaron's position as High Priest was very important in the service of God. His sons had important positions, too. No one else was allowed to be near to God in the way Aaron and his sons were. They had to carefully carry out the instructions God gave for His worship in the Tabernacle.

The fire on the great brass altar was never allowed to go out and the fire on the golden incense altar had to be kept going with embers from the brass altar. These were God's instructions.

Nadab and Abihu were two of Aaron's sons. They didn't think it was important to follow God's instructions. One day they used embers that were not from the brass altar to start the incense altar fire. God was very angry over their disobedience. Immediately He made a flame shoot out and burn them both to death.

When Moses was told of this punishment, he said to Aaron, "Now the people will understand what the Lord meant when He said that all who come near Him must do so with reverence, and with respect for His glory."

Moses wouldn't let Aaron come near the bodies of his sons. He called two relatives to take them out of the camp to be buried. Aaron and two of his other sons, Eleazar and Ithamar, were not even allowed to go to the funeral. They had to stay in the Tabernacle and see to it that God's instructions for worship were followed.

The Lord had a special message for Aaron, too. He warned him that neither he nor his sons must ever drink wine or other strong drink when they were on duty in the Tabernacle. If they did, the same thing would happen to them as had happened to Nadab and Abihu.

"I will display My holiness through those who come near Me. I will display My glory before all the people."

Leviticus 10:3

Ten against Two

Numbers 13:1–14:38

About a year after the Israelites left Egypt something happened that meant they were coming close to the land God had promised them. God told Moses to choose a man from each tribe. Those 12 men were to go spy in the land of Canaan. They were to find out about its riches and to see how strong the people who lived there were. Someday they would have to fight those people to win the land. Moses made Joshua the leader of the 12 spies. This was dangerous, but Joshua was a brave man.

The spies sneaked into Canaan. They searched through it from south to north. On their way there they passed through the land of the giants. On their way back they came to the brook of Eshcol where they found a wonderful grapevine. They cut off one branch of grapes from the vine. It was so heavy that it took two men to carry it on a pole between them. They also took pomegranates and figs to show Moses and the rest of the Israelites. They searched

the land of Canaan for 40 days. Then they went back to the Israelite camp and took the samples of fruit with them.

The spies reported that the land was truly a rich land. But most of the spies were afraid of the giant people who lived in Canaan. Ten of the spies could only think of the towns with high walls and the war-like tribes who lived in them. Only two spies, Caleb and Joshua, felt that they should take the land at once.

As usual the Israelites began to complain that if they had only stayed in Egypt they would not have to fight these giant, powerful people. The people even wanted to choose a different leader and head back through the desert to Egypt.

When they heard that the people wanted new leaders, Moses and Aaron threw themselves down on the ground and prayed to God for their people. Caleb and Joshua were so up-

The 10 spies return from Canaan. (Numbers 13:25-26)

set that they tore their clothes as they begged the people to trust God. Canaan was a good land and rich in food and water. If they were obedient, God would lead them into it safely. But the people didn't listen. Instead, they tried to kill Joshua and Caleb.

That's when God stepped in. He let the people see His glory shining above the Tabernacle to show them that He knew what was happening and to remind them of His promises. God told Moses that He was so angry with the people that He wanted to destroy all of them except Moses and his family. Moses begged God to be merciful and not to destroy the people. So God said He wouldn't, but He would punish all the ones who had rebelled against Him. They would not be allowed to go into the Promised Land. Of all the Israelite adults, only Joshua and Caleb would be allowed to go into the Land of Promise along with the children of the rest of the people. The punishment for not trusting God to give them the land was that for every day the spies had spent in the land, the Israelites would have to spend a whole year in the desert. That would be 40 years altogether.

The people were scared now. They said they would take the land like God had wanted them to do. But God wouldn't listen to them. They had to go back into the desert as He had told them. If they tried to capture the land now, He would not be with them.

The LORD now said to Moses, "Send out men to explore the land of Canaan, the land I am giving to the Israelites. Send one leader from each of the twelve ancestral tribes."

Numbers 13:1-2

The End of the Long Journey Draws Near

Numbers 20:1–22:1

Because they didn't trust God, the Israelites had to wander for 40 long years in the wilderness. But God took care of them. He made sure they had food to eat. The older Israelites who had not trusted God died and the young ones grew up. When the 40 years of punishment were nearly over, they arrived in the wilderness of Paran. Shortly after they had reached Kadesh-Barnea, Miriam, the sister of Aaron and Moses, died.

But there was another reason for unhappiness. The fountain where they had once got water had dried up and now there was no water to drink. The Israelites were upset and they started to complain. "If only we had died with the others in the desert or stayed in Egypt. Moses, why did you bring us out of Egypt into this terrible place? Just to die?" Moses and Aaron went to the Tabernacle to pray as soon as they heard the complaints.

God told them what to do. Moses had to take his shepherd's staff and go to the great rock in front of the camp. He had to speak to the rock while all the people watched. After Moses had called the people together, he struck the rock two times with his staff. This was not what God had told him to do. Even so, a stream of water burst out of the rock and there was enough water for the people and all their flocks and herds. Because Moses and Aaron did not obey exactly what God had told them, they too would not be allowed to go into the Land of Promise.

When they came to Mount Hor, east of Edom, God told Moses to take Aaron and Aaron's son, Eleazar, up into the mountain. There the High Priest's clothes were taken from Aaron and put on Eleazar, and then Aaron died. When Moses and Eleazar came back from the mountain without Aaron the whole Israelite nation mourned for him for 30 days.

The Israelites were near the land of Canaan. The king of the Canaanites, Arad, heard that they were coming toward his land. He sent out his army to attack the Israelites and some of them were taken prisoner. The Israelites asked God for strength and He helped them to defeat the Canaanites and destroy their towns. The name of that place was Hormah.

Although God had helped them, and kept all His promises to them, the Israelites still grumbled and complained when things got rough or unpleasant. They talked about the time when their fathers had lived in Egypt. They even grumbled about the special food, manna, God gave them every day. God got so angry at their complaints that He sent poisonous snakes. Many people were bitten and died. "Pray for us, Moses!" the people cried. Moses prayed and God told him to make a snake out of brass and hang it up on a pole. Then, if any Israelite was bitten by a snake, they were to look at the brass snake and the bite would be healed and they would not die.

After this the Israelites kept traveling. They had to fight many kings and armies who did not want them to pass through their lands.

Before long the children of Israel were camped near Jericho. Finally they could see the land of Canaan on the other side of the Jordan River. Their long wanderings were nearly over.

The Lord said to Moses and Aaron, "Because you did not trust Me enough to demonstrate My holiness to the people of Israel, you will not lead them into the land I am giving them!"

Numbers 20:12

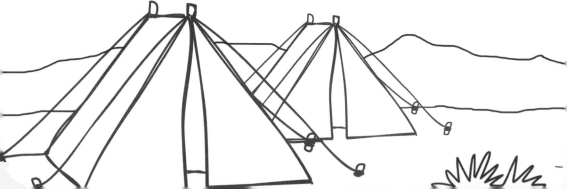

A Clever Man Learns from a Donkey

Numbers 22:2–25:18; 31:1–8

Small tribes lived along the edge of the land of Canaan. They saw what happened to nations who fought against God's people and they were afraid of what might happen to them.

Balak was the king of Moab and he was worried about the Israelites who were camped nearby. He thought of a plan, but he needed the help of a man named Balaam, who was a prophet – a man who could speak to God. Balak sent messengers to Balaam, and asked him to curse the Israelites. But God told Balaam not to do anything mean to the children of Israel, because He had blessed them. So Balaam told the messengers that God wouldn't allow him to do what they wanted.

Balak sent different men to Balaam and they promised him great rewards if only he would do what King Balak wanted. This time God told Balaam to go with the messengers to Balak, but to do just what God told him to do. Balaam wanted to obey God; however, deep in his heart Balaam also really wanted the money Balak promised him.

Balaam set out, riding on his donkey, when suddenly the donkey saw something that Balaam couldn't see. An angel of the Lord was standing in the road holding a sword in his hand. When the donkey saw the angel, it jumped off the road and ran into a field. Balaam grabbed a stick and beat the donkey until it came back onto the road. Next, the angel stood in a place where the road ran between two stone walls.

When the donkey saw the angel a second time, it jumped to the side and Balaam's foot was crushed against the wall. Balaam angrily beat the donkey again. Then the angel disappeared for a moment, only to appear again a little farther on. The donkey was frightened again, so Balaam beat the donkey very hard.

Then God did an amazing thing. He opened the mouth of that donkey so that it could speak. The donkey said, "What have I done to you that you should beat me three times like this?" Balaam was so angry that he didn't realize that his donkey was actually talking.

He answered, "I hit you because you wouldn't listen to me."

The donkey spoke again, saying, "Haven't I always served you faithfully? Have I ever given you trouble before?" Balaam had to admit that the donkey had always served him well.

Then God opened Balaam's eyes so that he could see the angel standing in the road with the sword in his hand. Balaam threw himself down on the ground and the angel asked him why he had beaten the donkey so badly. The donkey had actually saved Balaam by being frightened at the sight of the angel. Otherwise the angel would have used his sword on Balaam. Then Balaam was sorry that he had beaten the donkey, and offered to turn back home again if the angel was angry about where he was going. The angel told him it was alright to go with the king's messengers, but he must not say anything except what the Lord told him.

The next morning, Balak took Balaam up a high mountain so that he could look down on the Israelites' camp in the valley below. There Balaam told the servants of Balak to build seven altars and sacrifice seven young oxen and seven rams to God. After they gave the offerings, Balaam told Balak to stay near the altars while he went farther up the mountain to pray to God. When he came back, Balak immediately wanted to know what God had told him. He was angry when Balaam said, "He told me to bless the children of Israel, and I cannot change that."

Then Balak tried again to persuade Balaam to curse the children of Israel. But Balaam reminded the king that he had already told him that he had to do what God wanted. Balak wouldn't give up. He got Balaam to climb another mountain, build seven more altars and ask once more for God's word.

Balaam cannot see the angel and is angry that his donkey won't go where he wants him to. (Numbers 22:23-27)

This time the message was even more against what Balak wanted. As Balaam looked at the Israelite camps, God's Spirit told him what those people would be like in the future. Their nation would increase just like gardens growing by the riverside. Their kingdom would be great and they would destroy all their enemies.

Balak was so angry about what God said that he told Balaam to go back home immediately. But Balaam had another message from God. He told Balaam what God was going to do later with Balak's people. A Star would come out of the people of Jacob, and a Scepter out of the people of Israel, to stretch out over the land of Moab as her ruler. And the lands of Edom and Moab and Ammon would one day be under the control of Israel. Balaam still wanted the money that Balak had offered. So he thought of a plan to get it. He suggested that Balak have his people marry the Israelites and lead them away from worshiping God. They could teach them to worship the idols of the Moabites.

That's exactly the way it worked out. Then everything began to go wrong. More and more Israelites were turning away from God, so God sent a plague to remind them that He was their God. Thousands of Israelites died. Moses had the ringleaders who had led the people away from God put to death.

Then the Israelite armies, strong and trusting in God, fought the Moabites and their neighbors, the Midianites. The Moabites and Midianites were soundly defeated and their towns were destroyed. Their kings and princes were killed. One of the men killed was Balaam. God had spoken to Balaam and he was able to find out what God was going to do. But Balaam was greedy and wanted Balak's money. The price of that greed was death among the enemies of God's people.

Then the LORD opened Balaam's eyes, and he saw the angel of the LORD standing in the roadway with a drawn sword in his hand. Balaam bowed his head and fell face down on the ground before him.

Numbers 22:31

A Look at the Promised Land

Numbers 26, 32; Deuteronomy 31, 34

While the Israelites were camped east of the Jordan River, Moses counted all the people who were 20 years or older. There were over 600,000 men, not counting the women and children! Only three were over 60 years old: Moses, Caleb and Joshua.

Moses was already 120 years old. He would not cross into the Promised Land because he had disobeyed God. But God would let him see the Promised Land before He took him into heaven.

The Israelites controlled all the land east of the Jordan River. There was good grazing land there, especially in the part called Gilead. Just before the Israelites began to cross the Jordan, the leaders of the tribes of Reuben and Gad and of half of the tribe of Manasseh went to Moses. They asked permission to stay in those grazing lands. They owned great herds of cattle and felt that this was a good place for them. They would build houses for their wives and children, and pens for their cattle and sheep. Then the men would go with the rest of the Israelites and fight against their enemies until all the tribes were settled in their own lands. Moses was satisfied with their promise. Soon they were busy setting up homes for their families.

Moses gathered all the leaders together and told them that his work was nearly over. He would not go with them into Canaan, but before he was taken away he wanted to remind them of all God had done for their nation since they had left Egypt. He reviewed all the laws God had given them and reminded them that God wanted them to teach those laws to their children so they could become obedient servants of God. "Go the way He sends you," Moses said. "Always remember that God is forever, and His strong, everlasting arms will hold you safe, keeping you from danger."

Moses placed his hands on Joshua's head and appointed him as the new leader of the Israelites.

Moses blessed all the tribes, greeted their leaders, and walked through the camp and out across the plains of Moab until he reached Mount Nebo. He slowly climbed to the top and God showed him the Promised Land. Then Moses died and God buried him up in the mountains in a place no one has ever been able to find.

So be strong and courageous! Do not be afraid and do not panic before them. For the LORD your God will personally go ahead of you. He will neither fail you nor abandon you.

Deuteronomy 31:6

Job, the Man God Trusted

Job 1–2, 42

A long time ago, a good man named Job lived in the land of Uz. Job was very rich, with thousands of sheep, camels and cattle. He had many servants. He had seven sons and three daughters. Job loved God and served Him. He made special offerings for his sons just in case they had sinned against God

One day the angels came before God to bring their reports and the devil slipped in with them. God asked him, "Did you notice My servant Job? There is no one like him in the world. He is honest and upright, and avoids all that is wrong."

Satan was doubtful about Job's goodness. He said, "Why wouldn't he serve You? Isn't he blessed in every possible way? Take away his riches and see what happens. I'm sure he will curse God then." God said, "We shall see. Do what you wish with Job's possessions or his family, but do not touch Job himself."

The devil went right to work bringing trouble to Job. One day Job's eldest son threw a

Job's friends try to make him feel better. (Job 2:11)

big party. All his brothers and sisters were there.

Job was at home when suddenly a messenger came rushing in and said, "The Sabeans attacked us and stole all the oxen and donkeys. They killed all the servants who were there. I am the only one who escaped."

He had hardly finished speaking when another man rushed in with more bad news, "Lightning struck and killed all the sheep and the shepherds who were looking after them."

Then another messenger came running in, "The Chaldeans attacked us and took all the camels and killed all the herdsmen except me."

Then came the worst news of all. While Job's sons and daughters were enjoying their party, a strong wind had swept in from the desert, and knocked the house down. Everyone was killed ... all of Job's children were dead.

So in one day Job had lost everything he had. He threw himself down on the ground and cried out, "When I came into this world I had nothing; when I go from it I will not have anything either. The Lord gave, and the Lord has taken away. Blessed be His name." Even though Job had lost everything, he did not sin against the Lord.

A little while later the angels gathered again in heaven. Once more the devil slipped in with them. God challenged him again, "Have you seen My servant Job? There isn't another man like him in all the world. Even though you took everything from him, he has still not turned against Me."

But the devil mocked God, "A man will give all that he has for his own life. If Job's health is taken away from him, I am certain he will curse You."

God took that challenge. "I give Job into your hands. You can do with him what you will, but you cannot take his life." Right away the devil made Job very sick. He put painful boils all over his body, even on his feet and in his hair. Job felt so bad he went and sat among the ashes.

His wife was bitter about all that had happened. She said, "Has it helped you to serve God? You might as well curse Him and die."

But Job answered, "You speak like a person with no understanding. We have received many good things from God. How can we refuse to receive bad things?" Once again Job did not sin. The devil failed to snatch him away from God.

By this time the news of all Job's problems had spread. Three of his friends – Eliphaz, Bildad and Zophar – came to see him. But they were no help at all. They were sure that Job must have done something wrong. Job tried to explain that he had always done his best to keep God's commandments, but his friends were sure he must have sinned. In spite of all they said, Job stood firm. He did not understand why God was treating him this way, but he still trusted God.

Then God Himself told Job's friends that they were not speaking the truth about Him, as Job had done. They must bring a sacrifice to Him and Job would pray for them. Then God would forgive them.

Job prayed for his friends and when he had done that, God made him well again. Then God gave Job twice as many sheep and cattle as he had owned before. There was no richer man in all the land. God also gave him more children ... seven more sons and three more daughters.

"Should we accept only good things from the hand of God and never anything bad?" So in all this, Job said nothing wrong.
Job 2:10

The Sign of the Red Cord

Joshua 1–2

Joshua, the new leader of the Israelites, trusted God who had a special message of encouragement for him, "Lead the whole Israelite nation across the river into the land which I shall give to them, just as I promised Moses. As I guided and strengthened him, so I shall be with you; I will not fail you nor forsake you. Do not be afraid."

So Joshua told the people to prepare to cross the Jordan River into the land the Lord had promised to give them. Not far away, at the foot of a mountain range, was the city of Jericho. The people who lived there were called Canaanites.

Before they crossed the river, Joshua sent two men into Jericho to spy out the land. These two spies crossed the river and slipped into the city. In the evening they found a room in the house of a woman called Rahab. Her house was built right on the wall of the city. The next day some people went to the king and told him that there

were strangers in the city who were staying in Rahab's house. The king sent soldiers to Rahab who demanded that she turn the men over to them. But Rahab had hidden the spies under stalks of flax on the roof of her house. "There were two men here," she said, "but they left already. They went toward the Jordan River. If you hurry, you might still catch them."

The soldiers left right away to search for the spies. When they were gone, Rahab went to the two spies. She told them that the people of Jericho had heard of God's wonderful works for the Israelites. They also knew that God had promised to give Israel the land of Canaan. "Will you promise me that when the Israelites capture Jericho, you will spare my life?" Rahab asked the spies. They promised to keep her safe as long as she did not give them away.

When it was dark, Rahab lowered the spies down by a rope out of the window of her house.

Before they left, the spies told her that when the Israelite army came to take the city, she should hang a red cord from the same window that she had lowered them from. Everyone who was in the house would then be safe.

The two men went across the Jordan River, back to the Israelites. When they brought their report, the Israelites were encouraged because now they knew that the Canaanites were afraid of them.

"I will be with you as I was with Moses. I will not fail you or abandon you. Be strong and courageous, for you are the one who will lead these people to possess all the land I swore to their ancestors I would give them."

Joshua 1:5-6

The Dry Riverbed

Joshua 3–4

Once the spies gave their report, Joshua felt it was time to cross the Jordan River and head to Jericho. So the whole Israelite nation moved right to the bank of the river.

For three days they stayed there, getting ready to cross the river.

Joshua knew that God was going to do something wonderful to help them. He told the people to be ready for it. Early one morning, Joshua told the people to start moving. At the head of the long column of people, the priests took up the Ark of the Covenant. They marched down into the river until all the priests holding the Ark were standing right in the water.

Then God did a wonderful thing. The waters of the river stopped flowing! The river had been flooding and overflowing its banks. But suddenly the water upstream gathered in a great pool and did not flow down. Downstream the water flowed away toward the Dead Sea.

The riverbed in front of the Israelites was completely dry. The priests carrying the Ark of the Covenant stood right in the middle of the riverbed and all of the people crossed into Canaan, walking around the priests. Because of the marvelous miracle God had done, Joshua decided to put up a monument right where they had crossed.

One man from each of the 12 tribes went down into the riverbed and picked up a large stone from the place where the priests had stood. They carried them to the place where their last camp was before entering Canaan. They stacked the stones there as a reminder of the amazing way God had let them pass into the Promised Land. Another 12 stones were placed where the priests had stood, right in the middle of the riverbed.

After this had been done the priests climbed out of the riverbed and God let the river flow again.

When they came into Canaan, the Israelites saw corn growing in the fields. They were no longer in a barren desert! The women used corn to make flour and bake unleavened cakes. When they ate those cakes, God stopped giving them the manna from heaven. From then on they would eat the food of Canaan.

Meanwhile, the priests who were carrying the Ark of the LORD's Covenant stood on dry ground in the middle of the riverbed as the people passed by. They waited there until the whole nation of Israel had crossed the Jordan on dry ground.

Joshua 3:17

The Battle That Wasn't

Joshua 5–6

The Canaanite kings were afraid of the Israelites, especially when they heard how God had let them cross the Jordan River on dry ground. But the city of Jericho had a big wall around it. There were soldiers inside who would fight to protect their city! One day Joshua went to inspect the city and see what they would have to do to capture it. As he was nearing the city, he saw a soldier with a sword in his hand. Joshua challenged him, "Are you for us or for our enemies?" The man answered, "No, I am the prince of the Lord's armies, and I have come to help."

Joshua threw himself to the ground, worshiped God and said, "What has the Lord to say to His servant?" Joshua knew this was not just a man. He wasn't even an angel, but He was the Lord Himself! The Lord told Joshua to take off his shoes because he was standing in a holy place. Then He told him what the Israelites must do to capture the city of Jericho.

Joshua led the Israelites in doing everything just as God had instructed. Each day, led by the priests carrying the Ark of the Covenant and blowing trumpets made of rams' horns, the soldiers marched around the outside of the city. They didn't shout or make any sounds, but simply followed the priests.

On the seventh day, early in the morning, the priests and soldiers marched again. This time they circled around the city seven times. At the end of the seventh time, Joshua told them to shout a mighty shout. And when they did, the walls of the city fell down flat, except the part on which Rahab's house was built. The Israelite soldiers rushed into the city and killed all the people of Jericho except Rahab and her family.

There were great treasures in the city – gold, silver, copper, and iron, but the soldiers took nothing for themselves. Anything that was taken was for the treasure of God's Tabernacle.

The walls of Jericho fall, just as God had promised. (Joshua 6:20)

From that time Rahab became an Israelite and married one of the princes of Judah. One of her descendants many years later was David, the great king of Israel.

The LORD said to Joshua, "I have given you Jericho, its king, and all its strong warriors. You and your fighting men should march around the town."

Joshua 6:2-3

The Israelites Are Tricked

Joshua 9

Soon the news of the Israelite army's power spread to all the tribes in Canaan. Six of the tribes were the Hittites, Amorites, Canaanites, Perizzites, Hivites, and the Jebusites. Leaders of these tribes knew that each tribe on its own wouldn't be able to defeat the Israelites, so they joined together to fight as one army.

Not far from the Israelite camp there was a small tribe called the Gibeonites. These people were afraid of the Israelites, so they worked out a tricky scheme. They dressed up in old clothes, put on old shoes, saddled their donkeys and carried old sacks. They even took dry, moldy bread with them. They straggled into the Israelite camp as if they were from a country far away and begged the Israelites to make an agreement with them.

They were so convincing that the Israelites forgot that God had told them to drive out all the Canaanites and to destroy their cities.

Three days later the Israelites discovered they had been tricked, because these people were really their neighbors. At first they were angry, and wanted to go to war against the Gibeonites, but then they remembered the agreement they had made with serious promises. So they decided to leave them alone.

However, in the future the Gibeonites would end up serving

the Israelites by getting wood and water for them. They would have to do all the heavy work connected with the Tabernacle. So wherever the Israelites camped, some of the Gibeonites were there to do this hard work.

Joshua said, "Why did you say that you live in a distant land when you live right here among us? May you be cursed! From now on you will always be servants who cut wood and carry water for the house of my God."

Joshua 9:22-23

The Sun Stands Still

Joshua 10

The Israelite camp was near the city of Jerusalem. The king there was worried about the Israelites attacking them. He sent men to the kings of five other nations. The five of them made an agreement to join together and go to Gibeon to try to separate the Gibeonites from the Israelites.

When the Gibeonites saw the armies coming, they sent word to Joshua. They asked him to remember their agreement, and to come and help them.

God gave Joshua a special message. God told him not to be afraid, because He would see to it that the Israelites' enemies would be defeated.

During the night Joshua moved his forces to Gibeon. In the morning they defeated their enemies at a place called Beth-horon. The enemy soldiers ran away. God even sent a hailstorm that killed more of the fleeing soldiers than had died in battle.

On that day of battle, Joshua did a strange thing. He asked God to let the sun stand still in the sky so that the Israelites could defeat their enemies before it got dark. "Let the sun stand still over Gibeon; and the moon over the valley of Ajalon," he cried. And the sun and the moon did stand still. They didn't move at all.

There never was such a day before and there hasn't been a day like that since. It was a day when God listened to the voice of a man.

That day the strength of the Canaanites was broken in the southern part of the land. The Israelites moved in safely and turned to the north, heading to Mount Hermon. All the kings of the Canaanites were put to death, their cities destroyed, and their people scattered in all directions. After this Joshua divided up the Promised Land.

So the sun stood still and the moon stayed in place until the nation of Israel had defeated its enemies.

Joshua 10:13

Gideon and the 300 Men

Judges 6:1–7:8

Soon the Israelites were disobeying God again. God punished them by allowing them to be attacked by the Midianites. For seven long years the Midianites constantly attacked them and stole from them. Every year when the Israelites' crops were ready for reaping, the Midianites swept in and stole everything.

God told the Israelites why these things were happening to them. He sent a prophet to remind them of the wonderful things He had done for them when He brought them out of Egypt and into the land of Canaan. He also reminded them that He had warned them against worshiping the false gods in Canaan, but they had not obeyed.

One day Gideon, the son of Joash, was threshing wheat at the bottom of a winepress. Suddenly he saw an angel from God sitting under an oak tree nearby. The angel said, "The Lord is with you, brave man." But Gideon replied, "Oh my Lord, if the Lord is with us, why has all this happened to us? Where are the miracles the Lord once did to help our fathers when He brought them out of Egypt? But now the Lord God has turned away from us, and let us fall into the hands of the Midianites."

The angel replied, "Do not be afraid! You will help your people and save them from the Midianites. Do not think you are alone in the fight. I shall be with you."

Gideon ran to get unleavened bread, cooked goat's meat, and a pot of broth. He took this food to the angel. But the angel did a strange thing. He told Gideon to lay the meat and bread on the rock in front of him, and to pour the broth over it. Gideon did and the angel touched the food with his staff. Fire burst out of the rock, and the food was completely burned up. As this was happening, the angel disappeared. Terrified, Gideon cried out to God, "What shall I do? Because I have seen an angel face to face."

God knew he was scared so He comforted him, "Let peace be in your heart. Do not be afraid. You will not die."

The very same night, the Lord told Gideon what to do. His first job was to stop the Israelites from worshiping idols, because that made God angry. Gideon took 10 men and cut down the worship pole where the people worshiped the false god Asherah. They also broke down the altar to the false god Baal. Then Gideon set up an altar to God, and used the wood of the pole they had chopped down to burn a young bull as a burnt offering to God.

When morning came, the people of the town were shocked to see what had happened. They didn't know who had done it, but one of them guessed it must have been Gideon. The people rushed to Gideon's father, Joash, and told him they wanted to kill Gideon for what he had done. But Joash was not afraid. "If Baal is really a god," he said, "he can take care of himself. He will punish the person who broke down his altar." The people watched and when they saw that Gideon was not harmed, they began to turn back to the true God. After this Gideon sent messengers to ask the men of Manasseh, Asher, Zebulun and Naphtali to meet with him beside the spring of Harod.

Gideon prayed for God's help because he wanted to be sure that it really was God's will for him to lead His people against the Midianites. He prayed, "If it is Your plan to use me to save Israel, then give me a sign. I will put a piece of woolly sheepskin on the floor. In the morning, if there is dew only on the fleece and not on the ground around it, then I will know it is right for me to lead the people." In the morning that was exactly what had happened, and Gideon was able to squeeze a bowlful of water out of the fleece.

But Gideon needed more convincing, so he asked for another sign. This time he asked that the fleece be dry while all the ground around it was wet. In the morning, he saw that God did what he had asked. God proved He would help Gideon save his people. By now men from the other tribes had joined Gideon and the other men at Harod. The Midianite army was camped not far away.

God told Gideon that he had too many Israelite soldiers. God knew that if they defeated the Midianites, they would think it was because of their own strength and power, and they would forget all about God again. So God told Gideon to tell his men that anyone who was even a little bit nervous could go back home. Only about 10,000 men out of the original 32,000 stayed for the fight. But God said there were still too many. He told Gideon to bring the soldiers down to the riverbank and to tell the soldiers to drink water from the stream. Almost everyone knelt down to drink. Only 300 scooped up water with their hands. Those were the men God chose to be in Gideon's army. The rest of the men were sent back to their tents while Gideon prepared the 300 for the battle.

The Lord told Gideon, "With these 300 men I will rescue you and give you victory over the Midianites. Send all the others home."

Judges 7:7

93

Gideon's Victory

Judges 7:9-25

That night God told Gideon to call his servant Phurah. Gideon and Phurah were to creep down into the Midianite camp. Gideon heard an enemy soldier telling his friend about a dream he had had. In his dream he saw a cake of barley come tumbling down the mountainside, right against the side of a tent. It knocked the tent over. His friend said, "That cake of barley is Gideon, that man of Israel, because God has given the whole army of Midian into his hands." Gideon was pleased when he heard this. God made the Midianites afraid, so the victory would be much easier for the Israelites. Gideon went back to his 300 soldiers and divided them into three groups.

He gave every soldier a trumpet, an empty jar and a lamp. The lighted lamps were put inside the jars so that the lights couldn't be seen. Then the soldiers sneaked close to the Midianite camp. Each of the three groups moved to a different side of the camp. When Gideon gave the signal, they all blew their trumpets and smashed the jars and rushed into the camp with the lights showing. They shouted, "A sword for the Lord and for Gideon." The Midianites were so terrified they didn't even fight. Instead they ran as fast as they could to safety. Gideon sent messengers to the tribe of Ephraim, and they attacked the Midianites as they were running away. That was the end of the power of Midian.

Gideon remained a judge of Israel until he died. The Israelites loved him so much they wanted him to be their king. They wanted his family to become the royal family of the nation. But Gideon would not hear of it because he knew that only God could be King of Israel, and the people should always serve Him faithfully.

The LORD said, "Get up! Go down into the Midianite camp, for I have given you victory over them!"

Judges 7:9

Gideon and his 300 men chase the Midianites away. (Judges 7:19-21)

Samson, the Strongest Man in the World

Judges 13–14

The Israelites turned to God in the time of Jephthah, but it only lasted for a while. Before long they were worshiping idols again. There were three more judges after Jephthah, but they made no difference to the sinful ways of the people. The Philistines began to capture the land and rule over the Israelites. The Philistines lived near the Mediterranean Sea and their soldiers moved into the mountains to attack the Israelites. For 40 long years this went on.

As they usually did when they were in trouble, the Israelites turned back to God for help. Once again God sent an angel.

There was a man named Manoah who lived in the land of Dan. Manoah and his wife had no children. One day an angel appeared to Manoah's wife and told her that she would have a son, and that son would save his people from the Philistines. But as long as the boy lived, his hair must never be cut. When the baby was born, he was named Samson. As he grew up, he became a very strong man.

One day Samson went to a village called Timnah. While he was there, he met and fell in love with a Philistine girl.

One day he was walking outside the village when a young lion jumped out at him. Samson had no weapon to fight with. He grabbed the lion and tore it to pieces with his bare hands.

Some time later he went to Timnah again. He stopped to look at the skeleton of the lion he had killed. He was surprised to see that a swarm of bees had made their home inside and it was filled with honey he could eat.

Samson married the Philistine girl. There was a great feast that lasted a whole week. Thirty young Philistine men were selected to accompany Samson during the celebration. One day Samson asked them a riddle. He promised them 30 shirts and 30 suits if they could answer it.

But if they couldn't, they had to give him 30 shirts and suits.

The young men agreed and asked him to tell them his riddle. It was: "Out of the eater came forth meat, and out of the strong came forth sweetness." They tried and tried, but they couldn't come up with the answer. So they went to Samson's wife and said, "Get your husband to tell us the answer or we will burn down your father's house with you in it."

The poor young woman went to Samson, crying and begging him to tell her the answer. At first he wouldn't, but she cried and carried on so much that he finally told her. Of course, she went straight to the young men and told them. Just before the end of the feast, they went to Samson and told him the answer: "What is sweeter than honey? And what is stronger than a lion?" Samson knew immediately what had happened, and he said, "If you had not threatened my wife, you would not have found out my riddle." He left his wife and went to live with his parents.

The men of the town came to Samson with their answer: "What is sweeter than honey? What is stronger than a lion?"

Judges 14:18

Samson Sets Fire to the Philistines' Wheat

Judges 15

When the time came for the harvest, Samson had settled down and decided to go back to his wife. But he had been gone so long that her father had given her to another man to be his wife. He offered to give Samson his younger daughter but Samson was furious. He went out and caught all the foxes he could find until he had 300 foxes altogether. He tied them two-by-two together by their tails, and tied a burning piece of wood behind each pair. Then he chased them into the fields of the Philistines. Before long a fire was roaring through the fields.

When the Philistines realized Samson had done this, and why he was so angry, they burned down his father-in-law's house with the old man and his daughter inside. When Samson heard about that he got angry all over again. He went back to the village and killed everyone he could.

The Philistines were now so angry they decided to go to war against all the Israelites. They moved their army to attack the tribe of Judah, but Judah didn't have any weapons and they wanted to be left alone. They were afraid of war with the Philistines so they captured Samson and tied him up tight with two new cords. Then they handed him over to the Philistines at a place called Lehi.

The Philistines shouted at Samson and made fun of him. But God gave Samson great strength and he snapped the cords as if they were cotton threads. He picked up a jawbone of a donkey, and attacked the Philistines. Using just that bone, Samson killed 1,000 Philistines. After that amazing victory Samson was the judge of Israel for 20 years.

The Spirit of the LORD came powerfully upon Samson, and he snapped the ropes on his arms.

Judges 15:14

Samson and Delilah
Judges 16:1–22

Samson fell in love with another Philistine woman, named Delilah. When they heard that Samson was with Delilah, the Philistine leaders went to her and promised her lots of money if she found out how Samson got his great strength and how they could overcome him.

Delilah asked Samson three times about where his strength came from. He gave her a different answer each time she asked and each one was a lie. So each time the Philistines came to capture him, he got away from them easily. Finally Samson got so tired of Delilah's ques-

Delilah cuts Samson's hair. (Judges 16:19)

tions that he told her the real secret of his strength. He told her that if his hair was cut off, God would take away his gift of strength. That night, while Samson slept with his head on Delilah's lap, she called a man to come and shave off all his hair. This time when she shouted that the Philistines had come to capture him, Samson jumped up as usual, but he didn't know that the Lord was no longer with him. The Philistines took him to prison where he was chained up with brass chains. They made him do the hard work of grinding corn. But what they didn't notice was that Samson's hair was growing again. His strength was returning, too.

Then she cried out, "Samson! The Philistines have come to capture you!"

Judges 16:20

Samson's End

Judges 16:23–31

After Samson was captured by the Philistines, they called all their people together to make a great sacrifice to their god Dagon. They thought he had given Samson over to them. They dragged Samson in to make fun of him. The temple was packed with people. On the roof balcony alone there were 3,000 people watching. While the people were making their sacrifices, Samson asked the little boy who was his guide to place his hands on the great pillars that held up the temple roof. Samson prayed that God would give him strength one last time. Samson pushed the pillars with all his might. They tumbled down and the roof collapsed. More Philistines died that day than Samson had ever killed – but he died with them.

Then Samson prayed to the LORD, "Sovereign LORD, remember me again. O God, please strengthen me just one more time."

Judges 16:28

**Samson breaks the pillars and the temple
collapses on the Philistines. (Judges 16:29-30)**

Loving Loyalty

Ruth 1–4

During the time of the judges there was a terrible famine in Canaan – there was very little food for people to eat. Many people moved to other lands where they could find food. One man who moved was Elimelech from Bethlehem. He took his wife, Naomi, and their two sons, Mahlon and Kilion, and went to live in Moab. A few years later Elimelech died, leaving Naomi and her sons in Moab. The two sons married Moabite women, Orpah and Ruth.

For 10 years they lived happily together, but then Mahlon and Kilion both got sick and died. Naomi felt like a stranger alone in a foreign land, so she decided to go back to Judah, to her own family. She told Orpah and Ruth to go and live with their own families again.

But Ruth would not go. She hugged Naomi and said, "Please do not ask me to leave you; wherever you go, I will go, and wherever you stay, I will stay. Your people will be my people, and your God my God. I want to be buried where you are buried when you die. May God punish me if anything other than death parts us."

So the two women walked the long way from Moab to Bethlehem in Judah, back to Naomi's family.

Naomi and Ruth were very poor, and because they needed food so badly, Naomi sent Ruth to the wheat field of Boaz, who was a distant relative of Naomi. Ruth picked up the grain that the workers dropped.

On the very day that Ruth went to the field, Boaz himself came to see how the harvesters were doing. He liked Ruth right away and made her a very kind promise. He said that she could gather wheat in his fields as long as she wanted to, and no one would send her away. She could also drink water from the harvesters' wells if she was thirsty.

**Ruth brings the wheat she had gathered
in Boaz's field to Naomi. (Ruth 2:17-18)**

At the end of the harvest season, Naomi felt very sorry for Ruth because she had worked so hard to find food for them.

She told Ruth to go to the great harvest feast and explain to Boaz that Naomi was the widow of Elimelech who had been a relative of Boaz. Maybe Boaz would be willing to help them without Ruth having to work so hard to find food for them.

But when Boaz saw Ruth again, he fell in love with her at once. Before very long a marriage was arranged between wealthy Boaz and Ruth, the little widow from Moab. Naomi went to live with Boaz and Ruth in their great house.

God gave Ruth and Boaz a baby boy and they called him Obed.

When Obed grew up and was married, he and his wife had a son, too. That son was called Jesse. Jesse was the father of David who was a shepherd boy and later became the greatest king that Israel ever had.

"Wherever you go, I will go; wherever you live, I will live. Your people will be my people, and your God will be my God."

Ruth 1:16

The Boy Who Was an Answer to Prayer

1 Samuel 1–3

After the death of Samson, the strong man, the next judge of Israel was Eli. He was also the high priest in the Tabernacle at Shiloh. Eli was an old man and his two sons, Hophni and Phinehas, helped him.

There was a rich man named Elkanah who had two wives.

His favorite wife was Hannah, but she had no children. Each year they went up to the Tabernacle at Shiloh to bring an offering to God and to beg Him to bless them with a son.

One year when they were staying near the Tabernacle, Hannah went to the Tabernacle to pray by herself. She prayed and cried because she wanted a baby so much.

In fact, she wanted a baby so badly that she made a special promise to God, "Dear God, please give me a son. If You give me a son, as soon as he is old enough I will give him back to You to serve You."

Hannah prayed so hard, and cried so bitterly that Eli noticed her. Then he prayed with her that God would give her the son she longed for. Hannah was happy when she left the Tabernacle because now she believed that God would answer her prayer. That was exactly what happened. Hannah had a little boy. She named him Samuel, which means "asked of God."

Hannah didn't forget her promise to God. As soon as the little boy was old enough, she took him to the Tabernacle. She gave Samuel to Eli so that he could teach her son to serve the Lord.

One night Samuel had gone to bed, but he wasn't asleep yet.

Suddenly the Lord Himself called, "Samuel."

The little boy didn't know who was calling him. He ran to Eli because he thought that the old man had called him. But Eli said, "I didn't call you. Go back to bed."

So Samuel went back to bed. He had hardly lain down when the voice called once more. Again Samuel ran to Eli, and again the old man told him to go back to bed.

When it happened a third time, Eli realized that it was the Lord who was calling Samuel. He told the boy that if he heard the voice again, he should answer, "Speak, Lord, for Your servant is listening."

God did call again and Samuel answered. God gave Samuel this very important message, "I have seen how badly Eli's sons behave, and I have seen that Eli has done nothing to stop them. I will punish them. The priesthood will be taken away from them, and none of their descendants will have the right to act as priests ever again."

After hearing that sad message, Samuel lay wide awake on his bed until morning. He was afraid to tell Eli what God had said because he loved the old man very much. But in the morning Eli called him and made Samuel tell him what God had said. Eli was sad, but he knew that what God had said was right.

It was not long before all the people knew that God had spoken directly to Samuel.

That meant that Samuel was a prophet – God's spokesman to His people. The people respected Samuel very much. From then on God spoke to Samuel often, and in the Tabernacle he passed on God's messages to the people of Israel.

The LORD came and called as before, "Samuel! Samuel!" And Samuel replied, "Speak, Your servant is listening."

1 Samuel 3:10

God's Power in the Ark of the Covenant

1 Samuel 4:1–7:2

When Eli the priest was a very old man, the people of Israel were being attacked by the Philistines who lived along the coast of the Mediterranean Sea. There was a big battle near a place called Ebenezer. The Israelites were firmly defeated.

When they heard the terrible news, the elders of Israel met to decide what to do to keep the whole nation from being destroyed. They decided that the Ark of the Covenant must be brought from the Tabernacle to go into battle with the army. Then, they thought, all would be well. So they went to the Tabernacle and right into the Holy of Holies. But no one was supposed to go into the Holy of Holies except the high priest, and even he could only go in on the Day of Atonement. What made it worse was that Eli's two disobedient sons, Hophni and Phinehas, helped take the Ark to the army camp. When the Ark arrived in the camp, the soldiers gave a great cheer.

When the Philistines heard the shouting, they were very afraid. They were sure that the Israelites would defeat them. But when they fought, the Israelites lost again. Worst of all, the Ark was captured. Eli's two sons were killed in the battle.

On that day Eli was sitting on the side of the road, waiting for news. After the battle a man ran to Shiloh to tell the people what had happened. When Eli heard of the death of his sons, and especially of the capture of the Ark, he fell off his seat, broke his neck and died.

The Philistines were overjoyed that they had the Ark. They took it to the city called Ashdod and set up the Ark alongside an idol of Dagon, in his temple. When they came to the temple the next morning, the idol was lying on its face on the ground. They carefully set the idol up again, but the next morning they found that it had fallen down again. This time the head and both hands had broken off. There were more bad things to come. The people of Ashdod and all the people around suffered from a terrible disease, which made painful boils on their bodies. The Philistines were sure that all this had happened because they had taken the Ark from the Israelites. They decided to move it to the city of Gath. But that brought terrible problems to the people of Gath, too. When the Ark was sent on from Gath to Ekron, the sickness came to them, too.

For seven long months the Philistines suffered because they had the Ark. Finally they decided to send it back to the Israelites. They loaded the Ark onto a newly made cart, with two cows harnessed in front. They put offerings of gold on the cart to be a sacrifice to the God of Israel. No men led the cows, but they pulled the cart to the hills where the Israelites lived. The cows pulled the cart right into the valley of Beth-shemesh, where some of the people were harvesting wheat. When they saw what was on the cart, the people were excited. The Levites immediately built an altar and used the wood of the cart to make a fire. They offered the two cows to God as their sacrifice of thanksgiving.

But some of the people of Beth-shemesh were too curious for their own good. They wanted to see what was inside the Ark. They opened it, although they knew it was wrong to do so. God sent a great plague on them, and many people died.

The people who were left were afraid. They sent a message to the people of Kirjath-jearim, asking them to come and get the Ark. They did and for 20 years that was where the Ark remained – in the house of Abinadab.

They said, "Let's bring the Ark of the Covenant of the LORD from Shiloh. If we carry it into battle with us, it will save us from our enemies."

1 Samuel 4:3

Judge Samuel
1 Samuel 7:3-17

When Eli died, Samuel was too young to become the judge over Israel. But after a few years, when the Ark had been brought to Kirjath-jearim, Samuel began to tell the Israelites what they had to do if they wanted to defeat the Philistines. The Philistines were still raiding their villages and stealing their crops, making life very hard for the Israelites.

Samuel told the Israelites they had to stop worshiping the false gods of the Canaanites. He told them they had to destroy their ugly idols and turn back to the Lord, the only true God. When they did that, God would help them drive the Philistines out of their land.

The Israelites listened to what Samuel told them. Many of them met together at a place called Mizpah to fast and pray that God would deliver them. While they were there, Samuel was appointed judge over the nation and the people promised to serve God faithfully.

Before too much time had passed the Israelites were able to take back all the cities the Philistines had captured from them – from Ekron right up to Gath. From then on, during all the time that Samuel was judge over Israel, the Philistines were not able to trouble them anymore. Samuel set up his home in Ramah. From Ramah he traveled from town to town to judge and to settle disputes between the people.

Samuel said to all the people of Israel, "If you want to return to the LORD with all your hearts, get rid of your foreign gods and your images of Ashtoreth. Turn your hearts to the LORD and obey Him alone; then He will rescue you from the Philistines."

1 Samuel 7:3

"We Want a King"

1 Samuel 8:1–10:8

After Samuel grew to be an old man, there were two other judges in Israel. They were his two sons, Joel and Abijah. But just like Eli's sons before, they were bad men. They were greedy, and instead of judging honestly, they took bribes from people who wanted their own way. The people were very unhappy that their judges weren't honest.

One day the elders said to Samuel, "You are an old man now, and your sons are not judging in the way you did. All the nations around us have kings. We want you to appoint a king to rule over us, too."

Samuel was very sad about this, so he went to talk to God about it. God answered His faithful old servant and explained to Samuel that the people were not really turning against him, but were turning against God Himself. God told him to choose a king for them, so Samuel sent the elders back home and he set out to find a king for Israel.

There was a man from the tribe of Benjamin named Kish. He

had a strong, handsome son. The son was a tall man, head and shoulders above other people, and his name was Saul. Kish owned a herd of donkeys and one day the donkeys strayed away. Saul took a servant and went to look for them. They had traveled a long way without seeing any of the missing animals. When they had traveled as far as the land of Zuph, Saul decided they should go home in case his father was worried about them. However, the servant remembered that a wise man, a prophet of God, lived in a nearby town. That wise man was Samuel. The servant suggested that Saul go to see Samuel and ask him for help finding the donkeys.

As soon as Samuel saw Saul, God told him in his heart that this was the man that must rule over His people. Saul didn't know anything about this. He didn't even know who Samuel was. He just saw a man standing by the gate and asked him how to find the prophet's house. He was amazed when the man said, "I am the man you are looking for. Come and eat with me today, and tomor-row you may leave again. Do not worry about the donkeys. They have been found already. And for whom is all Israel longing? Is it not for you and for all your family?"

Saul hardly knew what to say, "I am a Benjamite. I belong to one of the smallest tribes of Israel. My family is one of the least important families in our tribe. How can you say that I'm the one Israel has been longing for?"

Samuel didn't answer, but took Saul and his servant into the dining hall. He made Saul sit in the chief seat between all the important people.

Before Saul left to go home the next morning, Samuel called him aside. The old man took some oil and poured it on Saul's head and said, "It is the Lord Himself who has anointed you to be king over His people. Now go on your way. When you come to Rachel's grave, just as you enter the land of Benjamin, you will see two men. They will tell you that the donkeys are found and that your father is not worried that you are lost. Go on from there and when you get to the oak of Tabor, you will meet three men going to sacrifice at Bethel. One of them will be carrying three young goats. Another will have three loaves of bread. The third will have a bottle of wine. They will greet you and give you two loaves of bread, which you will accept. After that you will meet a group of prophets playing musical instruments and prophesying in the name of God. You will see that they are filled with the Spirit of God. The Spirit will also come on you and you will be made a new man. All this will happen to prove to you that it is God who is calling you to be king. Wait for me in Gilgal and in seven days I will meet you there."

Everything happened exactly as Samuel had said. When the Spirit of the Lord came upon Saul, he became a changed man. Now he was no longer just a farmer's son, but a king.

Samuel took a flask of olive oil and poured it over Saul's head. He kissed Saul and said, "I am doing this because the LORD has appointed you to be the ruler over Israel, His special possession."

1 Samuel 10:1

Saul's Brave Son, Jonathan

1 Samuel 13:1–14:23

When Saul had been king for two years, he decided that the Israelites had to stop the attacks of the Philistines. He chose 3,000 men for the battle.

Of the 3,000 men, 2,000 were under Saul's command in Michmash and around Mount Bethel. The other 1,000 were under the command of Jonathan around Gibeah in Benjamin.

Jonathan, who was Saul's eldest son, led an attack against the Philistines and won.

This was the signal for Saul. He sent messengers throughout the land to call the people to an all-out war against the Philistines. By now the Philistines had many soldiers. The Israelites were terrified and they hid wherever they could. Some even ran across the Jordan River into the lands of Gad and Gilead.

Saul unhappily gathered his little army, which was now only about 600 men, and joined forces with Jonathan's troops.

Jonathan was a brave man and he was determined that the Philistines should be driven out of their land. One morning, without saying anything to his father, he called his armor bearer. The two of them quietly slipped away to spy on the Philistines' camp between Michmash and Gibeah.

Together they climbed up to the top of a rocky hill. There they stood up in full view of the enemy camp that was on another hill close by. When the Philistines saw them, they shouted, "Look, the Hebrews are crawling out of their holes in the ground. Come over where we are, and we will show you a thing or two!" Jonathan and the armor bearer rushed across and battled the Philistines. In that first attack they killed about 20 men. The battle was so fierce that the Philistines panicked and even began to fight each other.

When Saul and his soldiers saw what was happening, they rushed to join the battle and so did some of the Israelites who had been hiding in the hills and bushes nearby. One group of Israelites, who had been caught by the Philistines and had become their servants, broke out in revolt. Soon the mighty Philistine army was running away.

"Climb right behind me," Jonathan said to his armor bearer, "for the LORD will help us defeat them."

1 Samuel 14:12

The Downfall of Saul

1 Samuel 15

After the great victory against the Philistines, Saul took courage and led his men against the enemy nations on all sides. He led his army against the Moabites, Ammonites, Edomites, and the kings of Zobah, and once again against the Philistines. In every battle his men defeated their enemies.

The Amalekites lived in a land just south of the Israelites and caused many problems for Saul's people. They raided the farms and villages on the edge of the desert, stole things and killed some Israelites.

One day Samuel the prophet came to Saul with a special message from God. He said that Saul had to lead his people in battle against the Amalekites and destroy everything they possessed.

Saul's armies attacked the Amalekites and defeated them, killing all of them. But Saul did not obey the whole command of the Lord, which Samuel had told him. He did not kill Agag, king of the Amalekites. Saul also kept the best of the sheep and the cattle. It was only the worthless animals that he had killed.

Samuel was not with the armies. Because he was an old man he planned to follow them later. The Lord spoke to Samuel and said, "I regret that Saul was ever made king, because he has not kept My commandments." That night Samuel prayed all night long for Saul.

In the morning Samuel went out to meet Saul. When Saul met the prophet, he was very proud of the victory they had won. "I have done what the Lord commanded," Saul said.

But Samuel answered, "Then what is the bleating of sheep and lowing of cattle that I hear?"

Saul said, "We took some animals from the Amalekites. The people have spared the best cattle and sheep to offer them as sacrifices to God. We destroyed the rest."

Then Samuel said, "Let me tell you what the Lord told me last night. When you thought nothing of yourself, He made you king over all Israel. Then He sent you on a journey and told you to totally destroy the Amalekites. Why didn't you obey? Why did you try to gather riches for yourself instead of destroying everything as God had said?

"You speak of sacrifices. Do you think God is willing to receive them from you if you refuse to obey Him? To rebel against God is as bad as serving idols. Because you have refused to listen to God's word, God has rejected you as king."

Saul felt terrible when he heard Samuel's words. He begged Samuel to forgive him and to go with him to worship God, but Samuel wouldn't go because Saul had disobeyed God's commands. Saul grabbed Samuel's coat and held on so tightly that it tore. When that happened, Samuel said, "Just as you have torn away part of my coat, so God has torn away the kingdom from you and has given it to a neighbor of yours who is better than you. God does not lie. What He has said, He will do. You can be sure of that."

Saul kept begging Samuel not to shame him in front of all the people, so Samuel did go with him to worship God. Then Samuel returned to his home in Ramah and never went to see Saul again. From that day on, Samuel mourned for Saul.

What is more pleasing to the LORD: your burnt offerings and sacrifices or your obedience to His voice? Listen! Obedience is better than sacrifice, and submission is better than offering the fat of rams.

1 Samuel 15:22

Samuel reprimands Saul for not killing the sheep, as God had told him to. (1 Samuel 15:19)

A Shepherd Boy Becomes King

1 Samuel 16; Psalm 23

Samuel grieved every day for Saul who had disobeyed God. One day God told Samuel to go out and look for the new king who would replace Saul. He told Samuel to go to the home of Jesse in Bethlehem, because the new king would be one of his sons. Samuel had to take oil with him to anoint the man who would become king. The Lord also told him to take a cow to sacrifice in Bethlehem. When he got there, he was to ask Jesse to worship with him. God would point out which of Jesse's sons was to be anointed as king.

So Samuel went to Bethlehem. The elders of the town were terrified when he arrived. They thought he had come to punish them for some wrong they had done. But Samuel told them he had come in peace. He asked Jesse and his sons to come and sacrifice with him. When the young men came, Samuel looked them over very carefully to choose the new king. He saw the eldest son, Eliab, who was tall and strong, and Samuel was sure that he was the one God wanted. But God said, "Do not look at a man's height or his appearance. God does not see as man sees. Man looks on the outward appearance, but God sees the heart."

One by one each of Jesse's sons passed by Samuel, but God didn't point out any of them. Samuel was puzzled, so he asked Jesse if he had any other sons. Jesse said, "Yes, there is another, but he is very young. He is out in the field looking after the sheep." Samuel told Jesse to send for the boy. Samuel would not sit down to eat until the youngest son had come.

When David came into the house, the Lord said to Samuel, "Stand up and anoint him. This is the one I have chosen to be king." So Samuel poured oil on David's head and the Spirit of the Lord came upon the boy from that day on. David went back to his work of caring for his father's sheep in the hills around Bethlehem. He grew strong in body and in spirit. He was a young man who learned to know the Lord as his own special friend. More than once David had to kill lions and bears that attacked his sheep. He became an expert in the use of the sling with which he hurled stones at the animals that attacked the flock.

He became a good musician, playing on his harp. Because David loved God so much, he made up hymns praising God and sang them as he played his harp. We still have many of those songs of praise today. We call them the Psalms. One of the most beautiful of David's hymns is the Shepherd Psalm (Psalm 23):

The LORD is my shepherd;
    I have all that I need.
He lets me rest in green meadows;
    He leads me beside peaceful streams.
    He renews my strength.
He guides me along right paths,
    bringing honor to His name.
Even when I walk
    through the darkest valley,
I will not be afraid,
    for You are close beside me.
Your rod and Your staff

protect and comfort me.
You prepare a feast for me
    in the presence of my enemies.
You honor me by anointing my head
    with oil.
    My cup overflows with blessings.
Surely Your goodness and unfailing
    love will pursue me
    all the days of my life,
and I will live in the house of the LORD
    forever.

Out in the hills David drew closer and closer to the Lord. The Spirit of God taught him many things. But things were not going so well with King Saul. The Spirit of the Lord had withdrawn from him, and he was grumpy and unhappy.

Sometimes Saul behaved like he was crazy. His servants were afraid of him. After a while they discovered that if someone quietly played the harp when Saul was in a bad mood, he felt better.

One of the servants remembered a young man, a son of Jesse, who was not only a good harp player, but also an expert with weapons and a smart businessman. That young man was David. So David was brought to Saul, and Saul grew to love him very much. He made him his armor bearer.

David's harp music made Saul calmer so David went back to Bethlehem to be his father's shepherd as he had been before. No one knew that this young man had been anointed to become king in Saul's place.

The LORD said to Samuel, "Don't judge by his appearance or height, for I have rejected him. The LORD doesn't see things the way you see them. People judge by outward appearance, but the LORD looks at the heart."

1 Samuel 16:7

The End of a Giant

1 Samuel 17:1–52

Although Saul defeated the Philistines in several great battles, the war against them continued throughout the entire time he was king.

One time the Philistine soldiers gathered near Socoh in the land of Judah. The Israelite army was near the valley of Elah, not far away. The two armies were facing each other on opposite mountains with a valley between them.

One of the Philistine soldiers was a giant named Goliath. He came out into the valley each day and made fun of the Isra-elite soldiers and challenged them to come out and fight him.

Jesse's three oldest sons were soldiers in King Saul's army. Young David was still at home looking after the sheep. One day Jesse sent David to take food to his soldier brothers and to find out how they were. While David was in Saul's camp talking to his brothers, the Philistine giant came into the valley and made fun of the Israelites and of God Himself! The Israelites told David that if any man fought and killed Goliath, the king would reward him with

David fights Goliath. (1 Samuel 17:48-49)

great riches. The king would also give his own daughter to be that man's wife and the king would make his family a noble family in the land.

David asked his brothers why no one dared to go out and stop the giant from speaking against God. David's eldest brother, Eliab, got very angry with David. He felt David was calling King Saul's soldiers cowards. David felt strongly that Goliath had to be stopped. When he saw that none of the soldiers were brave enough to fight Goliath, he decided to ask King Saul for permission to fight the giant himself. At first the king said no because David was only a teenager. But David begged to be allowed to fight him. Finally Saul agreed. "Go," he said, "and the Lord be with you." Then he gave David his own helmet, metal armor and sword. But they were too heavy for David and he wasn't used to wearing them. He took them off, picked up his stick, shepherd's sling and five smooth stones from the stream. Then he headed to the valley to face the greatest warrior in the Philistine army.

When Goliath saw young David and the strange weapons he was carrying, he angrily shouted, "Am I a dog for you to come out against me with sticks? Come on, fight me and I will feed you to the birds of the air and the beasts of the field."

But David was not afraid at all. "You come out against me with a sword and a spear and a shield," he said, "but I come against you in the name of the Lord of hosts, the God of the armies of Israel, whom you have defied. Today God will give you into my hands. I will defeat you and cut off your head. The birds will feast on your body, so that all the world may know who is the Lord God, and that He has other ways of winning the victory than with spears and swords. This battle is the Lord's."

As Goliath ran toward him, David slipped a stone into his sling and hurled it right at Goliath. The stone hit the giant in the middle of the forehead and he fell down ... dead. David snatched Goliath's own sword and chopped off his head, just as he had said he would.

The rest of the Philistine army was watching and when they saw their soldier fall, they quickly ran away! The Israelites chased after them, driving them right back to their own city and killing thousands of Philistines during the battle.

David won the battle, but not because of his own strength. He won because he fought in the name of the Lord. All Israel knew how God had used the young David to free them from the hands of their enemies.

Everyone assembled here will know that the LORD rescues His people, but not with sword and spear. This is the LORD's battle, and He will give you to us!

1 Samuel 17:47

Saul Becomes Jealous of David
1 Samuel 17:53–18:30

David had played the harp for Saul many times in his palace to calm him when he was upset. But when the young man asked to be allowed to fight Goliath, Saul did not recognize David at all. After Goliath was killed, Saul sent his general, Abner, to find out who the boy was that defeated the giant. Saul wanted him brought to the royal tent. When he got there David told the king that he was the son of Jesse. Saul brought him into the royal household and made him a leader among the soldiers.

Of course the king was happy about the victory over the Philistines. But when the army returned home, his whole mood changed. The news of David killing Goliath had spread throughout the land and in village after village the women came out, singing and praising David for what he had done. "Saul has slain his thousands, and David his ten thousands," they sang. Saul was very jealous.

The very next day Saul was in one of his bad moods again. Once more David played his harp to calm him just as he had done in the days before the war. But this time Saul was holding a spear and his jealousy of David got the better of him. He threw it at David and tried to pin him to the wall. That happened twice, but each time David managed to jump out of the way.

Saul had promised to give his daughter to be the wife of the man who killed Goliath. But when the time came, Saul cheated David and gave his daughter to another man to be his wife. This happened while David was away fighting the Philistines again. Saul secretly hoped they would kill him. When David came back he found Saul's daughter was already married. Then Saul heard that his second daughter, Michal, loved David. Once again he sent David off to fight against the Philistines. This time when David came back the marriage had to be held and David became Saul's son-in-law.

David continued to succeed in everything he did, for the LORD was with him.

1 Samuel 18:14

David and Jonathan
1 Samuel 19–20

Saul's hatred for David grew so strong that he told all his servants, and even his son Jonathan, to look for a chance to kill David. Jonathan was very upset about that because he loved David. They had become best friends. Jonathan told his friend to hide from the king. David asked Jonathan what he had done to make Saul hate him enough to kill him. Jonathan tried his best to tell David that his father had promised to never hurt David. But David explained to him that Saul was hiding his evil plans from his son, because he knew how much Jonathan loved David.

The two friends made a plan. Jonathan would go back to the

palace and see how Saul felt about David. David was supposed to come to a feast with the king at the festival of the new moon, but he would not come. If Saul asked about him, Jonathan should say that David had asked permission to go home to Bethlehem for a family feast.

Out in the field that day the two friends made a special promise. They promised that they would not allow the king's anger at David to make any difference to their friendship.

Jonathan worked out a plan for letting David know how Saul felt about him. On the third day of the feast, Jonathan would come to the field where they were now standing, and bring his bow and arrows. He would also bring a boy to run and get the arrows. He would shoot three arrows and send the boy after them. David had to hide in the bushes nearby. If he heard Jonathan tell the boy that the arrows were on this side of him, that meant all was well. But if he shouted that they were farther away, then David had to get away as quickly as

possible because that meant that King Saul wanted to kill him.

So Jonathan went to the feast. On the first day, Saul didn't say anything about David's absence. On the second day, he asked Jonathan why David hadn't come to the feast. Jonathan told Saul that David had asked to be excused so that he could attend the family festival at Bethlehem. Saul was furious with David, and with Jonathan for being David's friend. He told Jonathan that as long as David was alive, Jonathan could never become king. Saul told him to get David immediately so they could kill him. But Jonathan asked, "Why should he be killed? What wrong has he done?" That made Saul so angry that he threw his spear at his own son.

Jonathan immediately left, afraid of the way his father had behaved. Early the next morning he went out to the field with his bow and arrows. He gave David the sign he had promised, telling him to run away. However, he loved his friend so much that he couldn't let him go without saying good-bye. So he sent the boy back to town with his bow and arrows. When David came out of hiding, the two friends cried together. Before they left each other, Jonathan blessed David with these beautiful words: "Go in peace; and the Lord will see that we keep the promise we have made to be friends to-gether, and our children after us, forever."

Jonathan said to David, "Go in peace, for we have sworn loyalty to each other in the LORD's name. The LORD is the witness of a bond between us and our children forever." Then David left, and Jonathan returned to the town.

1 Samuel 20:42

David Hides in a Cave

1 Samuel 22:1–5

David found a cave called the Cave of Adullam and he made that cave his home. Soon other men who were in trouble with King Saul or discontented with the way Saul was governing the land, came to David. In the end he was captain over about 400 men.

David was worried about the safety of his father and mother. He went to the king of Moab and asked him to allow his father and mother to stay there. He agreed so they went to live in Moab.

David was warned by a prophet named Gad to move away from his cave in case Saul discovered where he was. So David moved to Judah, and hid in a forest.

So David left Gath and escaped to the cave of Adullam. Soon his brothers and all his other relatives joined him there. Then others began coming – men who were in trouble or in debt or who were just discontented – until David was the captain of about 400 men.

1 Samuel 22:1-2

David Spares Saul's Life

1 Samuel 23–24, 26

Saul drove David out into the hills to hide, but that didn't mean David sided with Saul's enemies. When David heard that the Philistines were attacking the village of Keilah, he and his soldiers went to fight. They defeated the Philistines, killing many of them and taking their cattle.

One day a surprise meeting took place. Jonathan met David in a forest. The two friends renewed their promise of faithfulness to each other. After this they never saw each other again.

David found some caves on the rocky shores of the Dead Sea where his men could live.

Soon Saul discovered where they were. He gathered 3,000 of his best soldiers, and they hunted David and his little group of men. They searched in the mountain strongholds where they were hiding. One night Saul went into a cave. He didn't realize that David and his own best soldiers were hiding in cracks in the rocks and in smaller caves leading off the main one. Some of David's men whispered to him that now was his chance. But David did not wish to kill Saul. Instead, he crept into the main cave and quietly cut off a corner of Saul's robe.

After Saul had left, David ran to the cave's entrance and shouted out to Saul. He asked Saul why he kept on listening to men telling him that David wanted to hurt him. He told Saul that if he had wished to hurt him, he could have killed him there in the cave. Instead, he had only cut off a piece of Saul's robe.

When Saul heard what David said, he was so upset that he cried. Saul said, "Is that your voice, David, my son? You are more righteous than I am. You have behaved well toward me, but I have treated you badly. Today, when you could have killed me, you spared my life. May the Lord reward you greatly for the way you have dealt with me. But please promise me that when you become king, which I am sure will happen, you will not be unkind to my family, and will spare their lives."

David gave his word, and then Saul went home. But it wasn't long before Saul led another army of 3,000 men to hunt for David and his men in the wilderness of Ziph. David watched from his hiding place as their great camp was set up. That night he and Abishai, one of his warriors, slipped into Saul's camp under cover of the dark of night.

They crept through all the sleeping soldiers until they came to the very middle of the camp. Saul was sleeping in the middle of a circle of his carriages and chariots. Abner, his general, and some of the royal bodyguard were with him. The two brave men reached Saul's side. When they reached him, Abishai whispered to David, "Now God has delivered him to you. Just let me pin him to the earth with my spear. It will not need doing a second time!"

But David answered, "No! We have no right to touch the Lord's chosen king. Just grab his spear and the water bottle lying next to him, and we will take them with us."

As quietly as they had come, they crept between the sleeping soldiers and went back to their camp.

Early the next morning David stood on a hilltop a distance from Saul's camp. David shouted across to the king's soldiers and to Abner, his general, "Abner, why don't you do your duty and look after the king? Last night two of the king's enemies were right by his side. If they wished, they could have killed him. See, we have Saul's spear and water bottle."

King Saul recognized David's voice, and he cried out, "Is that you, my son, David?"

David answered, "Why do you hunt me, my lord? What have I done? If others have set you against me, may God deal with them." Saul was sorry once more for what he had done, and he confessed that he had sinned.

*"Here is your spear, O king,"
David replied. "Let one of your
young men come over and get
it. The LORD gives His own
reward for doing good and for
being loyal, and I refused to kill
you even when the LORD placed
you in my power, for you are
the LORD's anointed one. Now
may the LORD value my life,
even as I have valued yours today. May He rescue me from all
my troubles."*

1 Samuel 26:22-24

Saul's Sad End

1 Samuel 27–28, 31

David and his men were allowed to live in the Philistine
city of Ziklag, but the Philistines kept fighting the Israelites.

They finally decided to make
an all-out attack against Israel
and they called for their armies
to come from all parts of the
land.

In the meantime King Saul
pulled his Israelite armies together at Gilboa. But when
he saw how many Philistines
there were, Saul was afraid.

Samuel, who had given him
such encouragement, had died.
Saul himself was old and sick-
ly and he had driven David
away. So who could he turn

to for help? There was no one
who could bring him a message from the Lord.

That's when Saul showed
what he was really like in his
heart. Even though he had
commanded that all mediums
be driven away, he sent out
his servants to find a medium
who could talk to the dead.
They knew of one. She lived
not far from the camp, at a
place called Endor.

That night Saul disguised himself by putting on old clothes.
He took two of his men with
him to visit the medium. She
was afraid, but her mysterious visitor promised, in the
name of the Lord, that no harm
would come to her. She was

satisfied so she asked, "Whose spirit shall I call up?"

Saul answered, "Samuel's."

When Samuel suddenly appeared, the woman screamed in fear. Right then she realized who her visitor was. "Why have you deceived me?" she asked. "You are Saul." Saul told her not to be afraid, and asked her what she had seen. She told him she had seen an old man, who looked like a god. He had a long white beard, and was wearing a mantle. (A mantle was a sleeveless coat worn by prophets and kings.) Saul knew that it was Samuel, and he bowed down.

Suddenly out of the darkness Samuel spoke, "Why have you disturbed my rest?"

Shaking in fear Saul explained, "I'm in great trouble. The Philistines are making war against me. I get no answer to my prayers, and no promise of help from God. That's why I have called you, to ask you what I must do." Samuel answered, "If the Lord has turned from you and become your enemy,

then why are you bothering me? Didn't I warn you about this? Didn't I tell you that because of your disobedience the Lord would take the kingdom away from you, and give it to David? Tomorrow the Philistines will defeat Israel. By this time tomorrow night you and your sons will be with me."

When Saul heard that, he fell to the ground. The woman gave him food to strengthen him. Then he and his men returned to their camp, but all their courage had left them.

Early the next morning the battle began. The Philistines stormed the Israelite camp at Mount Gilboa and quickly defeated them. Before long Saul's three sons, Jonathan, Abinadab and Malkishua, were dead and the Israelite army was running away. Saul himself was hit by several arrows. When he saw how badly the fight was going, he asked his own armor bearer to kill him with his sword. But the armor bearer wouldn't do it so Saul threw himself on his own sword and died.

The reign of Saul came to an

end. It was a reign that began with great promise but, because Saul disobeyed God, it ended in tragedy.

Saul took his own sword and fell on it. When his armor bearer realized that Saul was dead, he fell on his own sword and died beside the king. So Saul, his three sons, his armor bearer, and his troops all died together that same day.

1 Samuel 31:4-6

David Becomes King

2 Samuel 1:1–5:5

David was very sad about the death of Saul and Jonathan. He wrote a lament, a song of sorrow, which he called "The Song of the Bow." Here are a few verses from the song:

Your pride and joy, O Israel,
    lies dead on the hills!
Oh, how the mighty heroes
    have fallen!
How beloved and gracious were
    Saul and Jonathan!
    They were together in life
    and in death.
How I weep for you, my brother
    Jonathan!
    Oh, how much I loved you!
Oh, how the mighty heroes
    have fallen!
Stripped of their weapons, they
    lie dead.

David decided to move away from the Philistine city Ziklag. He and his followers settled in Hebron where the tribe of Judah lived. The leaders there came to David, and anointed him king over their tribe. For seven years and six months David reigned as king.

In the meantime, Abner, who had been the commander of Saul's army, made one of Saul's sons king over all the tribes of Israel in the north. His name was Ishbosheth, which means "man of shame."

Under Abner's influence a very unhappy civil war broke out between David's followers and the followers of Ishbosheth. That meant there were two

129

kingdoms in the land, but David's kingdom grew stronger and stronger while Ishbosheth's kingdom got weaker and weaker. Eventually Ishbosheth's kingdom totally collapsed.

Two of Ishbosheth's men could see the way things were going and they decided to earn themselves David's favor.

One day Ishbosheth was lying on his bed. They crept in and stabbed him to death. Then they went to David to brag about what they had done. But David didn't react as they had expected. He had them put to death at once.

After the death of Ishbosheth, the leaders of all the tribes came to David and asked him to be their king.

David became king of Israel and reigned for 33 years over the whole land.

King David made a covenant before the LORD with all the elders of Israel. And they anointed him king of Israel.

2 Samuel 5:3

The Ark of the Covenant Is Brought Back
2 Samuel 6–7

For a long time the Ark of the Covenant had not been honored in Israel as it should have been. David decided that it should be brought back to Jerusalem, to a new tent, or Tabernacle, that would be set up there.

After this things were peaceful in Israel. David lived quietly in his palace, and God was worshiped in the Tabernacle. But David was not completely happy. It felt wrong to him that he lived in a palace lined with cedar wood while the Ark of the Lord was in a tent. He told Nathan the prophet how he felt and Nathan said that he should go on with his plan to build a better home for the Ark. Nathan said the Lord would bless him.

**David brings the Ark of the Covenant
back to Jerusalem. (2 Samuel 6:1-5)**

That night God gave Nathan a message for David. He said, "From the days that I led My people out of Egypt, the Ark of My presence has stood only in a tent. I have never told My people that they should build Me a house. But in David's heart I have such honor that he wants to do this for Me.

"David, I took you from herding sheep, and made you king over My people, and cut down your enemies before you. Now, because you have obeyed Me, I shall establish your family as the royal family of Israel. When you die, your son will become king, and he will build Me a house. To you and your children, and your family after you, I will give the throne and the kingdom forever."

Through this promise God was telling of the coming of Jesus, who would be a Son, a descendant of David.

"This is what the Lord of Heaven's Armies has declared: I took you from tending sheep in the pasture and selected you to be the leader of My people Israel. I have been with you wherever you have gone, and I have destroyed all your enemies before your eyes. Now I will make your name as famous as anyone who has ever lived on the earth!"

2 Samuel 7:8-9

A Crippled Man at the King's Table

2 Samuel 8–9

When David became king over all the people of Israel, the kings of the small nations near them were afraid. But instead of making peace with David, they raided his towns and villages so he had to go to war against them. David defeated several tribes, so the kings of other nations made treaties with him.

When peace came to the land, David had the chance to think of the promise he had made to his friend Jonathan, the promise to care for Jonathan's children and all his family. He decided to find out if any of Saul's family were still alive. He would show kindness to them for Jonathan's sake.

His men discovered that an old servant of Saul's, Ziba, was still alive and they brought him to David. The king asked him if he knew if any of Saul's family was still alive. Ziba answered that Jonathan's son was still alive and needed help. His name was Mephibosheth, and he was a cripple. When the terrible battle had taken place with the Philistines, in which Saul and Jonathan were killed, Mephibosheth had been a little boy. As the Philistines came pouring into the land, his nurse had tried to run away with him. But as they ran, Mephibosheth fell and hurt his legs. Now he was a cripple because his legs never healed properly.

David sent for Mephibosheth. The young man was afraid and he threw himself down before the king. But David said, "Do not be afraid, I will not harm you. For the sake of your father, Jonathan, who was my dear friend, I will be kind to you. All the land which belonged to your grandfather, Saul, I give to you. You will always have an honored place at the royal table in my palace."

Then David called Ziba and told him what he had given to Mephibosheth. Because Mephibosheth was a cripple, Ziba and his family were to take care of his land. Mephibosheth himself would live in the king's palace and be taken care of for the rest of his life.

This is how King David kept the promise he had made to his good friend Jonathan.

"Don't be afraid!" David said. "I intend to show kindness to you because of my promise to your father, Jonathan. I will give you all the property that once belonged to your grandfather Saul, and you will eat here with me at the king's table!"

2 Samuel 9:7

David Sins

2 Samuel 11:1–12:25

King David was a great general, but as his kingdom grew larger and his power increased, he didn't lead his armies into battle anymore. Instead, he sent Joab to be their leader while he stayed home to take care of the business of the kingdom.

One evening David went to the roof of his palace to enjoy the cool evening breeze. As he walked around, he looked over at a nearby house and saw a beautiful woman taking a bath. As soon as he saw her, David wanted her to be one of his wives. But when he asked his servants about her, they told him that she was Bathsheba, the wife of Uriah the Hittite, a soldier. Uriah was out fighting with Joab's army. David sent for Bathsheba and he loved her.

Then David had a terrible idea. He thought that if Bathsheba was a widow, he could marry her. He thought that he must somehow get rid of her hus-band, Uriah. So David wrote a letter to Joab. He even gave Uriah the letter to take to Joab after he returned from bringing a message to David.

In the letter David told Joab to put Uriah in the front rank, in the most dangerous part of the battle. Then he had to pull the other soldiers away from him so that he would be killed. That is exactly what happened. By the instructions of the letter he wrote, David became Uriah's murderer!

When Bathsheba's time of mourning for Uriah was over, she came to live in the palace, and became David's wife. But what David had done dis-pleased the Lord, so He sent Nathan the prophet to David to explain how He felt about David's sin.

Nathan told the king a story. "There were two men in a cer-tain town, one of them rich, and the other very poor. The rich man had many flocks and herds of cattle. The poor man had nothing except one little ewe lamb that he had bought and cared for. One day a traveler came to visit the rich man, but instead of taking one of his own sheep for their meal, the rich man stole the poor man's only lamb, killed it and used it as a meal for the visitor."

When David heard the story, he was very angry about what the rich man had done. He said, "The person who does such an awful thing deserves to die!"

Nathan pointed to David and said, "You are the man! This is God's word to you, 'I made you king over Israel and I rescued you from the attacks of Saul. I gave you all the riches you could wish for and a palace full of wives. Why did you do this horrible thing? You have murdered Uriah and stolen his wife. Because of this you will be punished. You will suffer, and know trouble and sorrow all your days. The child that Bathsheba bore to you will die.'"

Not long afterward, David and Bathsheba's son got very sick and died.

After their time of mourning had passsed, God gave David and Bathsheba another son. His name was Solomon. God loved Solomon and blessed him. He grew up to be a wise man and a great king.

David confessed to Nathan, "I have sinned against the Lord." Nathan replied, "Yes, but the Lord has forgiven you, and you won't die for this sin. Nevertheless, because you have shown utter contempt for the word of the Lord by doing this, your child will die."

2 Samuel 12:13-14

David's Son Steals the Kingdom

2 Samuel 15:1-23

God told David that he would pay for his sin and it would be painful. It wasn't long before painful things started to happen to David. He had many sons by his other wives. Not all of David's sons were good men. Some of them were really wicked.

One of his sons was named Absalom. He was the most handsome man in all the land and was very proud of his looks. But in his heart Absalom was an evil, selfish and cruel man. He had an evil plan to take the throne away from King David.

He had a very clever scheme, too. Each morning he got up early and waited beside the city gates for anyone who might come to talk to the king about their problems. He treated them like real friends, and because he was the king's son, the men felt very honored.

When they told Absalom their problems, he would say, "It's sad, but there isn't anyone who will listen to you from the king on down. If only I were king, I would see to it that there was justice for all."

Gradually Absalom turned the people of Israel against his father. Before long the whole nation had turned against David. The terrible news reached David and he told his servants to run for their lives. So they ran from Jerusalem – just a little group of servants with David's wives (especially Bathsheba and her young son, Solomon).

When they left the city gates, 600 soldiers under the command of Ittai, one of David's generals, went with them. So David's party crossed the Kidron River and went toward the desert.

David walked up the road to the Mount of Olives, weeping as he went. His head was covered and his feet were bare as a sign of mourning.

2 Samuel 15:30

By the Wayside

2 Samuel 15:32–37; 16:1–14; 17:15–29

When David reached the top of the Mount of Olives, he met Hushai, one of his best friends. Hushai was very upset over what had happened. As a sign of his sorrow he had torn his coat and rubbed ash in his hair. He was ready to go with David into the desert. But instead, David sent him back to Jerusalem to talk with Absalom's men and then pass on what he learned to the priests Zadok and Abiathar.

A little later, the king met Ziba, the servant of Mephibosheth. Mephibosheth was the crippled son of Jonathan who David had been so kind to. Ziba had brought two donkeys for the king, 200 loaves of bread; 100 clusters of raisins and a large amount of fruit for the rest of the men. But he also brought sad news.

Even after all David had done for him, Mephibosheth had gone over to Absalom's side, thinking that Absalom might become king. When he heard this, David gave Ziba all the land that had belonged to Mephibosheth. What David didn't know was that this was all a lie. Ziba was the real traitor, not Mephibosheth. The crippled prince *was* loyal to David.

The priests sent the news of Absalom's plans to David and he set up camp at Mahanaim in the land of Gad. He called his supporters to come there from all parts of the country. When they came, David was ready for any attack Absalom might make against him.

Absalom would ask where in Israel they were from, and they would tell him their tribe. Then Absalom would say, "You've really got a strong case here! It's too bad the king doesn't have anyone to hear it. I wish I were the judge. Then everyone could bring their cases to me for judgment, and I would give them justice!"

2 Samuel 15:2-4

David Returns to the Throne

2 Samuel 17:1–20:22

The people of Gad showed David great kindness. In fact, the very first to help him were people who didn't even belong to the nation of Israel. They brought bedding, dishes and food to help the poor people who ran from their homes. Before long all the people felt much better. Soon warriors were streaming in from all over to fight for the king.

David's army was not as big as Absalom's, but he split it into three divisions, each commanded by one of his trusty generals – Joab, Abishai and Ittai. David planned to go with his armies to fight, but the people wouldn't let him go. They knew that Absalom's men would try to kill David.

So David stayed back in the town of Mahanaim. From there, he directed the great battle. During the battle 20,000 of Absalom's men were killed.

Absalom was proud of his good looks, but he was most proud of his long, beautiful hair. It was that long hair that cost him his life. He was riding a mule when he saw some of David's soldiers and dashed under the overhanging branches of a big oak tree. His hair caught in the branches, and as the mule galloped away he was left hanging from the tree.

One of David's men saw what happened and raced to tell Joab, the general. When Joab heard the news, he asked the soldier why he hadn't killed Absalom. The man said that they had all heard David tell the three generals that no one was to harm his son Absalom.

But Joab said, "I have no time to stand and argue with you." Joab raced to the oak tree and drove three daggers into Absalom's heart while he hung helpless from the branches of the tree. Then Joab had the trumpet blown to call David's men back from chasing Absalom's soldiers. He had Absalom's body put in a pit in the woods and a great heap of stones was piled up over it.

A man was sent to give the news of Absalom's death to David. When he got close to the city, the watchman on the wall saw him and announced his approach. The messenger was a stranger, and he didn't understand how David would feel about Absalom's death. He blurted out the whole story, and David was very upset. "Oh, my son Absalom! My son, my son Absalom!" he cried. "I wish to God I had died instead of you, O Absalom, my son, my son!"

Though Absalom had rebelled against David and treated him badly, the young man was still his son.

When Joab heard how David was mourning and weeping, he had the victory celebrations turned into a time of mourning for the dead prince.

Joab went to David and said, "My king, you are doing a strange thing. Instead of praising the soldiers for what they have done for you, you cry just as if you were on Absalom's side and your own men have done something bad to you. Stand up and behave like a man. Let your soldiers know how happy you are over the victory they have won. If you don't, they will leave you, and the land will be worse off than it was when Absalom lived."

David wisely got up and went to sit at the city gate, which the king was supposed to do. After that he led his men back to the Jordan River where the tribe of Judah was waiting for him. They had a boat ready to take the king and his household across the river. When David crossed the Jordan, the first man to meet him was Shimei, who had made fun of him and thrown stones at him when he was running from Absalom. Now Shimei came to beg his forgiveness. Abishai wanted to kill Shimei, but David said, "Today no one will die in Israel. I am king again, and it is not necessary to kill."

The next man to come to King David was Mephibosheth, the crippled son of Jonathan.

David had been told that Mephibosheth was on Absalom's side, but that was a lie. Mephibosheth's hair was long, his beard ragged, and his clothes dirty and tattered, because he had been mourning ever since Absalom had driven David out.

Mephibosheth explained how his servant, Ziba, had tricked him by promising to go to the desert with Mephibosheth's family. But he was not angry with Ziba now, because the king had come back. David said that Mephibosheth and Ziba would have to divide the land that had belonged to Saul, but Mephibosheth said that Ziba could have it all.

The men of the tribe of Judah took care of him and welcomed him back into his own land. But the rest of the tribes of Israel were angry. "You act like you're the king's only friends," they said. "We also have a right to David."

The men of Judah told them that David belonged to their tribe, and they loved him. This made the rest of the Israelites angry. They listened to a man named Sheba, who convinced them not to listen to David. Pretty soon it looked like there might be another war.

David sent one of his warriors, Amasa, to stop Sheba's lies. But Amasa was so slow and unfaithful to David that Joab went after him and killed him. Then Joab cornered Sheba in the town of Abel. After several days of fighting, someone inside the town killed Sheba. Then Joab's army went back to Jerusalem. Once again there was peace in the land.

The king was overcome with emotion. He went up to the room over the gateway and burst into tears.

2 Samuel 18:33

David Disobeys

2 Samuel 24; 1 Chronicles 21:7-30

Some time after Absalom's death, David had the idea to take a census, which was a count of how many people lived in the land.

Joab warned David that if he did that he would be going against God's command. God didn't want His people to be filled with a feeling that they were powerful and then stop trusting Him.

But David was stubborn and wouldn't listen to Joab. His soldiers carried out his orders to count all the people of all the tribes. Nine months and 20 days later, they reported back to David. They told him that there were 800,000 men in Israel able to be soldiers and 500,000 from the tribe of Judah. The tribes of Levi and Benjamin were not included.

Once the counting was over, David got worried. He confessed that he had broken God's commandment, and begged to be forgiven for dis-

obeying. But it was too late. Joab had warned him and he hadn't listened.

Early one morning God sent the prophet Gad to David. He said, "The Lord offers you three things, choose one of them. Either three years of famine on the land, or for three months your enemies will take over the land, or for three days there will be sickness and terrible disease in the land." David was worried, but he didn't want his enemies to take over the land so he chose the three days of sickness.

When it came, it was terrible. In three days 70,000 people died. The angel of death arrived at the gates of Jerusalem, and came to the threshing floor that belonged to Araunah the Jebusite. David saw the angel of the Lord. He begged God to take away the sickness and spare Jerusalem.

David prayed, "O God, I am the one who sinned, not my

God sends fire to burn David's offering. (1 Chronicles 21:26)

people. Let Your punishment come on me and my family, but spare my people, who have done no wrong themselves."

Then the angel gave God's message to Gad the prophet who told it to David. God told David to build an altar on the threshing floor of Araunah the Jebusite. David immediately obeyed, but Araunah and his sons had also seen the angel and had hidden in fear. As David came in, the angel disappeared, and Araunah and his sons bowed down in front of their king.

David asked Araunah to name the price of the threshing floor so that he could buy it and build the altar. At first Araunah wanted to give the place to him and oxen for burnt offerings and the threshing instruments for firewood, and the wheat for a food offering. But David wouldn't take it without paying. This was his reason, "I must pay the full price, because I will not take somebody else's property for the Lord, nor offer Him burnt offerings without them costing me anything." So David paid 50 pieces of silver for the place and the oxen, and built his altar there.

He arranged the firewood on the altar and on top he placed special peace offerings and burnt offerings. God answered by sending fire from heaven to set the wood and the offerings on fire. From that moment on, the sickness stopped spreading, and David's punishment was over.

When David saw the angel, he said to the Lord, "I am the one who has sinned and done wrong! But these people are as innocent as sheep – what have they done? Let Your anger fall against me and my family."

2 Samuel 24:17

David Makes Solomon King

1 Kings 1:1–2:12

When David was an old man, he was a rich man. His greatest desire was to build a temple to the glory of God. But he was not allowed to build it. God honored him for his desire, but because he had been a man of war, he was not allowed to build the temple. That job would be done by his son Solomon, who would reign after him.

David was close to the end of his life. He was very weak and nearly blind. He spent much of his time in bed. This gave some of his enemies the chance they were looking for. His greatest enemy was once again one of his sons, Adonijah, the brother of Absalom who had rebelled against David before. Adonijah plotted with Joab and with Abiathar, one of the priests, to make him king even before David died.

But Zadok, the other priest, and Nathan the prophet and Shimei and others heard of this evil plan. They went to David's wife Bathsheba, the mother of his son Solomon, and told her what was happening. If she wanted to be sure of her and her son's safety, she had to make sure that David told all the people that Solomon would be the next king.

Bathsheba went to David, and while she was explaining to the old king what Adonijah was planning, the prophet Nathan came in with the same report. David got so stirred up that he raised himself up on his elbow, and said, "As surely as the Lord God lives, it is Solomon my son who is to follow me. This is my wish and the will of the Lord God."

Then he had them send for Zadok the priest and Benaiah the counselor. He told them to get the royal mule, which only the next king was allowed to ride. They had to place Solomon on its back and go to the part of Jerusalem called Gihon. Then Zadok was to anoint Solomon as king.

Then the trumpets were to be blown and in front of all the people they had to shout, "God save the King!" That is exactly what they did.

They caught Adonijah and his followers completely off guard. They were still having a feast when they heard shouting and great excitement. Then they realized what had happened. Solomon had already been proclaimed king. When the followers of Adonijah heard this, they were afraid and slipped away quietly to their homes.

Adonijah himself ran away to the temple and took hold of the horns of the altar so that he would be safe from any of Solomon's men who might want to kill him. Then he sent a message to the new king, asking for pardon. But Solomon was a wise man, "Yes," he said, "I pardon you. But if in the future you make one move against me, I will kill you."

Not long after this David called Solomon to his bedside to give him some advice about ruling the country.

The most important part of that advice is one to be remembered: "Keep the commands of the Lord your God, walk in His ways, and keep His statutes, His commandments, His judgments and His testimonies, as it is written in the Law of Moses. If you do this, you will prosper in all that you do, and wherever you go."

Not long after that David died. He had reigned over the people of Israel for a total of 40 years. The young King Solomon took the throne in his place.

Observe the requirements of the LORD your God, and follow all His ways. Keep the decrees, commands, regulations, and laws written in the Law of Moses so that you will be successful in all you do and wherever you go.

1 Kings 2:3

The Wise Young King

1 Kings 3–4; 2 Chronicles 1

When Solomon became king, his kingdom went from the Euphrates River to the border of Egypt, and from the Mediterranean Sea in the west to the great desert beyond Jordan in the east. There were not only Israelites living in his kingdom, but also people from the desert tribes and much of Syria as well.

To rule over a kingdom like that the young king needed to have great wisdom. He was also very young when he came to the throne so he certainly needed God's help.

A little while after he became king, Solomon went to Gibeon to worship God. He made 1,000 burnt offerings. That night God spoke to Solomon in a dream and told him to ask for some special gift. That's when Solomon showed his real greatness. He remembered how good God had been to his father, David, and how David had lived honestly and righteously with God. Then he thought about how difficult his own job would be to rule such a great kingdom with so many different people in it.

Thinking about all of that, Solomon asked for this gift: "Please give Your servant an understanding heart to judge Your people so I may tell the difference between good and bad. Because who in his own strength can rule such a great nation?"

Solomon did not ask for money, power or fame, but for wisdom. That pleased God very much and He gave Solomon what he had asked for. God said, "Because you have asked for this thing, and not for long life, riches or victory over your enemies, I shall give you what you asked for. But I will also give the things you did not ask for, riches and honor, so that to the end of your days there will be no king to compare with you. And if you keep My commandments as David did, I will give you a long life, too."

It wasn't long until Solomon had the chance to use the wisdom God had given him. Two women came to him with a tiny baby. One woman's baby had died in the night. They were fighting over whose baby had died and who the living baby belonged to. They wanted the king to decide which of them was really the mother of the living baby. The king was very wise. He told one of his guards to cut the living baby in two so that each mother could have half. He knew that the real mother would not let that happen. He was right! The real mother cried out, "O, my king, don't do it, please! Let her have the baby. Please do not kill him."

But the woman who was lying said, "Cut the baby in two, then it won't be mine, but it won't be hers either." Right away the king said, "Give the child to the mother who didn't want the baby killed. She is the real mother." Everyone in the palace was amazed at the clever way Solomon learned which woman was the real mother.

King Solomon wisely chose able leaders to help him govern the country. There were 12 main officers, and under them served many other officers. Part of their work was to keep the army strong. Solomon had 40,000 horses for his chariots and 12,000 charioteers. Besides this there were men who rode on camels and foot soldiers, too.

Great feasts were held in Solomon's palace. He passed on his wisdom to the people who feasted with him. He wrote 3,000 proverbs and 1,005 songs. The fame of Israel was greater than it had ever been before.

You showed great and faithful love to David, my father, and now You have made me king in his place. O LORD God, please continue to keep Your promise to David my father, for You have made me king over a people as numerous as the dust of the earth! Give me the wisdom and knowledge to lead them properly, for who could possibly govern this great people of Yours?

2 Chronicles 1:8-10

Solomon Builds the Temple

1 Kings 5–9; 2 Chronicles 3–8

The time had come for Solomon to build the Temple in Jerusalem. It was going to be built on Mount Moriah.

Hiram, king of Tyre in Syria, had sent gifts of cedar wood to his friend David when David built his palace. Now he sent servants to Solomon to promise his help once more. The new king told them what he planned to do.

Cedar and cypress logs were taken from the mountain to the sea. Here they were put on huge rafts and floated down the coast till they reached Joppa where they would be taken to Jerusalem.

The walls of the Temple were made of stone. All the blocks were finished at the quarry. On Mount Moriah they only had to be fitted together. So there were no sounds of hammering or chiseling heard there. The walls of the Temple were lined with cedar wood, and the beams and roof were made of cedar, too.

The Temple was designed in the same way as the Tabernacle tent in the wilderness, except now it could not be moved because it was an actual building. It was much bigger than the tent was, too. The Tabernacle had only one outer court, but the Temple had two.

One court was for the people of Israel. People from other nations, even though they worshiped the God of Israel, were not allowed in that court. The court behind it was only for the priests. Just inside the gate to the Holy Courtyard stood the great altar for burnt offering. The altar was made of rough stones that had never been shaped with a hammer or a chisel. Nearby was a great basin, or bowl made of bronze.

The basin stood on the backs of 12 bronze oxen. It was used for washing the offerings before they were laid on the altar. There were also 10 other bronze basins for washing.

Solomon stands by the finished Temple. (2 Chronicles 7:11)

Also inside this courtyard stood the Holy Place, the House of the Lord, which was the real Temple. It was made of cedar wood. At the front of it was a tower with special rooms for the high priest and his sons.

Behind this was a long hall where there was a table made of cedar wood covered with gold. It held the 12 loaves of showbread. There was also a golden altar for incense. In different places in the Temple hung 10 golden lamps burning the purest olive oil. Between this Holy Place and the Holy of Holies behind it, there hung a great heavy curtain embroidered with beautiful designs.

Inside the Holy of Holies was the Ark of the Covenant, which still contained the two stone tablets on which Moses had written the Law God gave him on Mount Sinai. At the two ends of the Ark were two beautifully carved cherubims overlaid with gold. Their wings stretched out over the Ark.

Two great carved pillars, which were called Jakin and Boaz, were at the entrance to the Temple. This Temple took seven years to build even though many thousands of people worked on it.

When it was finished, King Solomon held a great festival. A platform was built in front of the altar of burnt offering. Solomon stood on it and prayed for himself and his people.

Not long afterward, he had a dream, and in his dream God brought him a warning, "I heard your prayer, and I have made holy the Temple you have built. It will be My house, and I will live there. As long as you follow in the footsteps of your father David and keep My laws, your throne will continue safely. But if you turn away and stop following Me, then I will go out of the Temple and your enemies will take away all its glory."

And now arise, O LORD God, and enter Your resting place, along with the Ark, the symbol of Your power. May Your priests, O LORD God, be clothed with salvation; may Your loyal servants rejoice in Your goodness.

2 Chronicles 6:41

Solomon's Last Days

1 Kings 10-11

Solomon became famous for his great wealth and power, and for his amazing wisdom. The rulers of all the nearby nations came to see his wealth and ask his advice on things. One ruler was the queen of Sheba, who came to ask many questions to test Solomon's wisdom. She brought camel loads of treasures to make Solomon even richer. And, although she was a rich queen herself, she was amazed to see how grand his palace was.

After she had seen his palace and the city of Jerusalem, she said, "Everything I heard about your riches and wisdom was true. I didn't believe it so I came to see it for myself. Now I know that half was not told to me. Your servants who have the privilege of serving you are happy, and blessed be the Lord your God, who delights in you, and raised you up to be such a great king."

But everything was not good because Solomon wasn't paying attention to God's commandments. He had married many wives. Some of them did not believe in God. Solomon built them places where they could worship their false gods or idols. But the very worst thing was that he began to worship their idols with them. He still went to the Temple to worship God, but he also went with his wives to bow down before idols made of wood and stone.

One day God spoke His final words to Solomon, whom He had blessed so very much, "Because you do not keep My commandments, and have begun worshiping false gods, I am angry with you. I will take the kingdom away and give it to your servant. However, for the sake of My faithful servant, your father, David, I will not take away the kingdom in your lifetime. When I do take it away, I will leave one tribe, the tribe of Judah, in your son's control, for the sake of David, and for the sake of Jerusalem, the place I have chosen."

So God brought an enemy to the king of Israel. He was a young man named Jeroboam of the tribe of Ephraim.

One day Jeroboam was traveling from Jerusalem when he met the prophet Ahijah. Ahijah was wearing a new coat, and he did a strange thing. He tore the coat into 12 pieces. Then he took 10 of the pieces and gave them to Jeroboam, and said, "This is what God says to you, 'I will take the kingdom from the control of Solomon's family and will give 10 of the tribes to you. One tribe will be left with them, for the sake of David, and of Jerusalem. Solomon will remain ruler until the end of his life and then you will take his place. You will be blessed, if you obey My laws and do My will, and your kingdom will be great. Because of their disobe-dience, the family of David will be punished, but not for ever.'"

The news of this spread through the land, and when he heard it, King Solomon was angry. He wanted to kill Jeroboam. But the young man ran away to Egypt and lived there under the protection of Shishak the king.

For 40 years Solomon reigned in Jerusalem, and the kingdom of Israel was at its greatest. But Solomon was preparing the land for a terrible fall, all because he had stopped serving God and Him alone.

The LORD said to him, "Since you have not kept My covenant and have disobeyed My decrees, I will surely tear the kingdom away from you and give it to one of your servants."

1 Kings 11:11

Kingdom Split

1 Kings 12; 2 Chronicles 10

By the time Solomon died, Jerusalem had become a magnificent city, but the people of Israel were tired of the heavy taxes they had to pay to keep up the glory of the royal court. Solomon's son, Rehoboam, who was to be king after his father, was a foolish man.

All the elders of Israel met at Shechem to crown the new king. Jeroboam, the son of Nebat, came all the way from Egypt to be there. Before the crowning, they challenged the young prince, "Your father taxed us until it hurt. Lower our taxes, and we will serve you." Rehoboam sent them away for three days, and when they had gone he asked for help from his trusted advisers.

The old men warned him to be smart and promise to lighten the load of taxation. But Rehoboam was too foolish to listen. When the leaders came back on the third day, this is what he told them, "My father beat you with whips; I shall beat you with scorpions." By that he meant that he would be even harder on them than his father had been. When they heard that, the people said, "Forget about David's family. Why do we need them? Let's go home, Israel. Let David's family take care of themselves!" All that was left for Rehoboam to rule over were the men of his own tribe of Judah.

Solomon had once ruled over a great kingdom. Now Rehoboam ruled over only the tribes of Judah and Benjamin. Jeroboam was made king over all the rest of the land. In Solomon's time Syria, Moab, Ammon and Edom had all been part of Israel. Now they all left, so that there were six kingdoms instead of one.

Rehoboam tried to pull together an army to force the 10 tribes to join with Judah again, but God sent Shemaiah the prophet to forbid him to make war against his own people and Rehoboam obeyed.

So now the tribes of Israel were divided into two kingdoms: 10 tribes of Israel in the north under Jeroboam, with their capital at Shechem, and the kingdom of Judah in the south with its capital at Jerusalem.

To this day the northern tribes of Israel have refused to be ruled by a descendant of David.

The King Who Misled Israel

1 Kings 12:25–13:10

God gave Jeroboam wonderful opportunities when He made him king over the 10 tribes of Israel. But Jeroboam thought he was too important to obey God's commandments.

Jeroboam was afraid that if his people went to Jerusalem to offer sacrifices in the Temple, they might turn away from him and choose Rehoboam as their king. He worked out a plan to keep them from going to Jerusalem. He had two golden calves made. One of them he set up in Bethel and the other in Dan. Then he told the people, "It's too much trouble for you to go to Jerusalem. Here are the gods which brought you out of slavery in Egypt."

Jeroboam even arranged for priests to serve in the temples of the golden calves in Dan and Bethel. However, the men were not really priests, but dishonest people who didn't care about God at all. Then Jeroboam held a great feast at the very same time as the great feast in Jerusalem so the people would stay home instead of traveling to Jerusalem. At his feast Jeroboam decided that he would be the priest. That was against God's law, which said that no king was allowed to do the work of a priest.

When Jeroboam stood in front of the altar, a young man, a prophet from Judah, came to the Temple and spoke in God's name against this disobedi-

The altar bursts open before Jeroboam. (1 Kings 13:4-5)

ent king. He said that a child would be born in David's family, a boy who would be named Josiah, and he would offer up Jeroboam's false priests on the very altars the king had built.

Then he told the people a sign that would prove he was telling the truth. The altar would burst apart and the ashes on it would fall to the ground. Jeroboam exploded in anger. He pointed at the prophet and told his soldiers to catch him. But as he pointed, his hand withered and he couldn't lower his arm again. Just then, the altar burst open as the prophet had said it would and the ashes spilled onto the ground. Jeroboam begged the prophet to pray for

him. When the prophet did, the king's hand was made well again. Jeroboam was so pleased that he asked the prophet to come and eat with him in his palace. But the prophet refused. God had commanded that he not eat or drink until he was home again. Even if Jeroboam gave him half his riches, he could not stay. God also told him to travel home by a different road.

The king cried out to the man of God, "Please ask the LORD your God to restore my hand again!" So the man of God prayed to the LORD, and the king's hand was restored.

1 Kings 13:6

The Prophet Is Killed by a Lion
1 Kings 13:11–34; 14:20; 15:25–31

In that time there was an old prophet who lived in Bethel. His sons told him what had happened at the altar after the young prophet had spoken there. Immediately the old prophet rode after the young prophet. He found him sit-

ting under an oak tree by the road. The old prophet invited the younger man to come home and eat with him, but the young man told him that God had commanded him to go straight home. Then the old prophet lied and said that an angel had told him that he had to bring the prophet back to eat with him. So the young man went home with him to Bethel, and ate dinner. But the whole time he was unhappy. As they sat at the table, the Lord spoke to him through the old prophet.

"Since you have disobeyed Me, you will die. But your body will not be buried in the grave with the bodies of your fathers," the Lord told him.

Immediately after eating, the young prophet saddled a donkey and started home. On the way a lion attacked him and killed him. But then a strange thing happened. The lion did not tear up his body; it didn't attack the donkey either. The donkey and the lion stood looking at the dead body of the young prophet. People passing by were amazed at what they saw, and they went to the old prophet in Bethel and told him. The old man went out with his donkey and brought back the young man's body, and buried it in his own family grave. He felt so sad that his lies had caused this to happen that he asked that one day his bones should be laid beside those of the young prophet. He also told the people that what the prophet had foretold would certainly happen. In the time God chose, His servant Josiah, who was not even born yet, would come and destroy the false place of worship Jeroboam had built in Bethel and all the other idols he had built.

Jeroboam reigned for 22 years altogether. Then his son Nadab became king in his place. But Nadab was just as evil as his father. He reigned for only two years, and then he was murdered by one of his own servants, Baasha. Baasha saw to it that every remaining member of Jeroboam's family was killed.

The prophet said to his sons, "When I die, bury me in the grave where the man of God is buried. Lay my bones beside his bones. For the message the LORD told him to proclaim against the altar in Bethel and against the pagan shrines in the towns of Samaria will certainly come true."

1 Kings 13:31-32

Elijah, the Prophet of God

1 Kings 16:29–17:24

There were many evil kings after Jeroboam, kings who worshiped idols instead of God and led the people away from Him.

Ahab was the worst king of them all. He married a horrible woman named Jezebel, a heathen from the kingdom of Sidon. She brought with her idols of Baal and Ashtaroth, and taught the people of Israel to worship them. She hated those who loved the God of heaven and earth.

But there was also one great prophet. His name was Elijah. He went to King Ahab and gave him a message from God: "As the Lord God lives, there will be neither dew nor rain in this land until I give the word." So a drought settled on the land. There was no water and food didn't grow in the fields.

God told Elijah to go and hide himself beside the brook Kerith, which flowed into the Jordan River. He could drink water from the brook. Every morning and every evening God would send ravens to bring him bread and meat to eat.

After a while, because of the drought in the land, even the brook Kerith dried up. Elijah needed a new place to live. God sent him to a place called Zarephath. This was in the land of Sidon, the place the evil queen Jezebel had come from. God told Elijah that He had told a widow there to help His servant!

At the gate of Zarephath, Elijah saw a widow picking up sticks to make a fire. He said to her, "Please get me a drink of water." She went to get the water and he called out, "Please bring me a little piece of bread as well."

She replied, "Sorry, I do not have a single piece of bread, only a handful of grain in a barrel and a little oil in a jug."

Then Elijah said, "Bake me a little loaf of bread first, and after that bake some for yourself, because this is what God says to you, 'The grain barrel will not become empty and the jug of oil will not run out until I send rain again.'"

The widow did exactly as Elijah said and God kept His promise. Elijah and the widow and her son had all the food they needed until the rains came again.

One day the widow's son suddenly got sick and died. Elijah took the boy's body and went to his own room and laid the body on his bed. Then three times he stretched out over the body and prayed, "O Lord, You have brought great sorrow to this widow by taking away the life of her son. Please give him life again!"

God heard the prophet's prayer, and the boy came back to life again. Then Elijah took him to his mother. When she saw him alive again, she knew that Elijah was a man who walked very closely with God. She said to Elijah, "Now I know without any doubt that you are a man of God and that the word of God you speak is truth."

Elijah said to her, "Don't be afraid! Go ahead and do just what you've said, but make a little bread for me first. Then use what's left to prepare a meal for yourself and your son. For this is what the Lord, the God of Israel, says: There will always be flour and olive oil left in your containers until the time when the Lord sends rain and the crops grow again!"

1 Kings 17:13-14

Fire and Rain

1 Kings 18

The drought continued in Israel for three long years before God sent Elijah to King Ahab to tell him that rain was coming.

When Ahab saw Elijah, he angrily shouted, "Are you the one that has brought trouble to Israel?"

Elijah firmly answered Ahab, "I am not responsible for Israel's troubles. They are because you and your household turned away from God and began worshiping false gods." Then Elijah told him to call all 450 priests of Baal, which the evil Queen Jezebel had brought to the land, to meet him on Mount Carmel. The people of Israel came out to see what was going to happen.

When all the people had gathered on the slopes of Mount Carmel, Elijah cried out to them, "How long will you waver between two opinions? If the Lord is God, follow Him, but if it is Baal, then follow him." But the people were silent.

Elijah called for two bulls to be brought, one for him to offer up to God, and one for the false prophets to offer up to Baal. The offering would make the rain come. Elijah told the false prophets that they had to place the wood in position and then lay the meat of the bull on top. He would do the same. The wood was not to be set alight. They would pray and the god that answered by sending fire would be the true God.

The men of Baal did what Elijah said and prayed from early morning until noon. They jumped up and down, and shouted in front of the altar, but nothing happened.

Then Elijah said it was his turn. First he rebuilt the altar to God, which the Baal priests had broken down. He made it of 12 large stones, one for each of the tribes of Israel. He dug a deep trench around the altar. He laid the firewood on top of the altar, and then the pieces of the meat on top of that. Then he or-

God sends fire to burn up Elijah's offering. (1 Kings 18:36-38)

dered that 12 barrels of water be poured over everything on the altar.

At about three o'clock in the afternoon the work was done. Elijah began to pray: "Lord," he cried, "let it be known to-day that You are God in Israel, and that I am Your servant, and that I have done all these things in obedience to You. Hear my prayer, O Lord God, hear that these people may know that You are the Lord God, and may turn back to You."

As he finished, fire came down out of a clear sky and burned up the sacrifice and the water and even the stones that the altar was made of. When the people saw this, they threw themselves down on their faces and cried out, "The Lord, He is God! The Lord, He is God!"

"Kill the prophets of Baal," Elijah told the people, "don't let even one of them escape." Elijah told Ahab, "Go, eat and drink, because I hear the sound of great rains." Ahab left and Elijah went to the top of Mount Carmel and knelt down to pray. He told his servant, "Go, look out over the sea, and see if there is a cloud." The servant looked, and saw nothing. Elijah told him to go seven times to look. The last time he came back and said, "I see a cloud as big as a man's hand, rising from the sea."

Then Elijah said, "Hurry to Ahab and tell him to get his chariot and go down the mountain as fast as he can before the rain stops him." Even while he was speaking the clouds gathered above, black and heavy, and rain began to fall. Ahab drove his chariot as fast as he could to Jezreel. But the Spirit of the Lord was upon Elijah so that he held up his coat and ran, reaching the gates of Jezreel before Ahab.

In one day the power of Baal was broken in Israel, and the great drought came to an end.

Elijah stood in front of them and said, "How much longer will you waver, hobbling between two opinions? If the LORD is God, follow Him! But if Baal is God, then follow him!" But the people were completely silent.

1 Kings 18:21

God's Voice

1 Kings 19

When King Ahab told Queen Jezebel all that had happened, she was very angry. The queen sent a message to Elijah, saying, "I will see to it that you are as dead as my priests before another day is over." When Elijah heard that he did not stop to think how God had protected him in the past, but ran into the wilderness. He didn't stop until he was a whole day's journey away. Finally he sat down under a broom tree and fell asleep.

While he was sleeping, an amazing thing happened to Elijah. An angel touched him, and said, "Get up and eat." Then he saw a loaf of bread and a jug of water. Elijah ate and drank, and then lay down again. The angel woke him up again and there was more food and drink for him. This time the angel said, "Wake up and eat again, because there is a long journey ahead of you."

Elijah did as the angel said. The food and water was enough for a journey of 40 days and 40 nights to Mount Sinai, the mountain of God. This was where Moses saw the burning bush and where God gave Moses the Ten Commandments. Elijah found a cave on the mountain to live in. Then God asked him a question, "Elijah, why are you here?"

"O, Lord," Elijah answered, "I have loved You, and worked as hard as I could for You. The children of Israel have broken their promise to You, torn down Your altars and killed Your prophets. Now I am the only one left and they want to take away my life, too."

God said, "Go out and stand on the mountain, in the presence of the Lord your God."

While Elijah stood there, a fierce wind came up and pulled loose the rocks on the mountainside. But the Lord was not in that wind. Then there was an earthquake, but the Lord was not in the earthquake. After that a fire swept across the face of the mountain, but the Lord was not in that either. Then everything was quiet and Elijah heard a still, small voice. When he heard that voice, he hid his face in his coat and the Lord asked him, "What are you doing here, Elijah?"

Once more he answered, "Lord, I have served You with passion. The people of Israel have broken their covenant with You, torn down Your altars and killed Your prophets. I am the only one left, and now they want to kill me, too."

God said to him: "Go back the way you came. Find a man named Elisha and anoint him to become the next prophet." Elijah found Elisha, just as the Lord had said. Elijah went to him and without saying a word, he threw his own coat over Elisha's shoulders. Elisha knew that meant that Elijah had chosen him to be his replacement. He had to leave all his riches and his comfortable home, and go with the old prophet.

As Elijah stood there, the LORD passed by, and a mighty windstorm hit the mountain ... but the LORD was not in the wind. After the wind there was an earthquake, but the LORD was not in the earthquake. And after the earthquake there was a fire, but the LORD was not in the fire. And after the fire there was the sound of a gentle whisper. When Elijah heard it, he wrapped his face in his cloak and went out and stood at the entrance of the cave.

1 Kings 19:11-13

Naboth's Vineyard

1 Kings 21

King Ahab had his palace in Samaria, but he also had another palace in Jezreel. A man named Naboth owned a very fruitful vineyard near that palace. Ahab wanted Naboth's ground to make a vegetable garden for his palace. He offered to buy it, but Naboth wouldn't sell it.

When Naboth refused to sell his land, Ahab started pouting. He threw himself down on his bed and refused to eat.

His wife, the evil Queen Jezebel, asked him what was wrong. The pouty king told her that he wanted to buy Naboth's vineyard but Naboth wouldn't let him have it. Then Jezebel said, "You are the King of Israel! Get up, eat and be happy. I'll make sure you get Naboth's vineyard!"

Then Jezebel arranged to have Naboth accused of some crime he didn't really commit and then he was murdered. After that she told Ahab, "Get up and take over the vineyard that Naboth wouldn't give you, because Naboth is dead now."

In the meantime God gave Elijah a message for Ahab. Elijah gave Ahab God's message, which ended with these terrible words, "The family of Jeroboam was wiped out, and the family of Baasha, so also will the family of Ahab be wiped out. All because you have turned away from the Lord God."

Ahab was sad at this news and he was sorry for his sin. Then God spoke to Elijah and said, "Ahab has humbled himself before Me so I will not bring punishment on his family while he lives. But in his son's lifetime the punishment will come."

The LORD said: "Do you see how Ahab has humbled himself before Me? Because he has done this, I will not do what I promised during his lifetime. It will happen to his sons; I will destroy his dynasty."

1 Kings 21:28-29

Riding in a Chariot of Fire

2 Kings 1:1–2:15

After Ahab died, his son Ahaziah became king of Israel. But he only reigned for two years. One day he fell from a second-story window in his palace and was badly hurt. He sent messengers to the temple of the idol Baalzebub to ask the false god if he would get better.

But before the messengers could get to the temple, the angel of the Lord sent Elijah to meet those messengers. He asked them, "Shouldn't you go to the God of Israel instead of this heathen idol? Go back to Ahaziah and tell him that he will never get up from his bed. He will die."

When the messengers returned to the king, he asked them why they had come back so soon. They told him of their meeting with a strange prophet. They didn't know who he was, but described him as a hairy man with a belt of leather around his hips. Ahaziah said, "That was Elijah."

Ahaziah was angry at Elijah for saying what he did. He sent an officer with 50 soldiers to catch Elijah and throw him in prison. But when they found Elijah, he called down fire from heaven and they were all burned up. So the king sent another 50 men to get Elijah and the same thing happened.

The third time Ahaziah sent men, the captain in charge got down on his knees in front of Elijah, and begged him to spare his life and the lives of his men. This time Elijah went with them to see the king. He gave the same message to the king as he had first given to Ahaziah's messengers. Ahaziah died soon afterward.

Now Elijah's work was done and he knew that God would take him to heaven soon. One day Elijah was walking to Gilgal with his follower Elisha. He asked Elisha to wait for him at Gilgal while he went on to Bethel, where the Lord had sent him. However, Elisha felt that something unusual was going to happen so he refused to stay at Gilgal.

The two of them went on together to Bethel where they met a group of young men who were called the sons of the prophets. They were being taught by the prophets and when they were older, some of them would become prophets, too. The men ran to Elisha and said, "Don't you know that God is going to take your master away from you today?" Elisha answered, "Yes, I know. Be quiet now."

Then Elijah asked Elisha to stay at Bethel while he went on to Jericho. But again Elisha wouldn't stay behind, so they went on together until they came to Jericho. There a different group of the sons of the prophets came to Elisha and asked him the same question as the others had done at Bethel. Elisha gave the same answer.

At Jericho, Elijah told Elisha that the Lord wanted him to go to the Jordan River. Elijah asked Elisha to stay behind at Jericho. Once more Elisha refused, so the two of them went down to the river, followed by 50 of the sons of the prophets. There Elijah took off his robe, wrapped it in a long bundle and hit the waters of the river with it. The waters parted so that Elijah and Elisha could walk through to the other side on dry ground.

When they reached the shore Elijah said, "Elisha, tell me what I must do for you, before I am taken away."

Elisha answered, "I beg you, let a double portion of your spirit rest on me."

"You have asked a hard thing," Elijah said. "However, if you see me when I am taken away, you will be given what you have asked for. Otherwise you will not receive it."

The two of them walked on together for a little ways. Suddenly a chariot of fire and horsemen of fire appeared from heaven. Elijah was taken up in a whirlwind into heaven. Elisha saw what was happening and cried out, "My father, my father, the chariot of Israel and the horsemen of Israel!" And then Elijah vanished from his sight.

Elisha picked up Elijah's robe that had fallen from his shoulders and turned back to the Jordan River. He rolled it up and hit the waters of the river just as Elijah had done earlier. Once again the waters parted and he was able to walk through to the other side.

When the sons of the prophets saw Elisha come through the river like that, they cried out that the spirit of Elijah now rested on him. They ran to meet him, and bowed down in front of him.

Suddenly a chariot of fire appeared, drawn by horses of fire. It drove between the two men, separating them, and Elijah was carried by a whirlwind into heaven. Elisha saw it and cried out, "My father! My father! I see the chariots and charioteers of Israel!" And as they disappeared from sight, Elisha tore his clothes in distress.

2 Kings 2:11-12

Never-Ending Oil

2 Kings 4:1–7

God gave Elisha the power to do many wonderful things. Once one of the prophets died. His widow was left with two sons, no money and no food to give them. She came to Elisha and asked him to help her. She owed money to a man and since she couldn't pay him, he was going to take her two sons away to be his slaves. Elisha asked her what she had in her house. She told him there was nothing except a jar of olive oil. Elisha said, "Go to your neighbors and borrow as many empty jugs and jars as they can give you."

When she had gathered the jars, Elisha told her to take her two sons into the house and close the door behind them. Then she should pour oil from her jar into all the ones her neighbors had given her and put all

168

The oil doesn't run out as the widow fills each jar. (2 Kings 4:5-6)

the full ones to one side. She started pouring oil from her jar and it kept coming and coming! When all the borrowed jars were full, the oil stopped coming out of the jar.

"Now sell this oil and pay the man what you owe him," Elisha told her.

The widow did as she was told. Her sons kept bringing jars to her, and she filled one after another. Soon every container was full to the brim! "Bring me another jar," she said to one of her sons. "There aren't any more!" he told her. And then the olive oil stopped flowing.

2 Kings 4:5-6

Second Chance Jonah

Jonah 1–4

There was a prophet in Israel named Jonah. God spoke to him and said, "Go to the city of Nineveh and tell them to stop their wickedness."

But Jonah was afraid, because the people of Nineveh were the enemies of the Israelites. They would rather kill him than listen to him. He didn't want God to save the people of that evil city. So he ran away to the seaport town of Joppa to get on a ship that would take him to Tarshish, far from Nineveh. He boarded the ship and it set sail.

God knew what Jonah was doing. Once the ship was far out at sea, God sent a great storm with winds that blew so strong that it seemed as though the ship would sink. The sailors threw everything they could overboard to try to make the ship lighter. But nothing helped. Then each one cried out to his god for help, but the waves still tossed the ship about. All this time Jonah was asleep below deck. The captain woke him up and said, "How can you sleep at a time like this? Wake up and call on your God. Perhaps He can save us."

But the storm grew worse and worse until the sailors said to one another, "There must be

A big fish swallows Jonah. (Jonah 1:17)

someone on board who has caused this trouble for us. Let's draw lots to find out who it is." And when they did, they found out that it was Jonah.

He told them he was trying to escape from God. "What should we do with you?" they cried out. "While you are on this ship we are all in danger of dying."

Jonah told them to throw him into the sea. Then the sea would become calm and they would be safe. At first they wouldn't because they didn't want to let Jonah drown. But the sea didn't become calm, and, try as they might, they could not get the ship any closer to land. Finally they threw Jonah into the sea, and at once the waves calmed down and the wind stopped.

God sent a great fish to swallow Jonah. For three days and three nights Jonah was in the stomach of that fish. Every day he prayed, begging God to save him, and to forgive him for his sin of trying to run away. On the third day the fish spat him out onto a beach.

God spoke to Jonah again. He told him to go to Nineveh and preach the words God would give him. This time Jonah went.

Nineveh was a very large city. It took three days to walk around its walls. Many people lived there. When Jonah arrived, he shouted, "Another 40 days, and Nineveh will be destroyed." People gathered around to listen to him. Jonah told them about God's anger over the wickedness of their city. When they heard, the people were sorry for what they had done. Even the king believed, and led the people in prayer asking God to forgive them. They fasted, and cried over their sins. Not even the cattle were allowed to eat during the days of fasting. When God saw this, He forgave them.

When the 40 days Jonah had spoken about passed, the city was not destroyed.

Jonah was angry about this and he said, "O, Lord, isn't this what I said would happen from the beginning? This is why I ran away to Tarshish, because I knew that my work would be for nothing, and that in Your kindness and mercy You would forgive these people and spare their lives. Now take away my life. It would be better for me to die than to go on living."

But God was not angry. All He said to Jonah was, "Is it sensible for you to get upset about this?"

Jonah left Nineveh and a little way outside the city he made himself a shelter and sat in its shade to see what would happen to the city. While he sat there, God made a wild plant grow up over the shelter to make it cool. Jonah was very pleased. However, the next day God made a worm eat the stem of the plant until it withered and died. Then a hot wind began to blow. The sun beat down on Jonah's head until he was very angry and wished he were dead.

God asked Jonah, "Is it right for you to be angry about the plant dying?"

Jonah said, "Yes, it is right for me to be angry!"

But God said, "You are upset about the death of the plant, which really was nothing. You had nothing to do with its growth; it came up in a night and died in a night. Yet you do not want Me to spare the great city of Nineveh. There are more than 120,000 people in it and many cattle. Jonah, think this over again, will you?"

God's specially chosen people were the nations of Israel and Judah, but He showed love to other nations, too.

Then Jonah prayed to the LORD his God from inside the fish. He said, "I cried out to the LORD in my great trouble, and He answered me."

Jonah 2:1

The Victory of Jehoshaphat

2 Chronicles 17–20

After Asa, his son Jehoshaphat became king. Jehoshaphat was the strongest and wisest of all the kings the country had. He loved and served God. He watched carefully over the ways of his people. He sent his officials to all the cities to teach the people the law.

Jehoshaphat appointed judges in all the cities of Judah to see that the laws were properly kept. He warned those judges that they were not there to serve man, but to serve God. They had to be careful to never take bribes or give wrong judgments. God would punish them for these things.

Some time afterward, news reached Jehoshaphat that some of the nations around them were gathering armies to attack Judah. It was a rich country now, and they felt there were great riches to be taken. The Moabites, the Ammonites and other smaller nations had made an agreement with the Syrians. They planned to at-tack Jehoshaphat and his people. Jehoshaphat knew that his army was too small to fight against these big armies, but he knew where to turn for help. He proclaimed a day of fasting throughout the land. He called all his soldiers together in front of the Temple in Jerusalem. He prayed that God would help them in the great battles that would take place soon.

Then God spoke through a prophet called Jahaziel, one of the Levites; "Do not be afraid or worried because of these great armies. The battle is not yours, but God's. Go out to meet them tomorrow. Do not be afraid. You will not have to fight at all in this battle. The Lord will see to the victory." When they heard that, all the people bowed to the ground and worshiped God. Early the next morning the army moved out to meet the enemy. At the head of the column, singers and musicians from among the Levites marched to praise God as the army moved along. But when

**Jehoshaphat and all the people bow down
and worship God. (2 Chronicles 20:18)**

they reached the enemy camp, what a surprise they had. There was a terrible battle raging in the camp. The Ammonites and the Moabites were fighting against the rest. Some of the enemy soldiers were already running into the desert. There was no army for the men of Judah to fight. Without a single minute of fighting, they were able to take great piles of gold and silver and jewelry back to Jerusalem. They had so much that it took them three whole days to collect it all.

On the fourth day they gathered in a valley nearby to praise God for what He had done.

Ever since then the place has been called the valley of Beracah, which means "blessing."

After that wonderful victory, none of the nations around Judah dared to attack Jehoshaphat. There was peace in the land until the end of his reign, and the people praised and served God.

The king appointed singers to walk ahead of the army, singing to the LORD and praising Him for His holy splendor. This is what they sang: "Give thanks to the LORD; His faithful love endures forever!"

2 Chronicles 20:21

A Little Boy Becomes King

2 Chronicles 21–24

When Jehoshaphat died, his son Jehoram became the next king. Jehoram was married to the daughter of Ahab and Jezebel. She taught him to be a wicked man. As soon as he became king, he murdered all his brothers and many of the other princes of Judah. He reigned for eight years, and they were

very bad years. Elijah, the prophet who lived in Israel at that time, sent him a letter warning him of what would happen if he did not turn back to God. He told him that God would send an awful disease, which would strike all his family. Jehoram would have terrible pain and would die from it.

Then the Philistines and the Arabians in the south began to raid deep into the land of Judah. They even reached Jerusalem and they broke into the palace, stole the King's treasures, and took all his sons except Ahaziah.

The king was away at the time, but before long he got sick with the disease Elijah had warned him about. He died in terrible pain. His son Ahaziah was the next king. Ahaziah reigned for one year only. He went to visit his uncle Joram, the king of Israel, who had been wounded in a battle against the Syrians. They were both murdered at Jezreel by Jehu.

When his mother, Athaliah, heard the news of this, she ordered that all the other men in the royal family be killed. But the youngest son of Ahaziah, Joash, was saved by his aunt, who hid him in his nurse's bedroom. Later she secretly took him to the Temple where they hid him.

Athaliah made herself queen of Judah. Joash was hidden in the Temple until the seventh year of her reign. The queen stopped all the services in the Temple and built a temple for her idol, Baal. She made the people of Judah worship there. But while this was all happening, Jehoiada, the high priest, was planning to make Joash king of Judah. He arranged a special gathering of the leaders of the people in the Temple. He brought out the little boy, Joash, who was only seven years old. He anointed Joash and crowned him king. Soldiers stood around the Temple to protect the young king. When he stood there in front of them, the people shouted, "God save the king!"

When Athaliah the queen heard all this shouting, she came out of her palace to see what was happening. When she saw the young king standing there, she cried out, "Treason, treason!" Then Jehoiada called to the captains of the soldiers to take her and kill her because of her evil deeds. They took her away from the Temple to kill her so that the blood would not be shed in the house of the Lord. When they heard what had happened, the people of Jerusalem rejoiced,

**Athaliah orders the soldiers to kill all
the men in the royal family. (2 Chronicles 22:10)**

but they still needed a warning from Jehoiada. He warned Joash and all the people to be the Lord's people, and to serve Him. They were not to follow the false gods that Athaliah had served.

Then Jehoiada made a covenant between himself and the king and the people that they would be the LORD's people.

2 Chronicles 23:16

Three Kings of Judah

2 Chronicles 25–28

Amaziah was king of Judah after Joash. At first he served God, but in his heart there was always a longing to do what was wrong. In the reign of King Jehoram, the Edomites had rebelled against Judah. Now Amaziah decided that they had to be conquered again.

Amaziah led his men against the Edomites. With God's help Judah won a great victory against them. But Amaziah was very cruel and he murdered thousands of the people that were captured. He also showed what a faithless person he was by taking the idols of wood and stone that the Edomites had worshiped. He made them his own gods and the gods of his people. God was angry and sent a prophet to speak to Amaziah. "Why are you worshiping these gods which were not able to save the Edomites from defeat?" he asked.

The king flew into a rage and said, "Who asked you to give the king advice? Be silent, or you will be put to death."

The prophet answered, "I know that God will destroy you, because you have done this and will not listen to my advice."

Amaziah did not have to wait long for his punishment. The army from Israel had already attacked some of the towns of Judah and done a lot of damage. But now Amaziah listened to bad advisers and sent a challenge of war to Jehoash, king of Israel. Amaziah kept challenging him until the two armies met at Beth-shemesh. The Israelites soundly defeated the army of Judah and captured Amaziah himself. They broke down the walls of Jerusalem and took away all the treasures of the Temple and the king's palace. After this terrible defeat, Amaziah lived for another 15 years. He was such a hated man that in the end his own people drove him out of Jerusalem and killed him.

After Amaziah came his son Uzziah who was only 16 years old when he began to reign. Uzziah ruled for 52 years. For most of his reign he served God faithfully and did what was right in God's sight.

When Uzziah became king the land was very poor, but he began to build it up again. First of all he built up the seaport town of Eloth on the Red Sea to be a trading place. He attacked the Philistines and broke down the walls of several of their fortress towns to make the south of Judah safe from their attacks. Then he defeated the Arabians as well. When they saw how many victories he was winning, the Ammonites brought gifts to him and asked for peace. He repaired the walls of Jerusalem, which the Israelites had broken down during the reign of his father. He built strong, new watchtowers on the walls so that their enemies could not break into the city. Other watchtowers were built across the land, too, so that the watchmen could see from a long way off if any enemies were approaching.

Under the control of King Uzziah, Judah became so rich and so strong that people in all surrounding lands spoke of his greatness. But then Uzziah began to think too much of himself and to ignore God's commandments. He wanted to not only be king, but priest as well, and that was against God's Law.

One day he forced his way into the Temple to burn incense on the special altar of incense. Azariah, the high priest, went in after him with 80 of the other priests to try to stop him. Azariah said, "It is only the priests whom God has chosen who are allowed to burn incense here or to go into the holy place." That made Uzziah angry and he lifted up the censer to burn incense. But as he did it, a great white blotch came on the skin of his forehead. It was leprosy! From then on, Uzziah was not allowed to have anything to do with other people, because they might catch the disease. His son Jotham became king in his place. Jotham reigned for 16 years. He obeyed and served God faithfully all the time.

After Jotham came Ahaz. He was an idol worshiper, just like the kings of Israel. What a terrible time this was for the people of Judah! First the Syrians attacked them, took many of them as prisoners, and stole their possessions. Then Pekah, king of Israel, made war against them. After killing 120,000 men in one day's fighting, he took 200,000 women and children as prisoners to Samaria.

One of God's prophets reasoned with the Israelites there, "Judah was defeated in battle because God is angry with them for their sins. But you cannot make slaves of your own brothers, the people of Judah. You have also sinned against God. Listen to God's word and let our brothers go back to their own land."

The state of the country was worse than ever before. The Edomites had attacked them again. The Philistines had captured many towns in the south. It looked as though the whole country would be destroyed.

Then Ahaz asked the king of Assyria for help. The Assyrians came, but they didn't help. They took over the whole country. They stole all the treasures that were left and made Ahaz promise to pay great taxes every year to the king of Assyria.

Uzziah sought God during the days of Zechariah, who taught him to fear God. And as long as the king sought guidance from the LORD, God gave him success.
2 Chronicles 26:5

181

God Calls a Great Prophet

Isaiah 6

In the time of the three kings, Uzziah, Jotham and Ahaz, a young man lived in Jerusalem named Isaiah. God used that young man to bring His message to the people of Judah.

In the year that King Uzziah died, Isaiah was still a young man. One day when Isaiah was in the Temple praying, he had a vision.

It was as if he saw God sitting on a great throne, and around Him were angels. Before the throne stood angels called seraphims, each with six wings, two to cover their faces, and two to cover their feet, and two for flying. They cried out, saying, "Holy, holy, holy, is the Lord of hosts: the whole earth is full of His glory."

As they cried out, it seemed as though the whole Temple shook. It was filled with smoke. Isaiah was terrified, and he cried, "Woe is me, I am lost; because I am a man of unclean lips, and I live among a people of unclean lips; for my eyes have seen the King, the Lord of hosts." Then one of the seraphim flew toward Isaiah carrying the tongs that were used at the altar in the Temple. In them was a burning coal which he had also taken from the altar. He touched Isaiah's lips with the coal, saying, "This coal from God's altar has touched your lips, and now your sin is taken away and you are pure."

Then Isaiah heard the Lord Himself say, "Whom shall I send, and who will go for us?" Isaiah answered, "Here am I; send me."

Then God said, "Go and tell this people My message. They will listen, but never understand. They will look, but never see. Their ears will be blocked and their eyes shut. They will not see, or hear, or understand, and they will not turn to Me or be healed from their wrongs."

"For how long will this be, O Lord?" Isaiah asked. The Lord

said, "Until all the cities are destroyed and there are no people living in them anymore, and until the whole land is ruined. The people will be taken far away, but a tenth will be kept and brought back. Then the land will grow up again. "

Then I heard the Lord asking, "Whom should I send as a messenger to this people? Who will go for us?" I said, "Here I am. Send me."

Isaiah 6:8

Hezekiah the Godly

2 Kings 18–19; 2 Chronicles 29–32; Isaiah 36–37

When Ahaz died, his son Hezekiah became king of Judah. He was very different from his father. He tried to keep God's commandments, and to live as his ancestor David had lived. He started by making right all the wrongs Ahaz had done. He had all the heathen places of worship broken down and all the idols destroyed. In the very first month of his reign he had the Temple doors opened and the whole building repaired. Then he sent in the Levites to clean every part of the Temple. It took them 16 days to finish the work. When this was done, the sacrifices and services began again just as the Law of the Lord said they should be carried out.

For many years the Passover Feast had not been observed as the Lord had commanded. Hezekiah said this was the time to begin to keep the feast again. He felt that Israel and Judah should keep it together, so he sent messengers to the northern kingdom to invite the people to Jerusalem. But many of the Israelites were serving the idols of the Assyrians, and they only laughed at the messengers from Judah. But some of the people from Asher, Manasseh and Zebulun went to the feast in Jerusalem.

When Hezekiah became king, Judah, Israel and Syria were all in the hands of the Assyrians. Each of these nations had its own king, but all three kings were servants of the Assyrian king, and had to pay very heavy taxes to him every year. In the 14th year of his reign, Hezekiah felt that it was time for Judah to be free again. He didn't pay taxes to the Assyrian king. Instead he strengthened the wall of Jerusalem and prepared his soldiers to defend their country against any Assyrian attack.

When this happened, Sennacherib, king of Assyria, gathered great armies. Before very long many of the cities of Judah on the west side of the country had been captured. The Assyrians marched toward Jerusalem itself. Hezekiah saw that he had made a mistake. His country was not strong enough to fight against the Assyrians.

Hezekiah sent messengers to the headquarters of the king of Assyria to ask for peace. He promised to pay whatever tax the Assyrians wanted. The tax was so heavy that Hezekiah had to have the gold cut off the doors and the pillars of the Temple. This was the gold that Hezekiah had put on the Temple when he first became king.

Sennacherib, the Assyrian king, was not even satisfied then. He sent three of his princes with a powerful army to attack Jerusalem. When they came near to the city, the princes went ahead with a letter to Hezekiah. They also shouted insults to the soldiers defending the walls of Jerusalem.

When Hezekiah received Sennacherib's letter, he was upset, but he did the right thing. He took the letter to the Temple and laid it before the altar of the Lord. Hezekiah asked God to help His people in their time of need. Then he sent his own princes, Eliakim and Shebna, to the prophet Isaiah to ask if there was any message from God. This was the message they brought back, "The Lord says, 'Do not be afraid of what the Assyrians have said. The king of Assyria will not come into this city or even shoot an arrow into it, or attack it in any way. He will go back to his own land by the same way which he came. In his own land he will be killed by the sword. For the sake of the memory of My servant David, I will protect this city.'"

While this was happening, Sennacherib received news that a mighty army was coming from Ethiopia to attack him. To prepare for war against them, he called his men back from Jerusalem. Then a terrible thing happened to them. During the night an angel came from God and spread disease in the Assyrian camp. Before morning 185,000 soldiers were dead. When this happened, Sennacherib gathered all the men that were left

and he went back to Nineveh in his own country. A while later his own sons killed him with the sword while he was worshiping an idol. God had saved the city of Jerusalem and the people of Judah.

Be strong and courageous! Don't be afraid or discouraged because of the king of Assyria or his mighty army, for there is a power far greater on our side! He may have a great army, but they are merely men. We have the LORD our God to help us and to fight our battles for us!
2 Chronicles 32:7-8

Hezekiah Falls Ill

2 Kings 20:1-11; Isaiah 38:1-8

While the Assyrians were still in the land, Hezekiah got very ill. Isaiah came to him and said, "You must settle your affairs, because God says that this sickness will take away your life."

When Hezekiah heard that, he turned his face to the wall and prayed, "O God, remember that I have always served You

with my whole heart, and done what is good in Your sight. I beg You to save me."

God heard his prayer. He called Isaiah back and gave him a new message to take to Hezekiah. Isaiah had to tell the king that God had heard his prayer and seen his tears. God would make him well again. In three days he would be able to go to the Temple to worship. He would live for 15 more years. For all that time the Assyrians would not attack Jerusalem. Hezekiah was very happy to receive this message, but he wanted a sign to prove that God would really heal him. Isaiah asked him what sign he wanted. He asked, "Should the shadow on the sundial move back 10 steps or forward 10 steps?"

Hezekiah answered that it was an easy thing for the shadow to go forward. He said, "Let it go 10 steps backward." So Isaiah prayed to God. God brought back the shadow on the sundial by 10 steps so that Hezekiah could be sure of the truth of the promise.

For 15 years after that, Hezekiah continued to reign. There was peace in the land in all that time.

"Go back to Hezekiah and tell him, 'This is what the LORD, the God of your ancestor David, says: I have heard your prayer and seen your tears. I will add fifteen years to your life.'"

Isaiah 38:5

Manasseh Turns back to God

2 Kings 21; 2 Chronicles 33

After the death of Hezekiah, Manasseh became the king of Judah. He was only 12 years old when he came to the throne. He reigned for 55 years. But he was not at all like his father, Hezekiah. From an early age he encouraged the people of Judah to turn back to worshiping idols, and worshiping the sun, moon and stars. Even in the Temple of God he had altars built for all these false gods.

Because of all this, the Assyrians started attacking Judah again. During the war, Manasseh was captured and taken to Babylon. While he was in prison, Manasseh thought about his behavior. He began to realize that he had been wrong to turn away from God. He prayed for forgiveness. God freed Manasseh and had him taken back to Jerusalem. From that time on he served God.

When Manasseh died, his son Amon became king. Amon reigned for only two years and was very evil. He was murdered by his own servants.

While in deep distress, Manasseh sought the LORD his God and sincerely humbled himself before the God of his ancestors. And when he prayed, the LORD listened to him and was moved by his request. So the LORD brought Manasseh back to Jerusalem and to his kingdom. Then Manasseh finally realized that the LORD alone is God!

2 Chronicles 33:12-13

Young Josiah Becomes King

2 Kings 22:1–23:30; 2 Chronicles 34–35

The next king was Josiah, a little boy who was only eight years old when he became king. He was so young, but all the time he was doing his best to serve God in the right way. He commanded that all the idols and altars to false gods be broken down and burned.

He even crossed into Israel and broke down the altars there. When he came to Bethel, where Jeroboam had built a temple and made the golden calves for the people of Israel to worship many years ago, he broke the temple and the altar down. He burned everything that would burn. When all this work of cleansing was done, Josiah went back to Jerusalem. He made sure that all things that had anything to do with idol worship were taken away and destroyed.

While his workmen were busy around the Temple, Hilkiah, the high priest, found the Book of the Law. He took it to the young king at once. Shaphan, the king's scribe, read the Book to him. When the king heard the Law, and understood how much wrong had been done in the land, he was so upset that he tore his clothes. Then he told the Temple leaders to ask God what he and the people of Judah had to do to be forgiven, since they and their forefathers had broken His laws. He was sure that God would punish them for what they had done. The Temple rulers went to a prophetess called Huldah, and told her the king's request.

This was Huldah's answer: "This is what the Lord God of Israel says, 'Go and tell the man that sent you that I will cause great disaster to come upon this place and its people, because they turned away from Me and served idols. This land and this people must be punished for the evil they have done.

"'But because King Josiah has served Me faithfully and is sorrowful over all the sins of the nation, I will not punish Judah while he is alive. These terrible things will happen to Judah only after his death.'"

When he received this message, the king called the elders from all parts of the land and all the people of Jerusalem to a great meeting at the Temple gates. He stood beside one of the great pillars at the door and read to them the laws from the Book that had been found. They made a solemn promise to faithfully keep all the laws. For all of Josiah's life they were careful to live according to the laws and commandments of God. But the king didn't live for many years after that.

Josiah was eight years old when he became king, and he reigned in Jerusalem thirty-one years. He did what was pleasing in the LORD's sight and followed the example of his ancestor David. He did not turn away from doing what was right.

2 Kings 22:1-2

King Josiah listens to what the Book of the Law says. (2 Kings 22:10)

Jeremiah's Vision

2 Kings 24; Jeremiah 24, 29, 39, 43

After Jehoiakim, his son Jehoiachin became king. He was only 18 years old. In three months his reign was over because Nebuchadnezzar led the Babylonians against Jerusalem. They took Jehoiachin and his princes prisoner. They also carried away all the treasures still left in the Temple. They made Jehoiachin's Uncle Zedekiah king. Zedekiah was a wicked man who made fun of God's prophet Jeremiah.

One day, after Zedekiah became king, Jeremiah was sitting in the Temple when he saw a vision. In that vision God told him all that would happen to the people of Judah. He saw two baskets of figs. One was full of beautiful fruit, but the other had only rotten fruit not fit to eat. Then the Lord asked him, "What do you see, Jeremiah?"

Jeremiah answered, "I see figs. The good figs are very good, but the bad figs are so bad that they cannot be eaten."

Then the Lord said, "The good figs are the people who have already been taken to Babylon. I shall bless them and bring them back again to their own land. I shall make them love Me more and more. They will return to Me with all their hearts.

"The bad figs are Zedekiah and the people of Jerusalem and all Judah who have remained behind. They will suffer very much, with famine and disease and armed attacks. Those who are left will be scattered throughout the kingdoms of the world. None will be left in this land."

Afterward Jeremiah sent a letter to the prisoners in Babylon to encourage them by giving them a message from God. He wrote, "Build houses for yourselves and live in them. Make gardens and eat the fruit from them. Marry, and have children, and let your children marry, too. Pray for the peace of the city and the land in which you are living, because you and your children will live there for 70 years. After 70 years you will return again to your own land. It is God's plan to bless you with peace and prosperity. Pray to God and He will hear you. If you search for Him with your whole heart, you will certainly find Him."

At the same time Nebuchadnezzar and his armies were beating on the walls of Jerusalem. Soon the walls came tumbling down, and the soldiers swarmed into the city.

The king and his family tried to flee, but the Babylonians captured them and made them prisoners. Zedekiah was dragged in front of Nebuchadnezzar, chained and taken away to Babylon. In the meantime, all the buildings in Jerusalem were burned down. All the people, except the very poorest, were driven like a flock of sheep toward Babylon. That was the end of the kingdom of Judah. Zedekiah was the last king, and there were none to follow him.

Jeremiah chose to stay in Jerusalem, even though the city was destroyed. But the Egyptians captured Jeremiah and took him to Egypt where he died.

Jeremiah was often called the "Weeping Prophet." He often had to warn his people of the terrible fate that lay ahead of them. Jeremiah could not help feeling sorrowful about it. But he was faithful to God who called him to be a prophet. However, hard as it was, he gave God's messages to the people of Judah.

"I know the plans I have for you," says the LORD. "They are plans for good and not for disaster, to give you a future and a hope."

Jeremiah 29:11

Dry Bones Become Living People

Ezekiel 37

All that was left of the once great tribe of Judah was now a worn-out band of prisoners in Babylon. They had a long journey from the ruins of Jerusalem, through hot, dry desert. Many died on the way, but when they reached Babylon they were not treated cruelly. It was a fertile land, and they were even given plots of land on which they could grow food for themselves. Some of them went to work in the cities. A few even became important officials in the king's palace.

The best of all was that they were not made to worship the idols of the Babylonians but were allowed to serve the one true God of heaven and earth.

The Lord was good to these people. He did not turn away from them. He still gave them prophets as His messengers to the people. One was Daniel. Another was Ezekiel, who saw strange visions of angels and the throne of God.

Once in a vision, Ezekiel was taken into a wide valley. When he looked around, he found there were bones of people scattered all around, as if there had once been a great battle there. Then the Lord spoke to him, "Son of man, can these bones come to life?"

Ezekiel answered, "O Lord, only You know if they can come to life again."

Then God said, "Preach to the bones, and say to them, 'O dry bones, listen to the word of the Lord. This is what the Lord says to you, I will make the breath of life come into you again, and make sinews and flesh come on you. You will live. You will know that I am the Lord.'"

Ezekiel obeyed, and as he was speaking, there was a great noise. The scattered bones started moving together and sinews and flesh and skin formed on them. But there was no breath in them. Then God said, "Tell breath to come from the four winds, and make these bodies live." So Ezekiel did. And those bodies stood up on their feet, like a great army, filling the whole valley.

Then God said to Ezekiel, "Son of man, those bones represent the whole house of Israel. They feel that there is no hope for them any longer. But, as life has come into these dead bones, I will bring life into the house of Israel again. I will gather them from among the heathen. I will take them back to their own land. They will be a nation again. I will be their God, and they will be My people. Israel and Judah will not be separate anymore, but will live as one people in their own land."

When Ezekiel told his people this wonderful message from God, they were filled with courage and looked forward with joy to the day God would lead them home again.

"O My people, you will know that I am the LORD. I will put My Spirit in you, and you will live again and return home to your own land. Then you will know that I, the LORD, have spoken, and I have done what I said. Yes, the LORD has spoken!"

Ezekiel 37:13-14

Prisoners in the Palace of Babylon

Daniel 1–2

When Jehoiakim was king of Judah, King Nebuchadnezzar of Babylon attacked Jerusalem. When the city surrendered, Nebuchadnezzar took the king and some of the princes as prisoners to Babylon. When they arrived, Nebuchadnezzar told the ruler of the servants in his palace to select a group of young men from among the prisoners. They would be trained to work in the palace.

Among these young men were Daniel, Hananiah, Mishael and Azariah. These were their Jewish names. The ruler of the palace changed their names to Chaldean names: Daniel became Belteshazzar; Hananiah became Shadrach; Mishael became Meshach; and Azariah became Abednego. The king ordered that these men should have the very best food. He had some of the food from the royal table sent to them. Since this food had first been offered to the Babylonian idols, Daniel and his friends wouldn't eat it.

When they told the palace ruler they wouldn't eat the food, he was worried. He really cared about these young men. He was afraid that if they didn't eat the rich food the king had sent, they would get thin and weak and then the king would be angry with him.

But Daniel said, "Put us to the test for 10 days. Give us only vegetables and water. Then examine us, and see if we are thinner than the men who eat the meat that comes from the king's table. If we are then you can change the food we eat." He agreed and after 10 days he was amazed. The four young men looked fatter and healthier than all the others! He took them to King Nebuchadnezzar's throne room to be tested by the king.

The king asked them all kinds of questions. He found them to be 10 times more clever than all the magicians and astrologers in his kingdom. The king gave them the highest posts in the land.

One day the king called in all his wise men because he had a dream. He wanted them to tell him what it meant. But even though the dream worried him very much, he couldn't remember the dream. He told his wise men that if they couldn't tell him the dream and explain its meaning to him, he would have them all killed.

The wise men were very worried. How could they explain a dream that the king couldn't even remember? Then Daniel went to the chief of the royal guard and told him not to kill the wise men. After that he went to the king and asked to be given a little time. If given time, Daniel told the king, he would tell him the dream and explain it.

When the king agreed, Daniel went back to his friends, Hananiah, Mishael and Azariah. He

Daniel asks the guard to test them by only giving them vegetables and water for 10 days. (Daniel 1:11-15)

asked them to pray with him that God would show mercy to them and reveal to them the secret. God answered their prayer. That night in a vision God told the whole matter to Daniel.

In the morning Daniel asked to be taken to the king. The captain immediately took him to Nebuchadnezzar. The king asked, "Are you able to tell me what I dreamed, and what my dream means?"

Then Daniel answered, "The wise men of Babylon, the astrologers and magicians, cannot tell the king the secret of his dream. But there is a God in heaven who reveals secrets. He knows everything and has told me, His servant, the meaning of the dream. This is your dream. O king, you saw a great statue, which was beautifully made, but terrible to look at. Its head was made of gold, its chest and arms of silver, its stomach and sides of brass, its legs of iron, its feet partly of iron and partly of clay. While you watched, a rock not cut out by human hands smashed against the feet of the statue and broke them to pieces. The whole statue fell to the ground. The gold, silver, brass, iron and clay lay in pieces on the ground, and became like chaff on a threshing floor. The pieces were so fine that the wind blew them away. But the rock became a great mountain, and filled the whole world. This was the dream. Now I will tell you the meaning of it.

"God has given you this dream so that you will know what is going to happen in the future. You are the golden head of the image, for God has given you a great kingdom. The chest and arms of silver are a kingdom that will come after yours, but will not be so great. The third kingdom, of brass, will rule over all the world. It will be followed by a fourth kingdom, as strong as iron that will conquer all its enemies.

"But the feet of the image were partly clay and partly iron. They tell of a kingdom that will be partly strong and partly weak and easily broken. Each kingdom will be weaker than the one before it, until this last kingdom comes that will break to pieces when the rock not cut out by human hands smashes against it. That rock will be God's own kingdom that will not pass away. Like the rock in the image it will break to pieces all the other kingdoms, and will grow and grow, and take the place of all others. It will stand forever, a kingdom over the whole earth."

When Nebuchadnezzar heard this, he was so amazed that he threw himself down and worshiped Daniel as if he were a god. At the same time, he did not forget what Daniel had said. "Truly," he said, "your God is a God of gods and a Lord of kings and a revealer of secrets."

Then he made Daniel a great man in the land and ruler of the province of Babylon and gave him many gifts. Shadrach and Meshach and Abednego were not forgotten either. They were also made important officials in the province of Babylon.

Praise the name of God forever and ever, for He has all wisdom and power.

Daniel 2:20

The Golden Image and the Fiery Furnace
Daniel 3

Nebuchadnezzar knew the greatness of God, but he didn't understand that he should not worship idols. Not long after Daniel explained his dream to him, Nebuchadnezzar had his workmen make a great statue of a man. The statue was covered with gold from head to toe. It was 90 feet high and nine feet wide. Nebuchadnezzar had it set up on the plain of Dura near Babylon.

Then he sent men into the country to announce to all the important people that they must come to a great service where they would worship the idol Nebuchadnezzar had set up. When they got to the place, they would find musicians waiting. When the musicians played their instruments, all the people had to fall down and worship the statue. If they did not worship the idol, they would be thrown into a great furnace and burned to death.

When the music sounded, there were three men who stood there and would not bow down and worship the idol. These men were Shadrach, Meshach, and Abednego. Daniel was away that day. Some of the Babylonians went straight to tell the king and he had the men brought before him.

Nebuchadnezzar was furious with them for not obeying. He told them that he would have the trumpets sound again and the music played once more. If they did not do as he commanded he would certainly have them thrown into the furnace and no god would be able to save them.

But the three men were very brave. Without a moment's hesitation they answered, "O King, we are ready to give you our answer right now. If you have us thrown into the furnace, the God whom we worship is able to save us if it is His will. But even if it is not His will, we will not bow down and worship before your gold-en idol, nor any of the other gods of Babylon."

Nebuchadnezzar was very angry. He ordered that the furnace be made seven times hotter than usual. Then the three men were tied with ropes and thrown into the fire. When they were thrown in, the fire was so hot that the soldiers who threw them in were burned up by the flames. Shadrach, Meshach and Abednego fell right into the middle of the furnace.

The king was watching what happened. Suddenly he said in amazement, "Didn't we throw three tied-up men into the fire? Why do I see four men walking around in the fire, and not one of them is tied up? And the fourth man looks like the Son of God." As soon as the heat of the fire had died down, he went closer, and called out to the men, "Shadrach, Meshach and Abednego, you servants of the Most High God, come out of the furnace and come to me."

Only three men came out of the fire, and they were still in their clothes. Not one piece of clothing had even been burned

An angel of the Lord keeps Shadrach, Meshach and Abednego safe in the furnace. (Daniel 3:24-26)

a little. When the king saw this, he said to all the princes and other high officials gathered there, "Blessed is the God of these three men, who has sent His angel to save them from the fire because they would not serve any other god. I give a new commandment now that any person in Babylon, whatever his nation or language, who says anything against the God of Shadrach, Meshach and Abednego, will be put to death and his house will be torn down."

Then the king gave the three men even higher positions in the land than they had before. They became some of the most important men in Babylon.

If we are thrown into the blazing furnace, the God whom we serve is able to save us. He will rescue us from your power, Your Majesty. But even if He doesn't, we want to make it clear to you, Your Majesty, that we will never serve your gods or worship the gold statue you have set up.

Daniel 3:17-18

Handwriting on the Wall

Daniel 5

After King Nebuchadnezzar's death, the great Babylonian empire began to break up. Nebuchadnezzar's son was murdered and so were several of the men who followed him. Belshazzar was now king of Babylon.

As the Babylonian empire became weaker, another empire, further to the east, became stronger and stronger – the empire of the Medes and the Persians. While Belshazzar was king of Babylon, the Persian soldiers camped close by, waiting for a chance to break into the city.

One night Belshazzar held a great feast. He invited 1,000 of his important friends. Belshazzar sent for the gold and silver cups from the Temple, which Nebuchadnezzar had brought out of Jerusalem so that his guests could drink wine from them.

While the king and all his guests were eating and drinking, Belshazzar suddenly saw something that terrified him. He saw the fingers of a man's hand writing on the wall. There was no body attached. Just fingers writing! The king became pale with fright. He trembled all over. He called for the magicians and the wise men to be brought in at once to read the words and to tell him what they meant. He said, "If any man can explain this writing to me, I will clothe him in the richest robes and give him a golden chain, and make him third ruler in the kingdom." But no one could tell him.

Then the queen remembered Daniel. He was an old man by then and most of the people had forgotten the great work he had done while Nebuchadnezzar was king. But the queen still remembered and she suggested that Daniel be called.

When he was brought, Belshazzar promised him the same reward he had offered to the other wise men. Daniel didn't want the gifts, but he promised to explain the words. This is what he said, "O King, the Most High God gave your forefather, Nebuchadnezzar, a great kingdom. He had great power and so much money that it couldn't be counted. But he became proud and thought he had won all this by his own efforts. So God took away his kingdom and even his mind. He lived with animals. Only when he had learned that God is the Ruler of all, and gives the kingdoms of the world to those He wants, was he allowed to rule again.

"But you, O Belshazzar, have not humbled your heart, although you knew all about Nebuchadnezzar. You have become proud. You have even allowed the cups from God's Temple to be used for wine drinking. The words on the wall are God's message to you. These are the words: MENE, MENE, TEKEL, PARSIN. And this is what they mean: God has numbered the days of your kingdom and it will end. You are weighed in the balance and found wanting. Your kingdom will be divided and given to the Medes and the Persians."

Belshazzar gave Daniel the rewards he had promised, even though Daniel had said he did not want them. That very night the Persians captured the palace and killed Belshazzar.

While the feast was still going on, the Persian soldiers had already crept into the city and surrounded the palace.

God has numbered the days of your reign and has brought it to an end.

Daniel 5:26

Power over Lions!

Daniel 6

Darius the Mede was the next king of Babylon. He chose 120 princes to rule the different parts of his empire. There were three presidents over the princes. Daniel was the first of the presidents. He did his work faithfully and well, but the other two presidents and many of the princes were jealous of him. They wanted to get him into trouble with the king.

They came up with a plan to trap him. They would use his faithfulness to God against him, knowing that he wouldn't have anything to do with the worship of idols. This was

their clever plan: some of them went to the king and suggested that he make a special law that said no one was allowed to pray to any god or man except the king for 30 days. Anyone who broke the law would be thrown into the lions' den. The king liked this idea. He was glad they thought so much of him, so he signed the law without argument.

Daniel heard of the new law, but he wasn't worried. He had always been faithful to God, and he wouldn't change now. He went into his room and kneeled beside the open win-

**God sends an angel to shut the lions'
mouths and protect Daniel. (Daniel 6:22)**

dow, facing Jerusalem, to pray to God. He prayed three times a day, just as he had always done.

That was what his enemies were waiting for. They watched him pray. Then they told the king and demanded that Daniel be thrown to the lions. Darius was very unhappy. He tried his best to save Daniel, but there was nothing he could do. That evening at sunset, Daniel was brought to be thrown to the lions. But before that happened, the king spoke to him to encourage him. He said, "Your God whom you always serve will save you."

Then Daniel was put in with the lions and a big stone was put over the opening so that Daniel couldn't get out. The king and his nobles sealed the stone with their special signets so that no one could tamper with it. Then they went home.

Darius was very sad because he liked Daniel very much. He wouldn't eat, or listen to music from the royal musicians. That night he didn't sleep at all. Early in the morning, before anyone else was awake, he went to the lions' den. He called out sadly, "O Daniel, servant of the living God, was your God whom you serve so faithfully able to save you from the lions?"

He was thrilled to hear Daniel answer, "O king, may you live forever. My God sent His angel to close the lions' mouths. They have not hurt me. My God knew that I had done no wrong against Him or against you, O King!"

Then Darius told his servants to get Daniel out of the lions' den. The men who had tried to cause Daniel's death, along with their wives and children, were thrown in with the lions.

Darius had always loved Daniel, but now he knew the greatness of Daniel's God, too. He was never again cruel to those who served God.

My God sent His angel to shut the lions' mouths so that they would not hurt me, for I have been found innocent in His sight.

Daniel 6:22

The Jews Return Home

Ezra 1–3

King Cyrus of Persia was fond of the Jewish people. It had been 70 years since the first Jewish people were taken as prisoners by Nebuchadnezzar.

The Jewish people were not considered prisoners anymore. They lived in their own homes. They farmed their own land, but they were still not allowed to go back to Jerusalem. In the first year of the reign of Cyrus, the Lord put it into his heart to give the Jews permission to return to their own land. King Cyrus did even more than that. He issued a proclamation in which he said that God had commanded him to see that the Temple was built again in Jerusalem!

Jeremiah said many years before that the people would be taken away from Jerusalem and be in captivity for 70 years. Isaiah even said that the man who would send them home would be called Cyrus. There wasn't even a Persian army when Isaiah said that. Now it was all

happening. The 70 years were over. Most of the people who had been taken as prisoners from Jerusalem had already died, but their children still wanted to go back to their own country. How glad they were to hear Cyrus's proclamation!

This is what he said: "The Lord God of heaven has given me power over all the kingdoms on earth. He has told me to build Him a house in Jerusalem. Which of you among all His people wish to go back to your own land? May the Lord bless you, and bring you safely to Jerusalem to build His house there again. I command that wherever you stop on the way, the people of that place must help you with gifts of silver and gold and other goods, together with animals to carry these treasures. They must also bring you their offerings of money for the building of the Lord's house!"

Many of the Jews got ready to go back to Judah and the ruins of Jerusalem, but most of the rich men and the nobles decided to stay in Babylon. However, they did give big gifts to those who were returning. The king himself, although he was a Persian and not a Jew, gave them all the treasures which Nebuchadnezzar had brought back from the Temple when he had destroyed Jerusalem. There were 5,400 pieces altogether.

When the first group started the long journey to Jerusalem, there were 42,360 of them and what a joyful company they were. They even had 200 singers to provide them with music on the way. They traveled on horses, mules, donkeys and camels, and some on foot. They moved along slowly. In all the villages and towns along the way, they gathered more and more riches. Soon they were all settled in Judah.

After their arrival, all the men met together in the ruins of Jerusalem to bring sacrifices to God. They built the altar on its old site.

Every day, the morning and evening sacrifices were offered there, but the altar stood out in the open. There was no Temple as there had once been. Not even the foundations were left. But the work of rebuilding was soon begun. Money was paid to stonemasons and carpenters to begin setting up the new Temple. The leaders sent to Tyre and Sidon for more cedar wood.

In the second year after the Jews returned, the work was begun. The Levites and Zerubbabel were put in charge of rebuilding the Temple. They saw to it that everything was done correctly. One day the Jews would again be able to worship God as their fathers had done long ago.

This is what King Cyrus of Persia says: "The LORD, the God of heaven, has given me all the kingdoms of the earth. He has appointed me to build Him a Temple at Jerusalem, which is in Judah. Any of you who are His people may go to Jerusalem in Judah to rebuild this Temple of the LORD, the God of Israel, who lives in Jerusalem. And may your God be with you!"

Ezra 1:2-3

A New Temple Is Built

Ezra 3–6; Haggai 1–2; Zechariah 4

After the foundation of the Temple was completed, they held a special ceremony. All the men of Jerusalem gathered at the Temple site. The priests and Levites were there, dressed in their ceremonial robes.

When the stones were laid by the builders, the Levites made music with their cymbals. The priests sounded their trumpets. Then a song of praise was sung to the glory of God. This is what they sang to the Lord: "He is good! His faithful love for Israel endures forever!"

Everyone shouted with joy as the stones were cemented into place. But the old men who could still remember the beautiful Temple that Solomon had built and Nebuchadnezzar had destroyed, broke down and cried.

The work of building began with great joy and enthusiasm. But some people did not approve of what was being done. They were the enemies of Judah and Benjamin who lived nearby. They said that they served God, but they also served idols. They asked to be allowed to help with the building of the Temple.

But Zerubbabel said, "You have no part with us in this work. This is our work, and we have been commanded to do it by Cyrus, the king of Persia." That made them angry. From then on they did all they could to stop the work of the builders. They tried to frighten the people of Jerusalem by threatening to attack them. They even went so far as to send messengers to Cyrus to tell him he should stop the work in Jerusalem. They continued this for 20 years, even after the death of Cyrus.

When Artaxerxes was king, the enemies of the Jews sent a special letter to him, complaining about the building that was going on in Jerusalem. These are some of the things they wrote: "O King, this letter comes from your loyal people on the other side of the Euphrates River. We are worried about what is happening at Jerusalem. If that city is built again and the walls raised once more, the people of Judah will refuse to pay taxes. The king's revenues will be damaged. We advise the king to study the records of the empire. He will find that Jerusalem has been a rebellious city in the past. We believe that once it is built up again, the people of Judah will rebel once more. The king will have no kingdom on this side of the river."

Artaxerxes did not understand their hatred for the Jews. The answer he sent back was this: "Your letter was read to me. I have made my scribes search through the history of Judah. It is true, Jerusalem has rebelled against her rulers before. Go now, and command these men in my name to stop working on the building until I send instructions for the builders to begin again."

Their leaders, Rehum and Shimshai, were glad to receive the letter. They rushed off to Jerusalem to show it to the Jews and stop the work. Everything came to a standstill. Not another bit of work was done until the second year of the reign of King Darius.

When the Jews came back from Babylon, there was no prophet with them to bring them God's message. Now God used two men to pass on His word. Their names were Haggai and Zechariah. Their message to the people of Jerusalem was that they should continue building the Temple and the walls of the city.

God told Haggai to tell the people this: "Is this a time for you to live in your fine houses, while the house of the Lord lies in ruins? Consider your ways. Go up to the mountain, and bring wood, and build My house; and I will take pleasure in it, and be glorified. The first Temple was glorious. But this Temple will be greater still."

The other prophet, Zechariah, encouraged the people in the same way: "This is the word of the Lord to Zerubbabel, saying, not by might, nor by power, but by My Spirit. The hands of Zerubbabel have laid the

Some of the people celebrate the building of the new Temple, while others break down and cry. (Ezra 3:12)

foundation of this Temple; his hands also shall finish it."

Then Zerubbabel the prince and Jeshua the high priest began the work of building again, and the prophets worked with them. Soon after, Tatnai the Persian governor on the west side of the Euphrates River came to Jerusalem. He was worried by the stories the enemies of the Jews told him.

Tatnai wrote to King Darius of Persia to ask if King Cyrus had really ordered the Temple rebuilt. Darius's wise men looked through all the kingdom's records to see if Cyrus had really commanded that the Temple should be rebuilt.

Darius was a very kind-hearted man. When he learned that Cyrus had truly sent out such a proclamation, he did all he could to help the people in Jerusalem. Darius sent orders to Tatnai to leave Zerubbabel and his people in peace to build the Temple. He even said that part of the taxes from the province west of the Euphrates River had to be used for the work in Jerusalem.

Finally they were able to finish rebuilding the Temple. Zerubbabel and Jeshua were still in charge, just as God's prophets Zechariah and Haggai had said.

The new Temple was not as richly decorated as Solomon's Temple had been. There was no Ark of the Covenant in the Holy of Holies anymore, because it had been lost during all the fighting. It was never found again. In its place there was a white marble block. On that block the high priest sprinkled the blood of the sacrifice on the great Day of Atonement.

"This is what the LORD says to Zerubbabel: It is not by force nor by strength, but by My Spirit, says the LORD of Heaven's Armies."

Zechariah 4:6

The Beautiful Queen Esther

Esther 1–3

After King Darius died, Xerxes became king. One day King Xerxes planned a big party in his palace at Susa. It lasted for 180 days – nearly six months!

Princes from many different provinces were invited. The palace was beautifully decorated for the occasion. No two drinking cups were alike, except that they all were made of gold. While the princes feasted in the king's palace, a special feast was held for the ladies in the palace of the queen, who was named Vashti.

On the last day of the feast, when the king and his guests had all had too much to drink, Xerxes sent for Queen Vashti to come to his banquet hall. Xerxes wanted to show her beauty to his guests. But Queen Vashti refused to come. The king was very angry. He was embarrassed because his wife wouldn't obey him.

Xerxes called his wise men to tell him what to do. They said that if he didn't take firm action, the wives of all the other princes would become disobedient, too. So he sent Vashti away at once, and decided to make someone else queen in her place.

The king sent letters to all the provinces, commanding that the most beautiful young girls from all the villages and towns be sent to Susa so that he could choose his new queen.

A Jewish man named Mordecai lived in the fortress of Susa. He was raising his orphaned niece, Esther. She was a beautiful girl so she was taken to the palace, along with many other girls. Maybe she would be chosen as the next queen!

Hegai, one of the king's servants, took care of Esther at the palace. She stayed under his care until the day Xerxes came to choose his new wife. He chose Esther!

Now she had a beautiful palace to live in and all the riches she could wish for. But she couldn't see her beloved uncle, Mordecai, because the king owned her now. If she and her uncle wanted to tell one another anything, they had to secretly send letters through the palace servants.

Mordecai spent a lot of time sitting at the palace gates where many men gathered to talk. One day he heard two of the king's servants talking. They were planning to murder the king. Mordecai sent a message to Esther to tell her what was happening and she warned the king. Both men were put to death and the whole story of how Mordecai saved the king's life was written down in the royal history.

A while later, Xerxes promoted one of his men, Haman, to be the head over all the princes in the empire. All the people in and around the palace bowed to Haman whenever he passed by, except Mordecai. Mordecai was a faithful Jew and would not bow down to anyone except God. Haman got angry and decided that Mordecai must be killed. In fact, he wanted all the Jews in the empire to be killed as well. He didn't know that the queen herself was Jewish, because Mordecai had told Esther she must not tell anyone that she was a Jew.

Haman went to the king with his complaint against the Jews. Xerxes did not understand what this was all about, but he trusted Haman so he gave Haman permission to do what he wanted. Haman sent out a proclamation, sealed with the king's own seal, into all the land. The proclamation said that on the 13th day of the 12th month all the Jews would be killed – men, women, and even children. The proclamation said that all who helped to kill them could take the Jews' riches for themselves.

The king loved Esther more than any of the other young women. He was so delighted with her that he set the royal crown on her head and declared her queen instead of Vashti.

Esther 2:17

Esther Appears before the King

Esther 4–10

When Mordecai heard that a proclamation had been sent out announcing that all Jews would be killed, he was very upset. He tore his clothes, and put on sackcloth and rubbed ashes on his face to show how upset he was.

The queen didn't know about Haman's plan, but her servants came to tell her about how Mordecai was mourning. She sent clothes to him to put on instead of the sackcloth, but he wouldn't take them.

When Queen Esther's servants brought the clothes back, she asked one of the king's servants to find out what Mordecai was so upset about.

Mordecai told him about Haman's plans. He asked the servant to beg Queen Esther to ask the king to have mercy on the Jews.

Even though Esther was the queen, she was not allowed to go into the king's presence unless he sent for her. Anyone who broke this law could be put to death immediately, so Queen Esther was afraid to go to the king.

She reminded Mordecai about the law, but he sent a message back to her, saying, "You are a Jew. Don't think that you will be safer in the palace than the rest of your people are. If you say nothing, then the Jews will be saved in another way, but you and your family will be destroyed. And perhaps God has put you in the palace to save your people at just such a time as this."

When she received this message, Esther sent a message back to Mordecai. She asked him to get together all the Jews in Susa to fast and pray for her for three days. She and her servants would fast as well.

On the third day she would go to the king to beg for her people to be saved. The king might have her killed, but she was not afraid. Mordecai did exactly what she said.

So on the third day Esther put on her finest clothes and went to the king. When she stood in the doorway of the throne room, she looked so beautiful that he fell in love with her all over again. He stretched out his golden scepter toward her and asked her what he could do for her.

She invited the king to bring Haman to a special banquet that night in her palace. When the banquet was over, Xerxes asked Esther what she wanted. She said that they should come to another banquet the next evening and then she would tell the king what she wanted.

As Haman left the palace that day, he saw Mordecai beside the gate. As usual, Mordecai did not bow to Haman. When Haman's wife, Zeresh, heard this, she told him to have a gallows built that was 75 feet high, and to ask the king the next morning to have Mordecai hanged from it. Then he could go in and enjoy the queen's banquet. He

sent out his servants right away to build the gallows.

That night, King Xerxes couldn't sleep. He sent for one of his wise men to read to him from the book about his reign. When the man came to the part about when Mordecai had discovered the plot to kill him and had saved his life, Xerxes suddenly realized that he had never rewarded Mordecai for what he had done.

Xerxes asked if any of his princes were in the court at the time. Haman was there, waiting for a chance to speak to the king about hanging Mordecai. When the king sent for him, Haman was excited. Now was his chance!

The king asked him a question, "What should the king do for the man he wishes to honor?" Haman was thrilled. He was sure the king was talking about him. Wasn't he the king's favorite?

He was so sure it was him that he answered, "Let the royal robes be put on him, and let him ride on the king's horse,

Esther points out Haman as the man who ordered that all Jews be killed. (Esther 7:3-6)

and have the king's crown placed on his head. Let one of the king's greatest princes lead him through the streets of Susa and proclaim to the people that this is the man the king wishes to honor."

Haman was shocked when the king told him to do all this to Mordecai, the Jew. He had to do it! He had to hide his anger and go to Queen Esther's second banquet.

When that meal was over, King Xerxes asked Esther to tell him what her request was. He told her that she could have anything she asked for. The king loved her very much.

But Queen Esther said, "O King, if I have found favor in your sight, please spare my life and the lives of my people. Because I am a Jew, and it is ordered that we must all be killed."

"Who is the man who has ordered this?" asked the king, "Who would dare to order something like this?" Then Esther pointed to Haman and said, "This wicked man is our enemy." Haman was terrified, especially when the angry king got up and went out to the garden to walk around.

When the king returned, one of his servants told him about the gallows Haman had set up to hang Mordecai. Immediately the king ordered them to hang Haman from the gallows instead. So Haman died on the gallows he had made for Mordecai.

The law that had been sent out for the killing of the Jews on the 13th day of the 12th month was a law of the Medes and the Persians. That meant it couldn't be changed.

How could King Xerxes save Esther's people? He made a new law that said the Jews could defend themselves and their property if they were attacked. They could gather in groups and fight against their enemies.

When the 13th day of the 12th month came, very few people attacked the Jews. Those who did were defeated and many of them were killed.

Instead of a day of death and sorrow for the Jews, it became a day of rejoicing.

Even to this day the Jews keep it as a feast day, called Purim.

In the synagogues the rabbis read to the people the story of Queen Esther and of Mordecai who became a great prince in Susa.

Mordecai sent this reply to Esther: "Don't think that because you're in the palace you will escape when all other Jews are killed. If you keep quiet at a time like this, deliverance and relief for the Jews will arise from some other place, but you and your relatives will die. Who knows if perhaps you were made queen for just such a time as this?"

Esther 4:13-14

The People Learn God's Law Again

Ezra 7–10

While Artaxerxes was king, the Jews in Jerusalem had a very hard time. They were still being troubled by their enemies who stole their cattle and robbed their lands.

Some of the Jews were very poor and had borrowed money from richer people. Now they couldn't pay back what they owed, so they were taken as slaves in their own land.

Other Jews had married people from heathen tribes nearby and forgotten all about God's laws and worshiping Him. There was not a complete wall around the city of Jerusalem, so the people lived in constant danger of being attacked. Years after they had started their return from Babylon they were still not living in safety.

Then God sent Ezra, the priest and scribe, to help them. Ezra taught them God's Law again.

King Artaxerxes allowed Ezra to go to Jerusalem to help his people. Artaxerxes was kind to the Jews. He said that all the

Jews who wanted to could go with Ezra to Jerusalem.

Artaxerxes sent silver and gold with them from his own treasury. He even promised that if they needed anything for decorating the Temple, they could ask him. Everyone who served God in the Temple would be free from taxes. But all the people of Jerusalem and Judea must keep the laws of God.

When Ezra got to Jerusalem, he found that most of the people had forgotten that there even was a Law of God. He called the princes together and spoke to them very seriously. He pointed out that the men of Judah had married heathen wives and broken God's commandments. A very serious prayer time was held and Ezra begged God to forgive them and keep them faithful and obedient to His laws in the future.

Then all the people humbled themselves before God. They promised not to break His laws anymore. They sent away their heathen wives, and the children of those wives. All the men who had broken God's laws by marrying in this way were separated from the true people of God.

After Ezra's teachings the Law was faithfully taught in the Temple. A synagogue was built in every village and town and on every Sabbath day the elders taught the people from the Book of the Law.

Ezra, by God's calling, made the people of Judea God's people once more.

Praise the LORD, the God of our ancestors, who made the king want to beautify the Temple of the LORD in Jerusalem!

Ezra 7:27

The Walls of Jerusalem

Nehemiah 1:1–2:10

While Ezra the priest was teaching the people of Jerusalem the Law of God, God was preparing another man in Susa to rebuild the city walls. That man was Nehemiah, who was the cupbearer of King Artaxerxes in Susa and a faithful servant of God.

The news reached Nehemiah that his people in Jerusalem were very unhappy. He heard that the city walls were broken down, the gates had been burned, and the people were living in terrible poverty.

When he heard this, Nehemiah was very sad. He prayed that God would forgive the people for their sins, and show him how to help them.

He kept doing his job, which was to serve the king. The king noticed how sad Nehemiah was and asked him what was wrong. When Nehemiah explained his troubles, Artaxerxes asked how he could help.

Nehemiah prayed, and then asked the king to give him permission to go to Jerusalem to rebuild the wall. He asked the king to send messages to the governors of the provinces along the way to help him get safely to Jerusalem. The king and queen gave him permission to go. They also sent him to Asaph, who controlled the royal forests, to get all the wood he would need for the work in Jerusalem.

Then, with a team of helpers, and a large group of Jews who wanted to go back to Jerusalem, Nehemiah began the long journey through the desert.

The king granted these requests, because the gracious hand of God was on me.

Nehemiah 2:8

Nehemiah's Work in Jerusalem

Nehemiah 2:11–6:15

When Nehemiah reached Jerusalem, he didn't tell the people why he had come at first. For three days he was very quiet. Then one night he took a few men and secretly slipped out to inspect the wall and the gates of the city. When Nehemiah had seen the bad condition of the wall and gates, he went back to where he was staying.

The next day he went to the priests and rulers, and told them his plans for rebuilding the wall. He explained how God had answered his prayers, and that King Artaxerxes had promised to help. Then the people were encouraged and said, "Let us begin the work!"

Every family in the city had a part in the work. Each one had a section of the wall to work on or its gate to build. Each person worked very hard. It didn't matter how important the people were or what kind of work they did, everyone worked together to rebuild the city wall.

There was great enthusiasm among the people. Everyone looked forward to the work being finished and the safety of Jerusalem.

But there were some people who were angry at what was happening. Sanballat, Tobiah and Geshem made fun of the people and their work. They even tried to stop the work.

Sanballat laughed and said the Jews would never be able to make a wall out of the heaps of garbage in Jerusalem. Tobiah said that if a fox walked on top of it, their wall would fall over. But the Jews kept working.

This made the enemies of Israel so angry that they threatened to send men to attack the Jewish workers. But Nehemiah had a plan. While half the people of the city worked on the wall, the other half were armed and ready to fight off the attackers. Then Sanballat and his friends came up with another plan. They sent a letter to Ne-

**Nehemiah tells the people about his plan to
rebuild the wall of Jerusalem. (Nehemiah 2:16-18)**

hemiah. They asked him to meet them in a little village on the plain of Ono, so that they could discuss their differences.

Nehemiah was too smart for them, though. He knew that this was a trap. He knew they wanted to get him away from his people so they could kill him. He sent this message to Sanballat, "I'm doing important work and cannot leave. Why should the work be stopped while I come down to you?"

They sent invitations to him four more times, but they got the same answer from him each time. The fifth time they wrote that the people around Jerusalem said the wall was being rebuilt so the Jews could rebel against the Persian king. Nehemiah should come and discuss this problem with Sanballat so that they could prove this was a lie. But Nehemiah wrote back, "There's no truth in this. You have made up the story yourself."

But some of the Jews inside the city had been paid by Sanballat and his men to help them.

They tried to scare Nehemiah. They told him to hide in the Temple because his enemies were planning to kill him.

Nehemiah knew that this was another trap so he just laughed at them and said, "Should I hide in the Temple to save my life? I will not do it!"

After 52 days of hard work, the city wall was completed and the gates could be closed. Watchmen were set in all the watchtowers and the people were safe at last.

I told them about how the gracious hand of God had been on me, and about my conversation with the king. They replied at once, "Yes, let's rebuild the wall!" So they began the good work.

Nehemiah 2:18

The Biggest Bible Class Ever Held

Nehemiah 8–13; Malachi 1–4

When the walls of Jerusalem were finished, Nehemiah called the people of the city and of the towns and villages nearby to a meeting.

They met in the street, which led to the gate where the water carriers came in and out of the city. Men and women, even very young boys and girls, were there because this was a very important day.

A big wooden pulpit had been especially made and set up in the street. Ezra stood on the pulpit. He held a copy of the Book of God's Law. When he opened the Book, all the people stood up out of respect for the Word of God. Then Ezra blessed God's name and all the people said, "Amen." They bowed their heads and worshiped.

Sentence by sentence Ezra then read the entire Law of God to them. It took from early morning until the middle of the day. Every sentence had to be translated because the Law was written in Hebrew and the people spoke Aramaic now. It was the language of Palestine. Other men from the Levite tribe stood beside Ezra to help in the work of teaching the people.

Some of the people cried when they heard the Law, because they realized how often they had broken God's commandments. But Nehemiah, Ezra and the Levites comforted the people. They told the people they should consider this day a time for rejoicing. So the people held a great feast. They also sent food and drink to the poor who had none of their own.

The next day the leaders, priests and Levites held a meeting with Ezra so that he could explain the Law to them carefully.

For seven days, one after the other, Ezra taught them the Law. Then they went to teach the rest of the people.

When this week of teaching ended, the people confessed

their sins and the sins of their forefathers to God. Then they promised that they wouldn't allow their children to marry into the heathen nations.

They promised that they would keep God's Law and love Him with all their hearts. They would be careful to keep the Sabbath day. They would also bring sacrifices and offerings of money to the Temple as commanded in the Law.

All the promises were written down and the leaders, Levites and priests signed it in the name of the people.

Nehemiah felt that his work in Jerusalem was done, so he returned to the palace of the king of Persia to do his work as the royal cupbearer.

After a few years, though, he went back to Jerusalem to see how the people were getting along.

Nehemiah was sad to see that many people were working on the Sabbath, stomping grapes to make wine and bringing sheaves of corn into the barns, buying and selling just as on any other day. They had completely forgotten their promise to honor God.

Nehemiah angrily said, "Why are you doing such wickedness on the Sabbath day? Don't you remember how our fathers faced God's anger because of this same kind of behavior?"

Then Nehemiah made a new rule. Before dark when the Sabbath began, the city gates were closed. No one was allowed to bring in anything until after the Sabbath.

Because of this new rule, some traders had to spend the day outside the city walls until the gate was unlocked.

Nehemiah saw them from the wall and gave them a serious warning that if he saw them there again he would have them thrown into prison. After that they didn't come back on the Sabbath day again.

After the days of Ezra and Nehemiah, God sent His last prophet to Judah. His name was Malachi.

The most important thing he taught the people was about the Savior that God would send them one day.

This was what he said about the coming of the Savior and the one who would announce His coming, "Look! I am sending My messenger, and he will prepare the way before Me. Then the Lord you are seeking will suddenly come to His Temple. The messenger is surely coming … Look, I am sending you the prophet Elijah before the great and dreadful day of the LORD arrives. His preaching will turn the hearts of fathers to their children, and the hearts of children to their fathers. Otherwise I will come and strike the land with a curse (Malachi 3:1; 4:5-6)."

And those are the closing words of the Old Testament.

"I have always loved you," says the LORD.

Malachi 1:2

NEW TESTAMENT

God's Angels Bring Amazing News

Luke 1

About 400 years after Malachi taught the people, the Jewish country was a province of Rome called Judea. Although Judea had its own ruler, Herod, it was under the control of Roman Emperor Caesar Augustus.

At that time a priest named Zechariah lived in Jerusalem. His wife was Elizabeth. They didn't have any children, but had always wanted them. But now they were both old.

One day Zechariah was doing his job in the Temple when an angel appeared to him. Zechariah was frightened because he had never seen an angel before. The angel said, "Don't be afraid, Zechariah. Your prayers for a child have been heard. Elizabeth will have a son, and you must give him the name of John.

"He will be great in God's sight. His heart will be filled with the Holy Ghost from his birth. Because of his ministry, many will turn back to the Lord their God. He will help the people get ready for the Lord."

Zechariah was amazed. How could they have a son when they were both so old? He told the angel that, but the angel answered, "I am Gabriel. I come from God and have been sent to bring you His message. But to prove that the message comes from God, you will not be able to speak until the baby is born. This is because you did not believe my words." When Zechariah came out of the Temple, he couldn't speak a word.

Six months after this, the same angel, Gabriel, was sent by God to a young girl in a little town called Nazareth. Her name was Mary and she was a cousin of Elizabeth, the wife of Zechariah. Mary was engaged to marry Joseph, a carpenter, who was a descendant of David.

When the angel appeared to Mary, he said, "The Lord is with

An angel tells Mary that she will give birth to a Son
and His name will be Jesus. (Luke 1:30-31)

you, Mary, and you are blessed above all women." Mary didn't understand what he meant. But Gabriel comforted her, "Don't be afraid, Mary. God is very pleased with you. You are going to have a Son. You must call Him Jesus. He will be great, and will be called the Son of God. The Lord God will give Him the throne of His father David. He will reign over the house of Jacob forever. His kingdom will never come to an end." Then the angel told her that her cousin Elizabeth was going to have a baby, too, in about three months.

Then Mary said, "I am the Lord's servant. Let all this happen as God wishes." Then the angel left her.

Mary was very excited. She packed some clothes, and started the long journey to see Elizabeth and tell her what had happened. When Mary arrived, Elizabeth said, "Mary, you are blessed more than all women and the Son who will be born to you is blessed also! How is it that the mother of my Lord has come to visit me?"

Mary was filled with God's Spirit and sang a beautiful song of praise, which is still sung in many churches today. We call it "The Magnificat."

Three months later Elizabeth's son was born. When he was eight days old, their friends and family came to celebrate. They wanted to name him Zechariah after his father, but Elizabeth said, "No! He must be called John." The people said, "But there is no one in your family by that name!" Zechariah still couldn't speak, so he picked up a tablet and wrote, "His name is John."

As soon as he wrote, he was able to speak again. Not only did he speak, but he sang a song of praise to God, a song which, like Mary's, is still sung in churches today. It's called "The Benedictus." Zechariah's son became the greatest of God's prophets, John the Baptist.

Mary responded, "I am the Lord's servant. May everything you have said about me come true."

Luke 1:38

230

Zechariah writes on a tablet that his son's name is John. (Luke 1:62-64)

An Angel Visits Joseph

Matthew 1

Soon after John the Baptist was born, an angel came to Joseph in a dream.

Joseph was the carpenter from Nazareth who was engaged to Mary. Joseph was concerned because he knew that Mary was pregnant and was going to have a baby.

But the angel brought him an important message from God. "Don't be upset, Joseph," he said. "The Baby Mary is going to have is a special gift from God. It is God who has brought that Baby to life in her. She will have a Son. You must give Him the name of Jesus, which means 'Jehovah is salvation,' because He will save His people from their sins. All this is happening to fulfill the words of the prophets about the Savior God promised to His people a long time ago."

An angel of the Lord appeared to him [Joseph] in a dream. "Joseph, son of David," the angel said, "do not be afraid to take Mary as your wife. For the Child within her was conceived by the Holy Spirit. And she will have a Son, and you are to name Him Jesus, for He will save His people from their sins."

Matthew 1:20-21

A Baby in a Manger

Luke 2:1–38

Not long after Joseph and Mary were married, Augustus decided that all the people in his empire should be counted. He commanded Quirinius, the governor of Syria, to see that this was done. All the people were told to go to the town where their ancestors were from.

Joseph and Mary had to go to the little town of Bethlehem,

Joseph and a pregnant Mary travel to Bethlehem. (Luke 2:3-5)

even though it was almost time for Mary's Baby to be born. It was a long journey of about 80 miles, so Mary rode on a donkey. There were so many people in Bethlehem that there was no room for Mary and Joseph in the inn. The only place they could find to stay was in a stable.

They settled in to rest, but that very night Mary's Baby was born. There wasn't a bed for Him so they wrapped Him in strips of cloth and laid Him down on the straw in a manger.

A group of shepherds were in the fields near Bethlehem looking after their sheep. Suddenly a bright light shone around them, and they saw an angel from God. They were terrified, but the angel said, "Don't be afraid. I've come to bring you wonderful news, which will fill you with joy. Tonight in the city of David, in Bethlehem, a Savior has been born for you. He is Christ the Lord. This is how you will know Him. You will find a little newborn Baby, wrapped in cloths and lying in a manger."

And as the angel finished speaking, a great choir of angels appeared, praising God. This is what they sang: "Glory to God in the highest, and peace on earth to those with whom He is pleased!"

When the song was finished, the angels disappeared and once again the night was dark. The shepherds decided to hurry to Bethlehem. They wanted to see the Baby the angel told them about. When they got to the stable, they found Mary and Joseph and the Baby lying in a manger, just as the angel had said. They went out and told everyone they met about the wonderful thing that had happened.

When the Baby was eight days old, He was given the name of Jesus, just as the angel had told Joseph.

There was a law that after the first son was born in any family, the parents must go to the Temple in Jerusalem and offer a sacrifice of thanksgiving to God. Since Joseph was a poor man, the sacrifice he took was two pigeons.

Jesus is born in a stable. His mother wrapped Him in cloth and laid Him in a manger. (Luke 2:6-7)

When Joseph and Mary carried Jesus into the Temple, they met an old man named Simeon who was longing for the coming of the Savior God had promised. God's Spirit had told him in his heart that he wouldn't die until he had seen the Savior.

The same day Joseph and Mary took Jesus to the Temple, God's Spirit sent Simeon there, too. When the old man saw Jesus, he knew that He was the Savior. He took Jesus in his arms and praised God, "Now, Lord, let Your servant die in peace, as You promised. My eyes have seen Your salvation, which You have prepared in the presence of all nations."

Joseph and Mary were amazed at what was being said about Jesus. Then Simeon prayed for God's blessing on them both. He told Mary, "This Child will cause many in Israel to fall, but He will be a joy to many others. He has been sent as a sign from God, but many will oppose Him. As a result, the deepest thoughts of many hearts will be revealed. And a sword will pierce your very soul."

There was also an elderly woman called Anna in the Temple that day. She was a prophetess and brought God's messages to the people. She spent most of her time in the Temple, fasting and praying. When she saw the Baby in Mary's arms, she also praised God.

He was just a little Baby who was born in Bethlehem. But God's angels and His Holy Spirit told many people in Bethlehem and in Jerusalem that He was the Savior about whose coming all the prophets had spoken.

While they were there, the time came for her Baby to be born. She gave birth to her firstborn Son. She wrapped Him snugly in strips of cloth and laid Him in a manger, because there was no lodging available for them.
Luke 2:6-7

**An angel appears to the shepherds to tell
them that Jesus has been born. (Luke 2:8-12)**

Wise Men Come to Worship

Matthew 2

Not long after Jesus was born in Bethlehem, wise men from a country far to the east arrived in Jerusalem. Like many wise men, they studied the stars and they had seen one strange star, which seemed to move across the sky toward the west. They knew that this star would lead them to the new King of the Jews.

When they arrived in Jerusalem they asked everyone where they could find the newborn King, because they wanted to worship Him. King Herod heard that these men were looking for the new King. He was worried and so were many other people in Jerusalem. Herod called a meeting of the chief priests and the scribes. He asked them where the Scriptures said that the Christ, the promised King of the Jews, would be born.

They answered, "In Bethlehem in the land of Judah. The prophet wrote, 'And you, Bethlehem, in the land of Judah, are by no means the least among the leaders of Judah, for out of you shall come forth a Ruler, who will shepherd My people, Israel.'"

When Herod heard this, he spoke to the wise men in private and asked them to tell him when they had first seen the star that was leading them to the Christ. Then he asked them to come back and tell him when they found the Baby, "so that I can also go and worship Him." That's what he said, but he didn't really want to worship Christ at all. He had made an awful plan.

After they had spoken to the king, the wise men headed to Bethlehem. The star kept going on ahead of them so they knew they were on the right road. The star led them until it stopped right above the place where Jesus was.

When the wise men went inside the house, they saw the Baby Jesus with His mother, Mary. Immediately they bowed down and worshiped Him.

**The wise men follow the star to find
the new King of the Jews, Jesus. (Matthew 2:1-2)**

Then they gave Him the presents they brought: gold, frankincense and myrrh.

That night God warned them in a dream not to go back to Herod as he had asked them to do. They were to return to their own land by a different way.

When they left, an angel appeared to Joseph in a dream and told him that he must take Mary and the Baby and hurry to Egypt as quickly as possible. So that very night Joseph took Mary and Jesus, and slipped out of Bethlehem under cover of darkness. After a long and tiring journey they arrived in Egypt. They stayed there until an angel told them that King Herod had died. Then they went to Nazareth, where Joseph and Mary had lived before Jesus was born. The angel had warned Joseph to take his little family to Egypt for a very good reason: Herod had sent out his soldiers to murder all the little boys in Bethlehem who were two years or younger. He did that so the Baby who was born to be King would be killed. Then his own throne would be kept safe. But his plan didn't work because Jesus was safe in Egypt.

Jesus was born in Bethlehem in Judea, during the reign of King Herod. About that time some wise men from eastern lands arrived in Jerusalem, asking, "Where is the newborn King of the Jews? We saw His star as it rose, and we have come to worship Him."

Matthew 2:1-2

The Little Boy Grows Up
Luke 2:41–52

Every year Joseph and Mary went to Jerusalem to celebrate the Feast of the Passover. The year that Jesus turned 12, He went with them. At the end of the feast, all the people who had come to Jerusalem from Nazareth began the long walk home together. Joseph and Mary thought that Jesus was with the rest of the boys and girls. At the end of the first

Joseph, Mary and Baby Jesus escape to Egypt after an angel
warns them of King Herod's plan to kill Jesus. (Matthew 2:13-15)

day's traveling, they went to look for Him, but no one knew where He was.

So Joseph and Mary hurried back to Jerusalem, looking for Jesus as they walked. On the third day they found Him in the Temple, listening to the teachers of the law and asking them questions. Mary and Joseph were very upset. Mary went straight to Him and said, "Son, why have You treated us like this? Your father and I have looked for You all over. We were afraid."

But Jesus answered, "Why did you look for Me and why were you worried about Me? Don't you understand that I must be busy with the work My Father has given Me?" But they couldn't understand what He was telling them.

Then Jesus went with Joseph and Mary back to Nazareth and listened to them as a good son should listen to his parents.

Jesus grew in wisdom and in stature and in favor with God and all the people.

Luke 2:52

Preparing the Way
Matthew 3; Mark 1:1–15; John 1:19–29

Jesus of Nazareth didn't leave His hometown or begin to teach until He was about 30 years old. His cousin John preached to people about their sins against God. John was six months older than Jesus, but he had never met his cousin. Before he began to teach, John lived in the wilderness, away from other people, where he could think and pray. He even

ate locusts and the wild honey he was able to find in hollow trees and in crevices in rocks. His clothing was a robe made of camel's hair, with a leather belt around his waist. God spoke to John and gave him a message to preach to the people of Judea.

When John began to preach, the people came from all parts of

John baptizes Jesus and the Spirit of God descends on Jesus like a dove. (Luke 3:21-22)

the land to listen. This is what he told them: "I am the voice of one crying in the wilderness, 'Prepare for the coming of the Lord. Make ready your hearts to receive Him. Repent of your sins, and seek the forgiveness of God.'" And as they listened, many saw how wickedly they had lived, and were sorry for it. So they went to John near the Jordan River and he baptized them. That's why he was given the name of John the Baptist. Some of the people wondered, "Who is this man, John the Baptist? Could he possibly be the Messiah whom God had promised?"

But John said, "I am only a voice crying in the wilderness. I am the messenger the prophet Isaiah wrote about long ago who would come to prepare the way for the Messiah. After me comes One who is mightier than I am. I am not even fit to stoop down and untie the laces of His sandals. I baptized you with water, but He will baptize you with the Holy Spirit."

One day when John was preaching to a large crowd next to the Jordan River, he looked up and saw Jesus coming toward him. The Spirit of God told him who He was, and he cried out, "Look! The Lamb of God who takes away the sin of the world!"

John was very surprised when Jesus asked to be baptized as well. John protested, but Jesus told him this was all part of God's plan. So John baptized Jesus in the Jordan River.

Then an amazing thing happened. As Jesus came up out of the water, the heavens opened and John saw the Spirit of God descending on Jesus like a dove. A voice spoke from heaven: "This is My beloved Son and I am very pleased with Him."

He is a voice shouting in the wilderness, "Prepare the way for the LORD's coming!"

Luke 3:4

Jesus Is Tempted

Matthew 4:1–11

After Jesus was baptized by John in the Jordan River, the Spirit of God led Him into the wilderness to do battle against the devil. For 40 days and nights He ate nothing at all, and all that time the devil tempted Him. At the end of the 40 days, He was very hungry. Then the devil attacked Him more fiercely than ever.

First, the devil said to Jesus, "If You are truly the Son of God, command that these stones turn into loaves of bread."

But the Lord answered him, "It is written in God's Word, 'Man shall not live on bread alone, but on every word that comes from the mouth of God.'"

Then the devil took Him into Jerusalem to the highest place of the Temple and said, "If You are the Son of God, throw Yourself down from here; because it is written in God's Word, 'He shall give His angels charge concerning you, and they shall hold you up with their hands so that you do not strike your foot against a stone.'"

Jesus said, "On the other hand, it is also written, 'You shall not test the Lord your God.'"

Next, the devil took Him to a high mountain and showed Him all the world's kingdoms in their glory. Then he said, "I will give You all these things if You will bow down and worship me."

But Jesus said, "Get away from Me, Satan! For it is written, 'You shall worship the Lord your God only.'"

That was the end of the devil's attacks of temptation for the time being.

Jesus replied, "The Scriptures say, 'You must worship the LORD your God and serve only Him.'"

Luke 4:8

Jesus Chooses His Followers

Matthew 4:18–22; John 1:35–51; Mark 3:16–19

One day Jesus saw two men fishing. They were brothers, and their names were Simon Peter and Andrew. Jesus called to them, "Follow Me and I will make you fishers of men." They left their nets right away, and went with Him. A little farther on He saw two other brothers, James and John. They were in a boat with their father, Zebedee, busy mending the fishing nets. James and John followed Jesus as soon as He called them.

The next day in Galilee, Jesus met a man named Philip. When Jesus called him to come, Philip came with the other four who were already following Jesus. Philip went off quickly to speak to someone named Nathanael. When he found him, Philip said excitedly, "We have found the One Moses and the prophets wrote about, Jesus of Nazareth!" But Nathanael asked, "Can anything good come out of Nazareth?"

Philip just answered, "Come and see!" When Jesus saw Nathanael coming toward Him, He greeted him with these words: "Behold, a sincere Israelite, whose heart is altogether honest!" Nathanael answered in surprise, "But how do You know me?"

He was quite surprised when Jesus then said, "I saw you before Philip called you, when you were sitting under the fig tree." Nathanael could only say, "Teacher, You are the Son of God. You are the King of Israel!"

That's how the Lord Jesus began choosing His disciples. There were others – Simon the Zealot, James the son of Alphaeus, Matthew, Thomas, Philip, Judas Iscariot, and Thaddeus. These 12 men were with Him during the three years in which He preached and healed and did all kinds of miracles.

The next day Jesus decided to go to Galilee. He found Philip and said to him, "Come, follow Me."

John 1:43

Jesus calls His first disciples, Simon and Andrew, to follow Him so that He can make them fishers of men. (Mark 1:16-18)

Water Turned into Wine

John 2:1–12

One day Jesus and His disciples were invited to a wedding feast. The wedding was in the little village of Cana in Galilee. His mother, Mary, was there, too. The feast was a great party until they ran out of wine. It was a problem that there was not enough wine for everyone. But Mary had an idea. She went to Jesus and told Him that there was no wine left.

There were six large stone water jars in the house. Each of the jars held about 25 gallons of water. Jesus told the servants to fill them all to the brim with clean water. Then He told them to dip out some of the water and take it to the man in charge.

When the man tasted it, he was surprised. He had thought that the wine was gone, but now they brought him the best wine he had tasted so far. He didn't know where it had come from; but the servants knew!

The man in charge went to the bridegroom to ask about this delicious wine. "Usually," he said, "the best wine is served first, and afterward, when people have drunk a lot, they bring out the wine that isn't as good. But you have kept the best until last."

This was the first miracle that was performed by Jesus; later He would do many more.

This miraculous sign at Cana in Galilee was the first time Jesus revealed His glory. And His disciples believed in Him.

John 2:11

Jesus Teaches a Pharisee

John 3:1–21

When the feast was over, Jesus went down to Capernaum with His family and His disciples and spent a few days there. Then He went to Jerusalem for the Passover Feast in the Temple.

One night while Jesus was in Jerusalem, one of the Pharisees, a man called Nicodemus, came to see Him while it was dark and no one could see him.

The Pharisees were very strictly religious Jews. They were proud of the careful way they kept the law. Nicodemus was afraid of what the other Pharisees would say about him if they knew he had talked to Jesus, but he really wanted to talk with Him.

"Master," he said, "we know that You are a teacher who has come from God. No one could do the miracles You do." Jesus answered, "Truly, I tell you, unless a person is born again, they cannot see the kingdom of God."

Nicodemus didn't understand what Jesus meant, and that He was speaking about the new hearts we all need for God. "How can a person be born when they are old?" he asked. "How can anyone be born twice?"

Jesus answered, "I tell you that unless you are born of water and God's Spirit, you cannot enter into the kingdom of God."

He meant that we must be born of God's Spirit, otherwise we cannot become the children of God. He told Nicodemus that this was all very mysterious. Just as we cannot tell where the wind begins or where it is going, so we cannot tell how God's Spirit gives new birth. Nicodemus was still confused.

Then Jesus said, "As Moses lifted up the brass snake on a pole in the wilderness to save the people of Israel, so the Son of Man must also be lifted up so that all who believe in Him may have everlasting life. God so loves the world that He gave His only Son, so that whoever believes in Him should not die but have everlasting life.

"God did not send His Son into the world to condemn the world, but so that people could be saved. But those who will not come to the Son have condemned themselves already."

In this way Jesus was teaching how He would have to die on the cross to save His people from their sins.

"There is no judgment against anyone who believes in Him. But anyone who does not believe in Him has already been judged for not believing in God's one and only Son. And the judgment is based on this fact: God's light came into the world, but people loved the darkness more than the light, for their actions were evil."

John 3:18-19

John the Baptist Is Murdered

John 3:23–30; Matthew 14:1–12; Mark 6:14–29

When Jesus began to teach and do miracles, many of John the Baptist's disciples left him and went to follow Jesus. John expected this and he knew that it must happen. Once he told his followers, "He must increase, but I must decrease."

At that time, the wife of King Herod Antipas, whose name was Herodias, was a very wicked woman. She didn't like hearing of this man going around teaching people about God. She persuaded Herod to have John arrested and thrown into prison.

Herod himself was very interested in what John said, but Herodias hated him because he said that it was not lawful for Herod to marry her since she was really the wife of his brother, Philip. She disliked John so much that she wanted Herod to have him killed, but Herod was afraid to do that, because he knew that John was a holy man. Instead, he had John locked up in prison.

Some while afterwards, on Herod's birthday, the daughter of Herodias, Salome, came to dance for Herod. He enjoyed her dancing so much that he promised to give her anything she asked for as a reward. She asked her mother what she should request. That gave the terrible Herodias the chance she was waiting for. Herodias told Salome to ask for the head of John the Baptist on a plate. Herod was very upset, but because he had made a promise and didn't want to break it in front of his guests, he sent soldiers to John's cell to behead John and to bring his head to Salome.

That's how the life ended of the man Jesus called the greatest of all the prophets.

Later, John's disciples came for his body and buried it. Then they went and told Jesus what had happened.

Matthew 14:12

A Stranger at the Well

John 4:4–43

One day when Jesus was traveling through the land of Samaria from Judea to Galilee, He came to a city called Sychar. Just outside the city was a well that Jacob had made many centuries before. Jesus had traveled very far and it was hot, so He sat down beside the well. While He was sitting there, a Samaritan woman came from the city to draw water. He asked her to give Him some water to drink. His disciples had gone into the city to buy food and He had no way to get water out of the well.

It surprised the Samaritan woman that He would speak to her because He was a Jew. The Jews usually had nothing to do with the Samaritans because Jews considered them "unclean." She asked Him why He was speaking to her and this was His answer: "If you knew who was asking you for water, you would instead have asked Him for water, and He would have given you the water of life."

She answered, "But how could You get water? The well is deep, and You have nothing with which to draw water. Where could You get the water of life You speak about?" She did not understand what He meant.

Then Jesus said, "Everyone who drinks water from this well will get thirsty again, but whoever drinks of the water that I give will never be thirsty again. The water I give will become in them a fountain overflowing to eternal life."

The woman still did not understand what He meant. She said, "Sir, give me this water so that I will not get thirsty again, or have to walk this long way to get water."

Jesus only answer was, "Get your husband and come back." Ashamed, the Samaritan woman replied, "I have no husband."

Jesus said to her, "You're right. You have no husband. However, you have had five husbands. But the man you're living with now is not your husband."

The woman said, "Sir, I can see that You are a prophet." Then she tried to change the subject. "Please tell me which of us are correct, the Jews or Samaritans. You Jews say we must worship at Jerusalem in the Temple there, but our people believe we should worship here on Mount Gerizim."

But Jesus answered, "Woman, you do not know what you worship. The time is coming when God will be worshiped in many places other than this mountain or Jerusalem. God is a Spirit, and all who worship Him must do so in spirit and in truth and will be able to worship Him wherever they are." Then she said: "I know that the Messiah is coming. When He comes He will teach us all things. Then all of this will make sense."

Jesus said, "I am the Messiah!"

Jesus tells the woman at the well that if she drinks
the water He gives, she will never be thirsty again.
The water Jesus gives leads to eternal life. (John 4:13-14)

At about this time the disciples came back from the city. They were surprised that Jesus was talking to this woman, but they didn't say anything about it. In the meantime the woman left her waterpot and rushed into the city, calling excitedly to everyone, "Come and see a Man who told me all the things that I have done. Could He be the Christ?"

While this was happening, the disciples showed Jesus the food they had bought, and asked Him to eat. But He said, "I have food to eat that you do not know about." They wondered where He could have found food, but He said, "My food is to do the will of My Father who sent Me, and to complete the work He has given Me. Do you not say, 'There are still four months and then comes the harvest'? I say to you, open your eyes and look around. The fields are already white for harvest."

He meant that there were many people whose hearts were ready to receive the message of salvation. Already fruit was being reaped for eternal life.

For two days Jesus stayed on in Sychar, and many hearts were turned to God because of what He told them. Then He continued on His journey to Galilee.

Jesus replied, "If you only knew the gift God has for you and who you are speaking to, you would ask Me, and I would give you living water."

John 4:10

Jesus Heals in Capernaum

John 4:46–54

One of the officers in King Herod's court came to Cana from Capernaum just to see Jesus. He was worried about his son who was very sick back at home. The officer asked Jesus to heal his son. "Please," he asked, "Come to Capernaum before my son dies."

But Jesus said, "Go back home; your son is well." The officer believed Jesus and started home. On the way he met some of his servants who were looking for him. They told him that his son was getting better. The official asked the men what time the boy had started getting better. He discovered that it was at the exact moment Jesus had said, "Your son is well."

From that time on, the man and all his family believed in Jesus.

Then the father realized that that was the very time Jesus had told him, "Your son will live." And he and his entire household believed in Jesus.

John 4:53

Trouble in Nazareth

Luke 4:16–31

Jesus went on to Nazareth, the town where He grew up. On the Sabbath day He went to the synagogue as usual.

This time when it was time for the reading of the Bible, He took the scroll and began to read from the book of Isaiah. This is what He read: "The Spirit of the Lord is upon me, for He has anointed Me to bring Good News to the poor.

"He has sent Me to proclaim that captives will be released, that the blind will see, that the oppressed will be set free, and that the time of the Lord's favor has come."

Then Jesus said, "Today this Scripture is being fulfilled in front of you all." Then He began to preach to them. Everyone who heard Him was surprised at the grace of His words. They asked one another, "But isn't this Joseph's son?"

Jesus said to them, "No doubt you will quote the proverb, 'Physician, heal Thyself' – do here what we hear You did in Capernaum. But I say to you that a prophet is not honored in his own land. Let Me remind you that in the days of Elijah, when there was a drought for three-and-a-half years, there were many widows in Israel; but Elijah was not sent to any of them, but only to a widow in Zarephath in the land of Sidon. And there were many lepers in Israel during the lifetime of the prophet Elisha, but none of them were cleansed of their leprosy, except Naaman the Syrian."

When they heard this, the people in the synagogue were angry. They rushed forward and dragged Jesus out of the town to the top of the hill on which the town was built. They wanted to throw Him over the cliff and kill Him, but He miraculously passed through the middle of the crowd and escaped.

Then Jesus went to Capernaum where He taught in the synagogue each Sabbath day.

Everyone spoke well of Him and was amazed by the gracious words that came from His lips. "How can this be?" they asked. "Isn't this Joseph's son?"

Luke 4:22

Some of Jesus' Miracles

Mark 1:21–39; Luke 5:1–11

Jesus did some wonderful miracles when He was in Capernaum that showed His power was from God.

One day He was speaking in the synagogue and a man who had a demon in his heart shouted at Him. "Leave us alone," the demon called out. "What do we have to do with You, Jesus of Nazareth? Have You come to destroy us? I know that You are the Holy One of God."

Jesus spoke sharply to the demon. "Be quiet, and come out of him," He said. The demon threw the man down on the floor in a kind of fit. When the man woke up, the demon was gone and it didn't come back to him again.

The people who saw what happened were amazed. What power Jesus had – He just spoke and the demon left! Jesus' fame spread through all the countryside. Jesus taught with such authority that those who listened to Him were amazed.

He did not teach as the scribes did, using longwinded arguments. He spoke with power and truth that no one could argue against.

Jesus did many wonderful miracles. For example, Simon Peter's mother-in-law was in bed with a very bad fever. Jesus went to her room, took her hand and lifted her up. As He did that, the fever left her and she got up and prepared a meal for Jesus and the disciples.

That evening many people brought their loved ones who were sick or possessed by demons to the house where Jesus was and He healed them.

Jesus was very tired after that, so He went to a quiet place in the desert to pray and to get strength again from His Father in heaven.

A few days later as He walked near the Sea of Galilee, a huge crowd of people gathered to hear Him preach. The crowd was very big and the people pushed in around Him. It was so crowded that He could hardly speak.

There were two fishing boats that were not being used on the shore so He climbed into one that belonged to Simon Peter and taught from there. When He finished speaking He told Simon Peter to row the boat out into deeper water, and let down his nets to catch some fish. Simon Peter said, "We fished all night and caught nothing. But, since You told me to, I will let down the nets."

When Simon Peter and his helpers tried to pull in their nets, they were so full of fish that the nets began to break. Simon Peter called to the owner of another boat nearby to come and help. Both ships began to sink in the water because of the weight of the fish.

When Simon Peter saw the full nets he threw himself down in front of Jesus and cried out, "Lord, depart from me! I am too sinful for You to have anything to do with me." James and John, the sons of Zebedee, Simon Peter's partners, were also amazed.

But Jesus said to Simon, "Do not be afraid. From now on you will become fishers of men."

When they got their boats back to land, they left everything they had and followed Jesus.

Jesus replied, "We must go on to other towns as well, and I will preach to them, too. That is why I came."

Mark 1:38

More People Are Healed

Mark 1:40–45; 2:1–12; Matthew 8:1–4; 9:1–8

After His visit to Capernaum, Jesus went from village to village in Galilee, teaching and healing the sick as He went. Crowds of people followed Him, to hear Him teach and to see what miracles He did. The news spread quickly of how He had healed the sick in Capernaum.

One day a leper came to Him and begged Him to take away his terrible sickness. Other people who were nearby stood back. They were afraid the sickness might spread to them. But Jesus didn't turn away from the sick man. The leper worshiped Him and said, "Lord, if You are willing, You can make me clean."

Jesus stretched out His hand and touched him, saying, "I am willing; be cleansed." And immediately the horrible white, dead patches of leprosy disappeared from the man.

Jesus told him not to tell anyone what had happened but to go to the priest and offer God a sacrifice of thanksgiving.

But the man couldn't keep quiet about the amazing thing that had happened to him! The more people he told, the more people rushed to listen to Jesus. People brought their sick and demon-possessed friends and family to Him to be healed. So many came that Jesus couldn't even get into the villages because of the crowd.

After several days of being surrounded by the crowds, Jesus managed to get back to Capernaum. One day He was teaching in a house and many Pharisees and doctors of the law were there to listen. They had come from all the villages and towns around Galilee. Some even came from Judea and Jerusalem. As usual, many sick people were brought to Jesus to be healed. But some people couldn't get their sick friends into the house because it was so full.

A group of men had brought one of their friends for Jesus to heal. He was on a stretcher because he couldn't walk or even move his arms. But they couldn't get him into the house. How could they get him to Jesus? They had an idea! They went up onto the roof of the house, carrying their friend on his bed. They removed some of the tiles from the roof. Then they tied ropes to the stretcher and lowered their friend down right in front of Jesus.

When Jesus saw how much faith those friends had in Him, He turned to the sick man and said, "Son, your sins are forgiven!"

When the Pharisees heard this, they thought, "That is blasphemy! Only God can forgive sins. What right does this Man have to say such things?"

Jesus knew exactly what they were thinking and He said,

"Why do you think evil of Me in your hearts? Which is easier to say, 'Your sins are forgiven,' or 'Get up from your bed and walk'?"

Then Jesus turned again to the sick man and said, "But so that you may know that the Son of Man has the power to forgive sins, I say to you, get up, take your bed, and go back to your home."

At once the man got up, took the stretcher he had been lying on, and went home. He praised God all the way. Those who saw what the Lord did were amazed, and even a little bit afraid. They said, "We have seen strange things here today!"

But the Pharisees hated Jesus.

Seeing their faith, Jesus said to the man, "Young man, your sins are forgiven."

Luke 5:20

A group of men lower their friend through the roof of the house where Jesus was teaching so that Jesus could heal him. (Mark 2:4-5)

Sabbath Work

Matthew 12:1-14; Mark 2:23-28; 3:1-6

While Jesus traveled through the towns of Galilee and Judea, healing the sick and teaching and doing good to anyone who was in trouble, the Pharisees and some others who hated Him kept trying to find some way to destroy Him.

They accused Him of blasphemy when He told the paralyzed man in Capernaum that his sins were forgiven and healed him. One of their plans was to try to show that Jesus didn't keep the law and broke God's commandments.

Another favorite was to try to trick Jesus into breaking the Sabbath law, which said, "Remember the Sabbath day and keep it holy." The Pharisees had made many additions to the law and some of the additions were just ridiculous. The Pharisees were on the lookout to see whether Jesus broke any of their rules.

One Sabbath day, Jesus and His disciples were walking through a wheat field and they were hungry. They picked a few grains of wheat and ate them. When the Pharisees saw this, they said, "Your disciples are breaking the law on the Sabbath day."

He replied, "Haven't you read what David did when he and his followers were hungry? They went into the house of God and took some of the sacred bread that only the priests are allowed to eat. And haven't you read in the law that the priests break the Sabbath law in the course of their work in the Temple and are innocent?

"I tell you, there is Someone greater than the Temple here. If you understood what the Scripture means where God says, 'I ask for compassion and not a sacrifice,' you would not condemn the innocent. The Son of Man is also Lord of the Sabbath." However, Jesus' words did not silence them. Jesus went on to the synagogue and when

He got there, they brought a man with a crippled hand to Him. Once again, trying to trick Jesus, they asked, "Is it lawful to heal on the Sabbath?"

Jesus answered, "Which one of you wouldn't rescue his sheep if it fell into a pit on the Sabbath day? Isn't a man more valuable than a sheep! So then it is right and lawful to do good on the Sabbath." Then He looked at the man with the deformed hand and said, "Stretch out your hand!" He did and it was healed and became useful just like his other hand.

Instead of being happy for the man, the Pharisees continued planning to kill Jesus.

"Yes, the law permits a person to do good on the Sabbath."
Matthew 12:12

A Crippled Man at the Pool

John 5:1–18

After this, Jesus went up to the Passover Feast in Jerusalem. He went there every year.

Near the Sheep Gate in the city wall of Jerusalem was a pool of water that was famous for the miraculous way it healed sick people. At certain times the water was mysteriously stirred up by God's angel. The first sick person to step into the water after that was immediately healed.

Many sick people lay around the pool waiting for the water to be stirred. One man had been sick for 38 years. He was very crippled and couldn't get down into the water quickly enough. He didn't have any friends to help him get into the pool.

When Jesus came to the pool and saw the man, He said, "Do you want to get well?'

The man answered, "Sir, there is no one to help me down into the pool. The others get there before me when the water is stirred up."

Jesus said, "Pick up your bed, and walk." And at once the man stood up, and was well! This happened on the Sabbath. When the Pharisees saw the man who had been lame carrying his bed down the street, they told him angrily that he was breaking the law.

He said, "The Man who made me well again told me to pick up my bed and go home."

Then they said, "Who was this Man? Show Him to us." But Jesus had slipped away into the crowd, and the man did not know who He was.

Later Jesus found the man in the Temple and said to him, "You are well now, but be careful that you do not sin, or something worse will happen to you." Then the man left. When the Jews asked him who had healed him, he was able to tell them that it was Jesus.

Once more the Pharisees went to Jesus and accused Him of being a lawbreaker because He had healed a man on the Sabbath.

Jesus said, "My Father has worked until now, and I work also." That made them very angry. He was not only breaking the Sabbath law, but He was also saying that He was equal with God.

From then on, whatever Jesus did, the Pharisees tried to trap Him into doing wrong. They tried to plan a way to have Him killed.

Jesus told the man, "Stand up, pick up your mat, and walk!" Instantly, the man was healed! He rolled up his sleeping mat and began walking! But this miracle happened on the Sabbath.

John 5:8-9

Important Things Jesus Wants You to Know

Mark 2:13-17; Matthew 5-7

One day when Jesus was walking down the street in Capernaum, He passed a tax collector named Matthew. Jesus said to him, "Follow Me." Matthew stood up, left what he was doing, and without a moment's delay followed Jesus and became one of His disciples.

That night Jesus ate with Matthew at his house. Other tax gatherers came to the dinner, too. The tax collectors were hated and despised by the Jews because they collected money from their own people to give to the Romans. They often demanded more money than the people owed and kept the extra money for themselves.

When the scribes and Pharisees saw that Jesus was eating with the despised tax collectors, they asked His disciples, "Why does He eat with tax collectors and sinners?"

When He heard this, Jesus said to them, "Healthy people aren't the ones who need a doctor, but the sick do. I didn't come to call the righteous, but to call the sinners. I come to these people because they know their need. You think that you need nothing."

One day Jesus climbed a little way up the side of a mountain near the Sea of Galilee and sat down. He called His disciples to sit close to Him. Jesus told them how people who belong to the kingdom of God must live. He explained the principles, or rules, of the Kingdom.

We call what He said there the "Sermon on the Mount." Here is a part of the most beautiful passages from the Sermon. The entire Sermon can be read in the fifth, sixth and seventh chapters of Matthew in the Bible.

"God blesses those who are poor
  and realize their need for Him, for
    the Kingdom of Heaven is theirs.
God blesses those who mourn,
  for they will be comforted.
God blesses those who are humble,
  for they will inherit the whole earth.

God blesses those who hunger and thirst for justice, for they will be satisfied.

God blesses those who are merciful, for they will be shown mercy.

God blesses those whose hearts are pure, for they will see God.

God blesses those who work for peace, for they will be called the children of God. God blesses those who are persecuted for doing right, for the Kingdom of Heaven is theirs.

God blesses you when people mock you and persecute you and lie about you and say all sorts of evil things against you because you are My followers. Be happy about it! Be very glad! For a great reward awaits you in heaven.

And remember, the ancient prophets were persecuted in the same way."

It was also in the Sermon that Jesus taught the disciples to pray what we call the "Lord's Prayer":

"Our Father in heaven,
may Your name be kept holy.
May Your Kingdom come soon.
May Your will be done on earth,
as it is in heaven.
Give us today the food we need,
and forgive us our sins,
as we have forgiven those who sin against us.
And don't let us yield to temptation,
but rescue us from the evil one."

"Healthy people don't need a doctor – sick people do. I have come to call not those who think they are righteous, but those who know they are sinners."

Mark 2:17

More Amazing Miracles

Matthew 8:5–13; Luke 7:1–17, 36–50

When Jesus went back to Capernaum, one of the first men who came to Him was a Roman centurion, an officer who was in charge of a hundred soldiers. Actually, this man didn't come to Jesus himself, but he sent some Jewish elders to ask Jesus to come and heal his servant. The poor servant was paralyzed and in great pain.

The elders respected the centurion because he loved the Jewish people. He even had a synagogue built for them in Capernaum. The elders begged Jesus to go to the centurion's home and heal the servant.

Jesus started to the centurion's home, but before they got there they met some of his friends coming with a special message for Jesus. "Do not trouble Yourself further. The centurion doesn't feel worthy enough for You to come to his home. That's why he did not come to You himself. He was ashamed to trouble You. But he asks You only to speak the word because he knows that

then his slave will be healed. He is a man of authority, but he knows that You have even greater authority. If he gives orders to his servants, they obey. He knows that Your orders will be obeyed also. Please give the order and his servant will be healed."

Jesus was amazed at what they said. He told the people around Him, "I haven't found such faith as this man has even among the people of Israel." When the centurion's friends returned to his house they found the slave was well again. Jesus had heard the centurion's plea.

Soon afterward, something even more wonderful happened. Jesus went to a town called Nain. As He got close to the town, He met a sad procession coming toward them. It was a funeral procession.

A dead man was being carried out of the town to be buried. He was the only son of a widow, and she was very upset. When

Jesus saw her, His heart was filled with sorrow. So He went up to her and said, "Do not cry." Then He went and touched the stretcher that held the body and said, "Young man, get up." The young man sat up and began to speak and Jesus gave him back to his mother.

All the people who saw this were filled with fear and whispered among themselves, "A great prophet has arisen among us!" and, "God has visited His people." The news of what had happened spread very quickly through all the land.

One day a Pharisee named Simon invited Jesus to come and eat with him at his home.

As Jesus sat beside the table in the Pharisee's home, a woman came in. This woman had been a very bad person. She brought an alabaster jar of expensive perfume. She was crying as she knelt at Jesus' feet and kissed them, and dried them with her hair. Then she poured the perfume over them.

Simon saw this and he thought to himself, "If this man were really a prophet, He would know what a terrible kind of person this woman is and would have nothing to do with her at all."

Jesus knew what he was thinking and said to him, "Simon, I have something to say to you."

"Master, say it," replied the Pharisee.

Jesus told him a little story. "Two men owed money to a certain moneylender. The one owed him 500 days' wages, the other only 50 days' wages, but neither of them were able to pay. He kindly let them both off. Which of them will love him more, do you think?"

Simon answered, "I suppose the one who was forgiven the larger debt."

Jesus said, "Your answer is correct." Then He looked at the woman and said to Simon, "Do you see this woman? When I came into this house, you didn't even offer Me water to wash My feet. She has washed them with her tears and wiped them with her hair. You gave me no kiss of welcome, but she has not stopped kissing My feet. You didn't anoint My head with oil, but she has covered My feet with sweet perfume.

"I tell you, Simon, that her sins, which were many, are forgiven, for she loved much, but the one who is forgiven little, loves little."

Jesus turned to the woman and said, "Your sins are forgiven."

Those at table with Him looked at one another and asked, "Who can this be, who even forgives sins?"

But Jesus ignored them and said again to the woman, "Your faith has saved you; go in peace."

A sick servant was made well again and a widow's son was brought back from the dead. A sinful woman was saved and made His loving servant. Could anyone fail to believe in Jesus? But there were some who still hated Him.

When Jesus heard this, He was amazed. Turning to those who were following Him, He said, "I tell you the truth, I haven't seen faith like this in all Israel!"

Matthew 8:10

Parable of the Sower

Matthew 13:1–23; Mark 4; Luke 8:4–15

Jesus often told stories to the crowds of people who came to listen to Him. The stories were parables, or stories with a meaning. Jesus used them to teach the people truth from God's Word.

One day, when He was sitting beside the Sea of Galilee, a large crowd gathered around Him

to listen to His teaching. He told them what is perhaps the best known of all His stories, the Parable of the Sower.

"A sower went out one day," He said, "to sow seed in his field. As he scattered the seed, some of it fell on the pathway next to the field, and the birds came and ate it up. Other seed fell on the

The sower scatters the seed. Some of the seed falls on the pathway next to the field, some on the rocky places in the field, some in the thorn bushes, and some on good soil. (Matthew 13:3-9)

rocky places in the field, where the soil was not very deep. That seed grew very quickly; but the young plants didn't have strong roots because of the shallow soil. When the sun beat down on them, they withered away and died.

"Other seed fell among the thorn bushes, and the thorns grew up and choked the young plants. But some of the seed fell on good soil. Those young plants grew up and became a good crop. In some places there was 100 times as much grain as the farmer had planted. In other places there was 60 times as much and in others, 30 times. Let everyone that has ears listen to what I say."

Then Jesus explained to the disciples what the story of the sower meant. "The sower is a person who sows the seed of God's Word among people. The seed that falls on the pathway beside the field is like the Word of God sown in human hearts and immediately snatched away by the devil. The seed that falls in rocky places is like the Word sown in the hearts of people who accept it and are immediately full of joy, but before long they turn back to their old ways and do not grow in God's grace. The seed sown in thorny places is like God's Word being choked in people's hearts because they care more about riches and the things of the world.

"Then there are those in whose hearts the Word is sown and who honestly try to live by the Word. They produce fruit in their lives to God's glory, some 30, 60 or 100-fold."

"Listen! A farmer went out to plant some seed. As he scattered it across his field, some of the seed fell on a footpath, and the birds came and ate it."

Mark 4:3-4

The Good Seed and the Kingdom of Heaven

Matthew 13:24–30, 33–50

Another story Jesus told was about a man who bought good seed and sowed it in his field. At night while his servants were asleep, his enemy came and spread the seeds of a weed in the same field.

When the seed sprouted and the wheat came up, the servants were upset to see the weeds there, too. They went to their master and asked him how this could have happened. He told them that an enemy had done it.

The servants wanted to pull out all the weeds, but the master wouldn't let them. If they tried to get rid of the weeds, they would step on the wheat and kill some of it.

Wheat and weeds must be allowed to grow together until the harvest time. Then the harvesters would be told to gather the weeds into bundles first and burn them. After that the wheat would be gathered and put into his barn.

Jesus explained this story to the disciples: "The one who sowed the good seed," said Jesus, "is the Son of Man. The field is the world, and the good seed are those who belong to the kingdom of God. The bad seed and the weeds that grew from it are the sons of the devil. The harvesters are God's angels. The weeds in the story are gathered and burned, and that's what will happen at the end of the age. The Son of Man will send His angels into the world. They will gather all who have not served God and they will be thrown into everlasting fire. It will be terrible for them. But the righteous, those faithful to the kingdom of God, will come to heaven."

Jesus also described the kingdom of God as being like leaven, or yeast, which a woman took and mixed into dough made with three measures of flour. The leaven disappeared, but it made all the dough rise.

He also told them that the kingdom of heaven is like

**The man stops his servants from pulling the weeds
that had come up between the wheat. (Matthew 13:28-29)**

a treasure hidden in a field, which a man found. He then sold everything he had and bought the field.

The kingdom of heaven is also like a merchant looking for pearls, who, when he finds one pearl of great value, goes and sells everything he has so he can buy the pearl.

Here is another story Jesus told: "The Kingdom of Heaven is like a farmer who planted good seed in his field."

Matthew 13:24

"Peace, Be Still"

Matthew 8:23–27; Mark 4:35–41

Jesus was very tired so He asked the disciples to take Him to the other side of the Sea of Galilee where He could find some peace and quiet. It had been a long day of teaching, without time to rest or even to eat.

As soon as the boat left the shore, Jesus lay down on the cushion in the back of the boat and fell asleep.

Suddenly a big storm blew up on the sea. The little boat was tossed back and forth by the waves. The disciples were experienced fishermen, but even they were terrified at the strength of the storm. They woke Jesus up and cried out, "Lord, save us. We are going to die!"

Jesus said, "Why are you afraid, you men of little faith?" Then Jesus said to the storm, "Peace, be still!" The wind stopped blowing at once and the waves calmed down.

The disciples were amazed! "What kind of Man is this," they wondered, "that even the wind and the waves obey Him?"

The disciples were absolutely terrified. "Who is this Man?" they asked each other. "Even the wind and waves obey Him!"

Mark 4:41

Jesus tells the wind and the waves to calm down.
They listen and the storm disappears. (Matthew 8:26)

Jesus Heals People

Matthew 9:18–31; Mark 5:21–43; Luke 8:40–56

Jesus did wonderful things! He healed the sick and He even brought dead people back to life!

One time when Jesus was teaching in Capernaum, a ruler named Jairus pushed through the crowds to Him and cried out, "Lord, my daughter is dying, but I know that if You come and lay Your hands on her she will live again."

Jesus left at once to go to Jairus's home. But on the way someone else stopped Him who also had a very bad problem. It was a woman who had been sick for 12 long years. She had heard of Jesus' amazing power. So she pushed through the crowd that was around Him, and bent down and touched the hem of His robe. As she touched it, she felt the sickness going out of her. She had only touched His robe, but Jesus knew what had happened. He asked, "Who touched My clothes?" He look-ed around, and as His eyes fell on the woman, she started shaking in fright. She threw herself down in front of Him and told Him everything. Jesus kindly said, "Daughter, your faith has made you well. Go in peace, and be healed of your sickness."

Everyone was amazed at what had just happened, but then messengers came from Jairus's home and told him, "Your daughter is dead. Don't bother Jesus any more."

Jesus heard them and He said, "Don't be afraid, just believe." Then He told the rest of the people not to follow Him any more. He only took His disciples Peter, James and John with Him to Jairus's house.

When they reached Jairus's house, it was filled with people who were crying and grieving for the girl. Jesus made everyone leave the house, except Jairus and his wife. Then He took them and the three disciples into the room where the girl was lying. He took her by the hand and said to her, 'Little girl, I say to you, wake up!" She immediately awoke, got up and walked around. Her father and mother and the disciples were amazed! Then Jesus told the parents to give her something to eat.

After this miracle, Jesus left Capernaum again, but everywhere He went He healed sick people and taught those who gathered around Him. One day He found two blind men begging by the roadside. They cried out to Him to have mercy on them. He asked them only one question: "Do you believe that I am able to give you back your sight?" When they said they did believe, He gently touched their eyes and at once they could see!

Then Jesus took her by the hand and said in a loud voice, "My child, get up!" And at that moment her life returned, and she immediately stood up! Then Jesus told them to give her something to eat.

Luke 8:54-55

A Boy Shares His Lunch

Mark 6:30–44; Luke 9:10–17; Matthew 14:13–21; John 6:1–5

The disciples finished the job Jesus gave them of preaching in Galilee. Then they came back to Jesus. They went with Him to the little town of Bethsaida.

They needed quiet time after the hard work they had been doing, but crowds of people followed them. Jesus stopped on a hillside beside the Sea of Galilee to teach about the kingdom of God and to heal the sick people who came to Him.

By the time He was finished teaching it was late in the day. The people who were there to listen to Jesus had no food and the disciples said He should send them home to eat.

But Jesus shocked the disciples by telling them to give food to the people. The disciples didn't know where they could find enough food to feed 5,000 men and even more women and children. Then Jesus asked, "What food do you have for them?"

Andrew answered, "There is a boy here who has five barley loaves and two fish, but what good are they when we have so many people to feed?"

Jesus said, "Tell all the people to sit down." When all of them were sitting on the grass, Jesus took the five loaves of bread. When He had thanked God for it, He broke the bread and handed the pieces to the disciples to give to the people.

Then He did the same with the fish. Every single person there had as much to eat as they wanted. When they were finished, the disciples picked up the leftovers. There were 12 full baskets left over!

The people were amazed by this miracle and they said, "Truly this must be the Great Prophet sent by God."

Then they wanted to make Him king, but Jesus slipped away from them and went up into the mountains alone to pray.

Jesus took the five loaves and two fish, looked up toward heaven, and blessed them. Then, breaking the loaves into pieces, He kept giving the bread to the disciples so they could distribute it to the people. He also divided the fish for everyone to share.

Mark 6:41

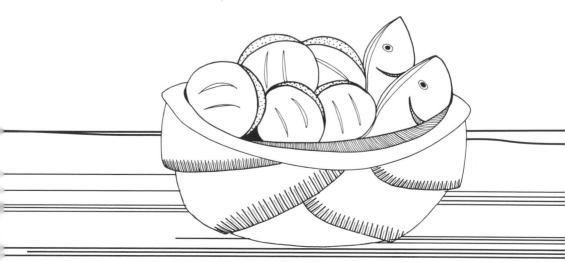

Jesus takes five loaves of bread and two fish from the little boy, and feeds more than 5,000 people with it. (Matthew 14:19-21)

Jesus Walks on Water

Matthew 14:22-33; Mark 6:45-52; John 6:16-21

It was just beginning to get dark when the disciples got into a boat and started to row across the sea to Capernaum.

The wind started blowing stronger, and the waves got bigger and bigger so that the disciples couldn't row across to the other side of the sea before it got completely dark.

They were rowing as hard as they could, but had only gone about three or four miles when they saw a man walking on the sea toward them.

They were scared because they weren't sure who it was or how someone could walk on top of the water. But then Jesus called out, "It's Me, Jesus. Don't be afraid."

Peter shouted, "Lord, if it is You, command me to come to You on the water."

Jesus said, "Come!" and Peter got out of the boat and walked on top of the water toward Jesus.

But then he noticed the roaring wind and saw the big waves and he got scared. The moment he got scared he started to sink. Peter cried out, "Lord, save me!" Jesus grabbed Peter and said, "O man of little faith, why did you doubt?"

When they both climbed into the boat, the wind stopped and the boat was at the place they had been rowing toward. The disciples worshiped Jesus and said to Him, "You are certainly God's Son!"

"Yes, come," Jesus said. So Peter went over the side of the boat and walked on the water toward Jesus.

Matthew 14:29

Peter walks on the water towards Jesus, but then he gets scared and starts to sink. Jesus saves him. (Matthew 14:29-31)

Jesus Is the Bread of Life

John 6:22–70

Jesus and the disciples landed at Gennesaret, a little village just south of Capernaum. When the people saw who had come, they sent the news to all parts of the district.

Soon Jesus was surrounded by a great crowd. Some people who had seen Him multiplying the loaves and the fishes on the previous afternoon were there. They asked, "Master, when did You come here?"

But He knew what was in their hearts, and gave them the answer they really deserved: "You have looked for Me, not because you saw signs that proved My authority, but because you ate the food and your stomachs were filled. Do not work for the food that goes away, but for life, which the Son of Man shall give to you. On Him, God the Father has set His seal."

At once they challenged Him. "Show us a sign to prove that God has sent You. Moses gave our fathers manna in the wilderness. What do You give us?"

Jesus answered: "It was not Moses who gave the manna, but My Father in heaven. And now again it is My Father who gives you the true bread from heaven. I am the Bread of Life, whoever comes to Me shall not hunger, and whoever believes in Me shall never thirst."

They asked Him many questions and tried to trap Him in what He said. Most of them turned away from Him and did not follow Him any more. Among the few who remained were the 12 disciples.

Jesus sadly said to His disciples, "You do not want to go away, too, do you?"

Peter answered Him, "Lord, to whom shall we go? You have the words of eternal life."

"I am the bread that came down from heaven."

John 6:41

The Answer to a Mother's Prayer

Matthew 15:21–30; Mark 7:24–37; 8:22–26

When Jesus and His disciples left Capernaum, He went to Tyre and Sidon and lived on the coast of the Mediterranean Sea. This was not Jewish country, but Phoenicia, a part of what is now called Syria.

While Jesus and His disciples were walking one day, a Canaanite woman came to them and began to cry out to Him, "Have mercy on me, O Lord, Son of David. My daughter is possessed by a demon." But Jesus didn't say anything to her. The poor woman kept crying out to Him.

She made such a fuss that the disciples said to Him, "Please, Lord, send her away, because she is making so much noise."

But He answered, "I was sent to the lost sheep of the house of Israel."

She bowed down in front of Him and said, "Lord, help me!" Jesus said, "It's not right to take bread from the children and throw it to the dogs." He was saying that He had come to help God's people, the Israelites.

But the woman wisely answered, "Yes, Lord, but even the dogs can eat the crumbs that fall from their master's table."

Jesus answered, "O woman, your faith is very great. I have heard your plea, and will do as you wish." At that very moment her daughter was healed!

One day a man who was deaf and had trouble speaking was brought to Jesus. The man's friends begged Jesus to lay His hands on the man and heal him. Jesus took him away from the crowd, and put His fingers gently into the man's ears. Then He touched the man's tongue. With a deep sigh He then looked up to heaven, and said, "Be opened!" Immediately the man could hear and he was able to speak clearly.

The people were amazed. They said, "Look, He does all things well! He even makes the deaf to hear and the dumb to speak."

At Bethsaida, some people brought a blind man to Jesus. After taking the man aside privately, Jesus touched his eyes with saliva and then laid His hands gently on the man. "Do you see anything?" He asked.

The man answered, "I see men but they look like trees walking around." So Jesus laid His hands on the man's eyes again. Then the man was able to see clearly. He was so glad that he wanted to tell everyone, but Jesus told him not to go into the town or tell anyone what had happened. Jesus wanted people to come to Him to hear His teaching and have their souls healed, not to think of Him only as a miracle worker who could make their bodies well.

Jesus told the crowd not to tell anyone, but the more He told them not to, the more they spread the news. They were completely amazed and said again and again, "Everything He does is wonderful. He even makes the deaf to hear and gives speech to those who cannot speak."

Mark 7:36-37

Glory Shines from Jesus' Face

Matthew 16:13–23; 17:1–9; 18:1–3; Mark 8:27–33; 9:1–10, 33–35;

Jesus made a special point of explaining to His disciples who He was and what He Had come to do.

One day, Jesus asked His disciples a question, "Who do people say that I am?" They answered, "Some say John the Baptist come to life again. Others say Elijah. Some others say Jeremiah or one of the prophets."

Then Jesus asked, "But who do you say that I am?"

Simon Peter, always the first

to speak, said, "You are the Christ, the Son of the living God."

Then Jesus answered, "You are truly blessed, Simon, because flesh and blood did not reveal this to you, but My Father, who is in heaven. I also say that your name is now Peter, which means rock, and on this rock I will build My church. The gates of hell shall not have power over it."

What He meant was that He would build His church on the foundation of the faith that Peter had – faith that Jesus was the Christ whom God had sent.

There were other things that Jesus taught His disciples that they just couldn't understand. For instance, He told them about terrible things that were going to happen to Him before long. "The Son of Man must go up to Jerusalem," He said, "and suffer many things at the hands of the elders and chief priests and scribes. They will hand Him over to the Gentiles, and He will be spit on and made fun of, beaten and eventually killed. But on the third day He will rise again from the dead."

Peter was horrified to hear these things. He firmly said, "God forbid it, Lord! This shall never happen to You."

But Jesus turned to him and said, "Get behind Me, Satan! You are a hindrance to Me, because you look at everything from man's point of view, and not God's."

Jesus came to save His people from their sins by dying for them on the cross. If He didn't do that, there could be no salvation for anyone. That's why He spoke so sternly to Peter.

Then Jesus turned to the disciples and spoke very seriously to them, "If anyone wishes to follow Me, he must deny himself and take up his cross and come after Me. For whoever tries to save his life will lose it, and whoever gives up his life for My sake and the gospel's will save it. What good is it for a man if he gains the whole world but loses his own soul? What could a man give in exchange for his soul? If anyone is ashamed of Me and My words, then I will be ashamed of him when I come on the Day of Judgment."

About a week later, Jesus took Peter, James and John with Him to a quiet place at the top of a high mountain. While Jesus was praying there, the three disciples fell asleep.

Suddenly they awoke and saw the Lord Jesus had been transformed before them. His clothes had turned to a shining white, whiter than anything on earth. Then Elijah and Moses appeared and began talking with Him.

Peter wanted to build a shelter to cover them. But a voice from heaven said, "This is My dearly loved Son, who brings Me great joy. Listen to Him." The disciples were frightened and fell face down on the ground.

On another occasion, Jesus' disciples began arguing about which of them was the most important. They each wanted the best place in heaven. Jesus called them to Him and said, "If anyone wants to be first, let him look upon himself as the least of all, and be their servant."

Jesus picked up a little child and said, "Everyone who receives a small child like this in My name also receives Me. And whoever receives Me is not just receiving Me, but also Him who sent Me. Unless you become as humble as this little child, you will not enter the kingdom of heaven. "

Then a voice from the cloud said, "This is My Son, My Chosen One. Listen to Him."

Luke 9:35

Jesus tells His disciples about His coming death and His resurrection three days later. (Matthew 16:21)

How Often Must You Forgive?

Matthew 18:21–35

Peter had a question for Jesus, "Master, how many times must I forgive my brother if he hurts me? Is seven times enough?"

Jesus said, "No, not just seven times, but up to 70 times seven." He explained how the disciples should speak to another believer who had hurt them. He told them the parable, or story, of the unforgiving servant. It showed them that they should always be ready to forgive others.

This is the story: There was once a king who was owed money by his servant. He decided that it was time the servant paid him, so he called him in. But the man didn't have the money to pay the king, so the king commanded that he and his wife and children be sold into slavery. The man fell on his knees and begged the king to have patience with him.

The king felt sorry for him and forgave the whole debt. But the man was not such an unforgiving man. He found another man who owed him a small amount of money. He demanded that the man pay him, but the man had no money to pay. The second man begged the first man to have patience with him. Instead, the first man had him thrown into prison until he could pay back what he owed.

The king heard about this and was very angry. He sent for the man whose debt he had forgiven and said to him, "You wicked man! I forgave your debt when you begged me. Shouldn't you have had mercy on your friend as well? Since you didn't, now you will go to prison until you pay back all you owe me."

Then Jesus said, "This is how My heavenly Father will treat you, if you do not forgive your brother from the heart."

Then his master was filled with pity for him, and he released him and forgave his debt.

Matthew 18:27

288

The man is very happy because the king decided to forgive him all of his debt. (Matthew 18:26-27)

Jesus Continues His Ministry

Matthew 8:18-22; Luke 9:51-62; 10:38-41; 17:11-19; John 7:10-46

Jesus went to Jerusalem to celebrate the Feast of Tabernacles, but He didn't go with His disciples. He sent them ahead and then He followed secretly later on. Just before Jesus and the disciples left Capernaum, a man came to Him and said, "Teacher, I will follow You wherever You go."

But Jesus answered, "Foxes have holes to live in, and the birds have nests, but the Son of Man has no home."

Jesus called another man to follow Him. But the man had all kinds of excuses. "Let me go and first bury my father," he said.

But Jesus said, "Let the dead bury their own dead; but your job is to go and tell people the news of the Kingdom of God."

Another man said, "I will follow You, Lord, but I must first go and say goodbye to the people at home."

To him Jesus said, "No one who has once put his hand to the plow and then looks back is fit for the kingdom of God."

Before the disciples left Jesus to go to Jerusalem, they went with Him through Samaria. This was unusual because the Jews hated the Samaritans and would have nothing to do with them.

One day Jesus sent some of the disciples ahead into a Samaritan village to find a place for them to spend the night, but the Samaritans refused to help them. When James and John saw that the people wouldn't help them, they asked Jesus if He wanted them to pray for fire to come down from heaven and destroy that village. But Jesus stopped them and said, "You don't understand that the Son of Man has not come to destroy men's lives, but to save them." So they went on to another village where the people gave them a nicer welcome.

As Jesus and His disciples walked from Samaria to Galilee, they came upon a group of 10 lepers. The lepers stayed away from them, but called out, "Jesus, have mercy on us!"

When Jesus saw them and heard their cry, He said, "Go, show yourselves to the priests." As the 10 men went, they were cured of their terrible sickness.

One of them, when he realized what had happened, came back and praised God loudly. He threw himself down in front of Jesus. The healed man thanked Jesus for what He had done. That man was a Samaritan.

Jesus turned to the disciples and said, "Weren't there 10 men healed? Where are the other nine? Is the only one who praises God this foreigner?" Then He said to the Samaritan: "Get up and go your way; your faith has made you well."

After this, the disciples went on to Jerusalem, while Jesus stayed behind for a few days. When He arrived in Jerusalem,

the Feast of Tabernacles had already been going on for several days. He went to the Temple and taught the crowds there. On the last day of the festival, the custom was for the people to take offerings of water into the Temple as a reminder and thanksgiving for the way God had given their ancestors water in the wilderness.

On that day Jesus called out, "If anyone is thirsty, let him come to Me and drink. Whoever believes in Me, rivers of living water will flow from his heart."

Many people were very worried about what He said, but others were sure in their hearts that He was really the Christ. However, the chief priests and elders sent soldiers to arrest Jesus. But the men didn't dare to even touch Jesus. They went back and told the chief priests that they had never heard a man speak like this Man!

Whenever Jesus went to Jerusalem, He spent time with three very dear friends: two sisters, Martha and Mary, and their brother, Lazarus. They lived in the little village of Bethany, on the Mount of Olives, just outside the city.

Martha was very proud of her home. She took great care that Jesus was made as comfortable as possible whenever He came to visit. Her sister, Mary, was not like Martha. She was content to just sit at Jesus' feet and listen to His teaching. Martha became very irritated about this. She was so busy with her preparations that she was annoyed to see Mary just sitting there. She went to Jesus and said, "Lord, don't You care that my sister is making me do all the work? Please tell her to help me."

But Jesus answered, "Martha, Martha, you are worried about too many things! But really only one thing is necessary. Mary has chosen the good thing, and it cannot be taken away from her."

"Anyone who believes in Me may come and drink! For the Scriptures declare, 'Rivers of living water will flow from His heart.'"

John 7:38

The Eyes of the Blind Are Opened

John 9

One day, while Jesus was walking down the street in Jerusalem, He saw a man who had been blind his whole life. All the people, including the disciples, believed that all sickness came as a direct result of someone's sin. They asked Jesus about this blind man. "Master, who sinned? Was it this man or his parents that caused him to be born blind?"

The answer surprised the disciples: "Neither this man nor his parents' sin caused his blindness," Jesus said. "His blindness happened so that the work of God might be shown in him. We must do the work of God as long as it is day. The night is coming, when no one can work.

The man was born blind, but Jesus heals
him so that he can see. (John 9:6-7)

While I am in the world, I am the light of the world."

After Jesus said this, He spat on the ground and made mud with the saliva. Then He touched the blind man's eyes with the mud. Jesus told him to wash in the pool of Siloam.

The blind man's friends led him to the pool and when he came back he could see as well as anyone else. All the people who had known this man when he was a blind beggar were amazed.

"How did this happen?" the people asked. "How were your eyes opened?" He answered, "The man called Jesus made mud and put it on my eyes then told me to wash in the pool of Siloam. I did what He said, and now I can see."

The people took him to the Pharisees, who asked him the same questions. But they were angry because it was the Sabbath. They said that Jesus could not have come from God or else He would not have healed on the Sabbath!

"What do you have to say about the Man who healed your eyes?" they asked him.

He answered them, "He must be a prophet." But the rulers didn't believe that Jesus had really done this miracle. They even refused to listen to the man when he said that he couldn't see before Jesus had healed his eyes.

They called his parents and asked them about it, too. "Is this your son?" they said, "do you say he was born blind? How come he can now see?"

His parents answered, "Yes, this is our son; yes, he was born blind. We don't know how it has happened that now he can see. We don't know who healed him. But he is old enough to answer. Ask him yourselves!"

They talked with the man again. "We know that this Jesus is a sinner." But the man had the answer for them, "Whether He is a sinner, I don't know. But one thing I do know, I once was blind, now I can see."

Then they said, "But what did He do to you? How did He heal your eyes?"

"I told you already," he said, annoyed, "but you won't listen. Why do I have to tell you again? Do you want to become His disciples?" That made them even more furious. They made fun of him. "You are His disciple, but we are Moses' disciples."

But the man said, "Now that's a strange thing. This Man opened my eyes, yet you don't know where He is from! If this Man were not from God, He could not have healed me."

They said, "You were born entirely in sin. Now you dare to teach us?" Then they threw him out of the synagogue.

Jesus heard how they had treated the man and He went to look for him. When He found the man, He said, "Do you believe in the Son of Man?"

The man didn't understand what Jesus was trying to say. The man asked Jesus, "Who is this Son of Man, that I may believe in Him?"

Jesus answered, "You've seen Him, and He is talking to you at this moment."

Then the man said, "Lord, I believe," and he worshiped Jesus, the Son of Man.

"It was not because of his sins or his parents' sins," Jesus answered. "This happened so the power of God could be seen in him."

John 9:3

Parable of the Good Samaritan

Luke 10:25–37

Later, when Jesus was teaching in Capernaum, one of the scribes asked Him a question. This scribe was a lawyer, in fact he was an expert in the law. He asked, "Master, which is the greatest commandment in the law?"

Jesus answered, "You shall love the Lord your God with all your heart and with all your soul and with all your mind. This is the first and greatest commandment and the second greatest commandment is like it: You shall love your neighbor like yourself. The whole law and all the writings of the prophets depend on these two commandments."

The lawyer knew that he had not kept the first commandment very well so he tried to argue with Jesus about the second one. "But who is my neighbor?" he asked. Jesus told him a story to help him understand. That story is known as the Parable of the Good Samaritan.

A man was traveling from Jerusalem to Jericho. On the way he was attacked by robbers. They stole his clothes and beat him and left him on the side of the road, barely alive.

Soon, a priest came along on his way to Jericho. When he saw the man lying there, he crossed to the other side of the road and kept going.

Then a man who worked in the Temple came along and he also crossed over to the other side and kept going.

Finally a Samaritan came by and his heart was filled with pity for the man. He bandaged the man's wounds. Then he put the man on his own donkey's back and took him to the nearest inn.

The Samaritan paid an innkeeper to take care of the man. He promised that when he came back, if it had cost more to look after the man, he would pay the difference.

**A despised Samaritan stops to help the
injured man on the road. (Luke 10:33-35)**

"Which of these three men behaved like a neighbor to the man attacked by the robbers?" Jesus asked.

The lawyer answered, "I suppose the one who felt bad for him and took care of him."

Jesus replied, "Go and behave in the same way."

That's how Jesus taught that to please God we must be ready to help anyone who is in trouble or need.

"'You must love the Lord your God with all your heart, all your soul, all your strength, and all your mind.' And, 'Love your neighbor as yourself.'"

Luke 10:27

Lazarus Lives Again

John 11

Mary and Lazarus were very good friends of Jesus who lived in the little village of Bethany near Jerusalem. One day Lazarus got very sick. His sisters sent a messenger to find Jesus, asking Him to come.

Jesus loved these three, but when He got the news about Lazarus, He did a very strange thing. He stayed where He was for two more days! On the third day He started the journey to Judea. The disciples were worried because they knew that the Judeans disliked Him and were planning to kill Him. But Jesus said, "Our friend Laza-rus is sleeping and I am going to Judea to wake him up."

The disciples didn't know what He meant. They said, "Lord, if he is asleep, that's good news. It means he's getting better."

But then Jesus put it plainly. "Lazarus is dead, but I am glad for your sakes that I was not there to help him so that you may believe. Let us go to him."

When Jesus reached Bethany, Lazarus's body had already been in the tomb for four days. There were many people at Martha and Mary's home trying to comfort them. When Martha heard that Jesus was coming, she went out to meet Him, but Mary stayed behind in the house crying.

When she got to Jesus, Martha said, "Lord, if You had been here, my brother would not have died. But even now I know that God will give You whatever You ask from Him."

Jesus answered quietly, "Your brother will rise again."

Martha said, "Yes, Lord, I know that he will rise again at the great resurrection on the last day."

Then Jesus replied, "I am the resurrection, and the life. Whoever believes in Me will live, even if he dies, and whoever lives and believes in Me will never die. Do you believe this?"

Martha said, "Yes, Lord, I do believe that You are the Christ, the Son of God, who was promised by the Father."

Martha called Mary to come and speak to the Lord, too. When she told Mary that Jesus was there, Mary quickly slipped out of the house. All of the people in the house saw her leave and they followed her. They thought she was going to the tomb to cry.

When Mary reached Jesus, she threw herself down at His feet and cried out, "Lord, if You had been here, my brother would not have died."

When Jesus saw her tears, and her friends crying, too, He was very upset. He asked, "Where have you put Lazarus's body?" They told Him and Jesus went to the tomb. As He went, Jesus wept.

When the people saw His tears, they said, "Look at how much He loved Lazarus."

But others said, "If this Man could open the eyes of the blind, couldn't He also have kept Lazarus from dying?"

Jesus got to the tomb, which had a great stone covering the opening. Jesus said to the men standing by, "Move the stone." Martha was very upset because Lazarus had been in the grave for four days already! Jesus said, "Didn't I tell you that if you believed, you would see the glory of God?"

So the men moved the stone, and then Jesus prayed, "Father, I thank You that You hear Me. I know that You hear Me, but I have said this for the sake of the people standing around so they may understand that You really have sent Me."

Then He called out, "Lazarus, come forth!" As Jesus spoke, Lazarus came walking out of the tomb. His hands and feet were still wrapped in the burial cloths. Jesus told the men standing by to unwrap him and let him go home.

The people saw Jesus' miraculous power and many believed in Him, but others went to the Pharisees and told them what Jesus had done. The Pharisees immediately called a special council. They discussed how they could put a stop to Christ's work. Some of them even said, "This Man is doing many wonderful things. If we let Him go on like this, all the people will follow Him. There could even be a rebellion about it. Then the Romans will take away the few rights we still have left."

But Caiaphas, the high priest, knew what they should do. He said, "It is better that one man should die rather than that the whole nation be wiped out. We must see to it that this Man is stopped." He did not realize it, but in his anger against Christ he was actually telling a great truth. Christ had come to die, so that many people, not only from among the Jews, but in all the world, should not have to die eternally.

From that time on, the Jewish leaders focused on putting Jesus to death. And from then on, Jesus stopped His public ministry.

Jesus told her, "I am the resurrection and the life. Anyone who believes in Me will live, even after dying. Everyone who lives in Me and believes in Me will never ever die."

John 11:25-26

Jesus brings Lazarus back to life. (John 11:41-44)

Parable of the Lost Sheep

Matthew 10:37-38; 18:12-14; Mark 8:34; Luke 9:23

One day, when a big crowd had gathered to listen to Him, Jesus warned them what it would really mean to follow Him. "If anyone does not love Me," He said, "more than even their father and mother and spouse and children and brothers and sisters, yes, even than their own life, they cannot be My disciple. Whoever is not willing to carry their own cross and come after Me, is not fit to be My disciple. I am telling you this, so that you know exactly what it means to follow Me. If you want to be My disciples, you must be ready to give up everything for My sake."

Many tax gatherers and outcasts were in the crowds who went to listen to Jesus. Sometimes He shared a meal with them so that He could teach them. The Pharisees grumbled about this, "This man spends time with sinners and even eats with them." Jesus told them several stories to show them how silly they were being.

"Which one of you," He said, "who owns a hundred sheep and has lost one of them, will not leave the 99 and go out and look for the lost one? When the shepherd finds it, he will carry it home across his shoulders, and then call his friends and neighbors to celebrate with him. In the same way there will be more joy in heaven over one sinner who repents than over 99 righteous people who do not need to repent."

"If a man has a hundred sheep and one of them wanders away, what will he do? Won't he leave the ninety-nine others on the hills and go out to search for the one that is lost?"

Matthew 18:12

When the shepherd sees that one of his sheep has gone missing, he leaves the other sheep to look for the one lost sheep. (Matthew 18:12-14

Parable of the Prodigal Son

Luke 15:11–32

Jesus told them another story. It's called the Parable of the Prodigal Son. A certain man had two sons. The younger son got tired of living at home. He went to his father and asked to be given his share of his father's riches, which he would inherit one day.

The father gave the boy his share of the inheritance and the young man went to a faraway country. But when he got there, he wasted his money on wild living.

About the time he ran out of money, there was a severe drought and famine in the land, and he had no food. He found work in the fields feeding pigs. Things went from bad to worse for him and he even considered eating the pigs' food because he was so hungry. All this made him begin to think about his father's house. Back at home, even his father's servants had all the food they needed. Here he was, a rich man's son, dying of hunger! He decided he would go back to his father, and say, "Father, I have sinned against heaven, and against you. I am not fit to be called your son. Just let me be one of your servants."

After a long journey, he could finally see his father's house. Before he actually got there, his father came running out to meet him. The father sent his slaves to bring out the best robe and put it on his son, and a ring on his finger and sandals on his feet. Then he told them to kill the fattest calf he had and to get ready for a great feast, so that they could rejoice that his son was home. He said, "My son was dead, and now he is alive again. He was lost, and has been found!" So the feast began.

The older brother was annoyed when he heard what was happening. He refused to go to the feast, but said to his father, "Look! I have served you for many years. I have listened to everything you told me, but

**The prodigal son returns home and
his father is happy to see him. (Luke 15:20)**

you have never held a feast for me so that my friends could come and enjoy it with me. But now my brother, who wasted all your money on wild living, gets a feast?"

But his father answered, "My son, you have always been with me and all that I have is yours. But your brother was dead and now he lives again; he was lost, but now is found."

The message of this story was that Jesus had come to save those who were lost.

"His father said to the servants, 'Quick! Bring the finest robe in the house and put it on him. Get a ring for his finger and sandals for his feet. And kill the calf we have been fattening. We must celebrate with a feast, for this son of mine was lost, but now he is found.'"

Luke 15:22-24

Parable of the Rich Man and the Beggar

Luke 16:19–31

A rich man lived in a beautiful home and had a great feast every day.

A poor beggar named Lazarus sat by the gate of the rich man's house. The beggar's body was covered with sores. He was very hungry and longed to have even the crumbs that fell from the rich man's table for his empty stomach.

The beggar died, and the angels carried away his soul to heaven. Not long afterward the rich man also died. He woke up in hell in great misery. A long way off he saw Abraham standing next to the beggar who had sat at the rich man's gate. He cried out to Abraham: "Father Abraham, have mercy on me and send Lazarus to bring me water, because I am in agony in this heat."

But Abraham said, "Before you died you lived in luxury and comfort, while Lazarus suffered from sores and hunger. Yet you did nothing to help him. Now he is being comforted, and you are suffering. Besides that there is a great gap between you and us which cannot be crossed."

The rich man cried out, "Father Abraham, I beg you to send Lazarus to my father's house. I have five brothers there. Warn them not to come to this place of torment where I am."

But Abraham said, "They have the writings of Moses and the prophets. Let them pay attention to what they read there."

But the man cried out in agony, "No, Father Abraham, but if someone goes to them from the dead, they will listen."

Then Abraham ended the conversation with these words, "If they do not listen to Moses and the prophets, their ways won't change if someone returns to them from the dead."

"Abraham said, 'Moses and the prophets have warned them. Your brothers can read what they wrote.'"

Luke 16:29

Parables of Riches

Luke 16:1–13; Mark 10:17–31; Matthew 19:23–26

When Jesus taught the people, He used words they could easily understand. He didn't want them to miss the lessons He was trying to teach them. That was why He told them stories.

One of them was the story of the dishonest steward. There was once a rich man who paid another man to be his steward and look after his possessions. But the rich man was told that

the steward was wasting his property by not taking care of it. He sent for the steward and asked him about it. "Give me a report of your work," he said, "because you cannot be my steward any longer."

The steward said to himself, "What shall I do now? I am ashamed to beg. I must figure out something, so that when I am released from the job of stewardship, I will have friends to take care of me."

So he called all the people who owed his master money and reduced the amount each of them owed. When the master heard what the steward had done, he praised the dishonest steward for his cleverness in getting friends by what he did.

When Jesus had finished telling this story, He said to the disciples, "People who don't serve God are sneakier than people who do serve Him. If that man was clever enough to ensure he would have friends in his time of need, how much cleverer you ought to be who are the children of righteousness! Take care that people who do not care for the things of God do not put you to shame by their enthusiasm."

Jesus was not praising the steward's dishonesty, but warning all His disciples to be more serious about doing good than the ungodly were about doing evil. We cannot serve two masters. We must either serve God, or the things of this world.

Another time a rich young man came to Jesus and asked Him what he must do to get eternal life. Jesus told him to keep God's commandments. The young man replied that he had kept the law since he was a child, but he felt that he was still missing something. Then Jesus said, "If you really want eternal life, sell all that you have and give the money to the poor. Then you will have treasures in heaven. Then come and follow Me." But the rich man was very attached to all his possessions. He went away unhappy.

Jesus said: "It is easier for a camel to go through the eye of a needle than for a rich man to enter the kingdom of God. But with God it is even possible for a rich man to be saved."

Jesus said to His disciples, "It is very hard for a rich person to enter the Kingdom of Heaven. I'll say it again – it is easier for a camel to go through the eye of a needle than for a rich person to enter the Kingdom of God ... Humanly speaking, it is impossible. But with God everything is possible."

Luke 16:23-24, 26

Don't Worry, Jesus Will Provide

Matthew 6:19–34; Luke 12:22–34

Jesus said to His disciples, "Do not be anxious about your life, or what you will eat, or what you will wear. Life is more than food, and the body is more than clothing. Think for a moment about the ravens. They don't sow or reap or build storerooms to put away food, but God feeds them. Are people not more important than birds? Think about the lilies. They don't work, but I tell you that Solomon in all his glory was never dressed like one of these. If God clothes the grass in the field like this, which is here today and gone tomorrow, how much more will He clothe you! The people of the world worry about these things, but God knows all your needs. Trust in Him. Instead of being anxious about such things, seek first God and His righteousness. Then all your needs will be given to you. Do not be afraid. It is the Father's joy to give you the Kingdom.

Give your riches to help the poor. Provide for yourselves treasures in heaven where no thief can steal it, and no moth can destroy it. Where your treasure is, there your heart will also be."

"Look at the lilies of the field and how they grow. If God cares so wonderfully for flowers that are here today and thrown into the fire tomorrow, He will certainly care for you."

Matthew 6:28, 30

309

Parables of Humility

Luke 18:9–17

Jesus would often tell stories to warn the people that they should be careful not to think they were better than other people. One of them was the story of the Pharisee and tax collector, who went to the Temple in Jerusalem to pray. The Pharisee stood up and prayed, "God, I thank You that I am not like other people – like cheaters, liars, dishonest people, or even like this tax collector. I fast twice a week and pay Temple tithes for all I get."

But the tax collector stood a way off with his eyes cast down and said, "God, be merciful to me, a sinner!"

"The tax collector," said Jesus, "went back home forgiven, but not the Pharisee. Everyone who glorifies himself will be cast down, and everyone who humbles himself will be lifted up. Let this be a lesson to you all."

Just after this some mothers brought their children for Jesus to bless. When the disciples saw this, they grumbled and tried to send the children away.

When Jesus realized what they were doing, He was annoyed with the disciples. He said, "Let the little ones come to Me. Don't stop them, because the kingdom of heaven belongs to those with hearts as humble as theirs. Truly, if you do not receive the kingdom of heaven like a child, you shall not go into it."

"Those who exalt themselves will be humbled, and those who humble themselves will be exalted."

Luke 18:14

Jesus embraces the children and says that only people who are like these children can enter the kingdom of God. (Luke 18:16-17)

Jesus Visits Jericho

Mark 10:46-52; Luke 18:35-43

Jesus and His disciples began their sad journey to Jerusalem. The road went through the city of Jericho. As He neared the city, Jesus showed His power again.

A poor blind beggar called Bartimaeus was sitting by the roadside. He heard the crowds coming along the road and asked what was happening. They told him that Jesus of Nazareth was passing by. The poor man began to cry out, "Jesus, Son of David, have mercy on me!"

The people in the crowd told him to be quiet, but he cried out louder than ever.

Then Jesus stopped and told them to bring the blind man to Him. They did and Jesus asked the man what he wanted.

The blind man said, "Please, Lord, I'm blind. I want to see."

Jesus said to him, "Receive your sight. Your faith has made you well again." Instantly the man could see and he followed Jesus.

Jesus said, "All right, receive your sight! Your faith has saved you." Instantly the man could see, and he followed Jesus, praising God. And all who saw it praised God, too.

Luke 18:42-43

Jesus Meets Zacchaeus

Luke 19:1-10

A very rich man called Zacchaeus lived in Jericho. He was the chief tax collector. He heard that Jesus was coming and he wanted very much to see Him. But Zacchaeus was short and could not see over the crowd of people. He had a great idea, though. He climbed up into the branches of a tree

**Jesus tells Zacchaeus to climb down out of the tree because
He wants to spend some time with him. (Luke 19:5)**

that was beside the road. He could look down from there to see Jesus pass by. When Jesus reached the tree, He looked up and said, "Zacchaeus, come down, because I must stay in your house today."

Zacchaeus climbed down from the tree and went with Jesus to his house. The he said, "Lord, I will give half of my possessions to the poor. If I have taken anything dishonestly from a per-son, I will give him back four times as much."

Jesus said to him, "Today salvation has come to this house. You have shown yourself to be a true son of Abraham. I came to seek and to save the people who are lost."

"The Son of Man came to seek and save those who are lost."

Luke 19:10

Parable of the Pounds

Luke 19:11–27

As Jesus and His disciples drew nearer to Jerusalem, He knew that His followers expected Him to establish the kingdom of God. So He told a story to try to help them understand that He must first go away from this world for a time. The story was about a nobleman. The nobleman went to a country far away. Before he left, he called his 10 servants and gave each of them one pound. They were to use the money to do business for him until he came back.

When the nobleman came back, he called the servants he had given the money to. He asked them how much money they had earned by trading.

The first said that he had earned an extra 10 pounds with his money. When the nobleman heard that, he said, "Well done, you good servant. Because you have been faithful in this, I will make you the ruler over 10 cities in my kingdom." The second reported that he had earn-ed an extra five pounds. The

The servants bring the money they had made to the nobleman. (Luke 19:16-21)

nobleman also compliment-
ed him, and made him ruler
over five cities. But the third
servant said, "Master, here is
your pound. I hid it because I
was afraid of you. I knew you
are a hard man, so I did not risk
losing the money if I invested
it."

The nobleman said, "You knew
you should have at least put
my money in the bank where
it could have earned interest."
Then he said to the other
servants, "Take the pound
from him, and give it to the
man who brought 10 pounds."
The other servants objected,
"But Master, that man has 10
pounds already!"

He said, "Those who use well
what they have been given will
be given even more. But from
those who do nothing, even
what little they have will be
taken away."

Jesus told His disciples this
story in order to warn them
that He must go away from
them, but in His absence they
must serve Him faithfully and
fruitfully.

*To those who use well what
they are given, even more will
be given. But from those who
do nothing, even what little
they have will be taken away.*
Luke 19:26

316

Preparations for the End

Matthew 21:1-13; 26:6-10, 14-16; Mark 11:1-11; 14:1-11; Luke 19:28-40

Just outside Jerusalem was the little village of Bethphage. When Jesus and His disciples reached it, He sent two disciples into the village on a special errand. As soon as they entered the village He told them they would find a donkey tied up with her colt alongside her. They were to untie them, and bring them to Him. If anyone stopped them and asked what they were doing, they should say that the Lord needed the donkeys. This was done to fulfill the words of the prophet Zechariah, who said, "Say to the daughter of Zion, 'See, your King is coming to you, gentle, and mounted on a donkey.'"

The disciples brought the donkeys to the Lord. Then they spread their coats on the back of the donkey and Jesus got on her. As He began to move slowly along the road into Jerusalem, the crowds that were watching spread their coats on the road. Others cut palm branches and spread them on the road in front of Him. As He went, they shouted out His praises, "Hosanna to the Son of David. Blessed is He who comes in the name of the Lord; hosanna in the highest."

When they reached the outskirts of Jerusalem, the people who saw them and heard the shouts of praise were puzzled and asked, "Who is this?" The crowds following Jesus shouted back to them, "This is the prophet Jesus from Nazareth in Galilee."

Some Pharisees were in the crowd. They were angry at what was happening and they said to Jesus, "Master, tell Your disciples to be quiet."

He answered, "I tell you this. If these people were to be still, the very stones on the road would cry out!"

Jesus went right to the Temple in the middle of the city. He found men there buying and selling doves and small animals for the people to use to make sacrifices. They were exchanging money for special Temple coins, but were cheating the people by charging too much. And this was on the Sabbath day, too!

This made Jesus very angry. He said to the traders, "In the Scriptures it is written: My house shall be called a house of prayer, but you have made it a robbers' lair." He turned over the tables of the money changers. He drove out all the men who were dishonoring God's house with their crooked businesses. Then the blind and lame people ran to Him and He healed them in the Temple.

When the people saw the miracles He was doing, even the little children gathered around Him and cried out, "Hosanna to the Son of David." The children knew their King, but the chief priests and the scribes were angry over what they saw and heard. They went to Jesus and said, "Don't You hear what they are saying?"

Jesus answered, "Yes, but have you never read the Scriptures? They say, 'Out of the mouths of babes and infants You have prepared praise for Yourself.'"

That night the Lord Jesus and His disciples went back to the little village of Bethany outside Jerusalem.

As Jesus and His disciples lay on low benches around the dinner table, a woman came into the room with an alabaster jar of very expensive perfume. She poured it on Jesus' head, and some on His feet, and wiped them dry with her own hair.

Some of the disciples were annoyed by what she had just done. They thought she was doing something very wasteful. One of them, Judas Iscariot, said, "Why wasn't this ointment sold and the money given to the poor? It would have made a lot of money." The truth was that Judas wasn't really interested in helping the poor. He was a thief and wanted to steal from the moneybag, which Jesus had entrusted to him.

Jesus said to him, "Leave her alone. She has done this to

Jesus enters Jerusalem on a donkey. (Matthew 21:5-6)

prepare Me for My burial. The poor are always with you. You will have many chances of helping them, but I will not always be with you. Truly, I tell you that wherever this Gospel is preached from now on, what this woman has done will be remembered to her honor."

Then Judas left and went to see the chief priests. He said to them, "What will you give me to deliver Jesus to you?" They paid him 30 pieces of silver. From then on, Judas looked for a good time to deliver Jesus Christ into the hands of His enemies.

"You will always have the poor among you, but you will not always have Me."

John 12:8

One Last Temple Visit

Matthew 21:18–22; Mark 11:12–14; Luke 20:20–26

The next morning Jesus returned to Jerusalem. On the way He saw a fig tree beside the road, but there was no fruit on it. Then Jesus said, "This tree will never again bear any fruit!" The disciples thought that was a strange thing for Him to say, especially when they saw that the leaves of the tree began to die right then and there.

Jesus explained why the tree immediately started to die the moment He spoke to it: "If you have faith in God, and do not doubt, you will not only do what I have done to this fig tree, but if you say to this mountain, 'Go into the sea,' that's what will happen. Whatever you ask for in prayer, really believing that God will give it, you will receive."

Once again Jesus went to the Temple. Again the priests and elders came to argue with Him. By this time the Pharisees and priests were doing everything they could to trap Jesus into saying something wrong. They were looking for a reason to drag Him before the courts and have Him condemned to death.

They sent some of their followers and the servants of Herod to ask Him a question. "Tell us," they asked, "is it right to pay tax to the Roman Caesar, or not?"

This was a tricky question. If He said it was right to pay tax, it would anger the people who hated the Romans. If He said that it was not right, then He would be guilty of treason against the Roman rulers. But Jesus saw the trick. He asked them to give Him a coin. He held it up in front of them and asked, "Whose picture is on this coin?"

They answered, "Caesar's."

So He said, "Then give to Caesar the things that belong to Caesar and to God the things that belong to God." The priests and Pharisees were speechless. They just did not know what to say.

Jesus said, "Give to Caesar what belongs to Caesar, and give to God what belongs to God." So they failed to trap Him by what He said in front of the people. Instead, they were amazed by His answer, and they became silent.

Luke 20:25-26

The Lord Will Come Again

Matthew 24; 25:1-13, 31-45; Luke 21:5-38

As they left the Temple gates, Jesus pointed to the big Temple buildings and said to His disciples, "See the greatness of these buildings? I tell you that not one stone of these buildings will be left standing. It will be totally broken down."

Then the disciples asked, "When will these things happen? What will be the sign of Your coming and of the end of the world?"

Jesus sat down with His disciples and explained what would happen in the future. He told of the destruction of Jerusalem, and of events that would take place before His return to judge all the world. He spoke of wars between the nations, famine and earthquakes, a hatred for all who trusted in Him, false prophets who would come and claim to be the Christ, and then, when all these signs were over, of how He would come again in glory with His angels to make the whole world bow before Him.

To explain what He meant, Jesus told His disciples the Parable of the Ten Young Bridesmaids. He told them that in those days the kingdom of heaven would be like 10 young bridesmaids who took their lamps and went to meet the bridegroom as he came to the marriage feast. Five of the bridesmaids were wise, and took spare oil with them for their lamps. The other five were foolish and didn't take any extra oil.

The bridegroom took a long time to come, and all the brides-maids fell asleep. But suddenly there was a shout, "The bridegroom is here! Come out to meet him." Then all of them got up and trimmed the wicks of their lamps to brighten the flame, but the foolish brides-maids discovered that their lamps were going out because there was no oil left in them. They asked the other girls to give them some of their oil, but they refused because then there wouldn't be enough for their own lamps. They told the foolish bridesmaids to buy some oil.

While they were gone, the bridegroom came and the five wise bridesmaids went in with him to the feast and the door was shut. When the other five got back, they knocked on the door and asked to be let in, but the master answered that he didn't know them. They had to leave in the darkness of the night.

"This is a warning to you," said the Lord, "to be watchful all the time, because you don't know the day or the hour when I will come again."

Jesus told the disciples that when He came back, He would come to judge between the godly and the ungodly. This is what it will be like: "When the Son of Man comes in glory, attended by all the angels in heaven, all the nations will be brought before Him. He will separate the good from the bad, just as a shepherd separates the sheep from the goats. Those who are His sheep, He will put at His right hand. The others He will put at His left hand. Then He will say to those at His right hand, 'Come, you blessed of My Father, the Kingdom He has prepared for you from the beginning of the world is yours. When I was hungry, you gave Me food. I was thirsty, and you gave Me something to drink. I was a stranger, and you took Me in. I was naked, and you gave Me clothes. I was sick, and you visited Me. I was in prison, and you came to Me. As you helped one of these brothers who believed in Me, you also helped Me.' After that, He will say to those on His left hand, 'Go away from Me, cursed ones, into the eternal fire that has been made ready for the devil and his angels.' He will say to them, 'Since you did not help one of the least of these brothers of Mine who believed in Me, you did not help Me.' And those people will go into eternal punishment, but the righteous will have eternal life."

"The King will say, 'I tell you the truth, when you did it to one of the least of these My brothers and sisters, you were doing it to Me!'"

Matthew 25:40

The Last Supper

Mark 14:12−41; Luke 22:7−38; John 13, 17

On the first day of the Passover Feast, the disciples came to the Lord Jesus. They asked Him where He wanted them to prepare to eat the Passover. He said, "Go into the city and you will find a man carrying a jar of water. Tell him that the Master says that His time is at hand and He wants to keep the Passover at his house with His disciples. The man will understand."

Peter and John went into the city and met a man carrying a jar of water, just as Jesus had said. They followed him to his home and prepared for the meal. Then they waited until evening for Jesus to come. The Passover lamb was cooked and the meal prepared by the time He arrived.

Before they began the Passover meal, Jesus said to His disciples, "I wanted to eat this Passover meal and drink this cup with you before I suffer. I tell you that I will not eat a Passover meal, or drink a cup of wine with you again, until the kingdom of God comes." Then He stood up and broke the bread into pieces. After saying a prayer of thanksgiving, He gave the pieces of bread to them and said, "This is My body, which is being given for you. Do this in remembrance of Me." Then He took a cup of wine. After He had given thanks to God for it, He gave it to them one by one, saying, "This cup is My blood, which is shed for you. Every time you drink it, you must do it in remembrance of Me."

Then Jesus picked up a towel and a bowl of water. He began to wash the disciples' feet and dry them with the towel. When He came to Simon Peter, the disciple said to Him, "Lord, You are going to wash my feet? No, it cannot be!" But Jesus answered, "You cannot understand now what I'm doing, but later you will understand."

When Jesus had washed their feet, He said, "Do you understand what I have done to you?

Jesus gives thanks at the Last Supper. (Matthew 26:26-29)

You call Me Master and Lord, and you are right, because I am. But if I, the Master and Lord, have washed your feet, you should also wash one another's feet. I have given you an example of how you should treat one another."

As He sat there talking to them, Jesus suddenly became very sad, and said, "I tell you, one of you will betray Me. I tell you this beforehand, so that when it happens, you may believe that I am really God, as I have said." The disciples looked at one another, and wondered which one of them He was talking about. One after the other, they asked, "Lord, will I be the one to betray You?"

Jesus answered, "It is the one I give this piece of bread to." Then He took the piece of bread and gave it to Judas Iscariot. Jesus sadly said to him, "What you have to do, do quickly!" The rest of the disciples didn't understand, but Judas left and went to turn Jesus over to the priests. After Judas had left, Jesus said to the other disciples, "I will be with you only a little while longer. You will look for

Me, but where I am going you cannot come." Simon Peter said, "But Lord, why can't I follow You? I will lay down my life for You."

But Jesus sadly said to him, "Peter, I tell you that before the rooster crows, you will deny three times that you don't even know Me." Then to the rest of the disciples, He said, "Not one of you will remain by My side, but I will not be alone, for My Father will be with Me."

Then He gave a comforting message to the confused disciples, "I am going to prepare a place for you in My Father's house. One day I will come for you again. In the world you will have troubles, but be brave, I have overcome the world." After this He prayed a beautiful prayer for Himself and the disciples.

"My prayer is not for the world, but for those you have given Me, because they belong to You. All who are Mine belong to You, and You have given them to Me, so they bring Me glory."
John 17:9-10

Jesus washes the disciples' feet. (John 13:4-5)

The Beginning of the End

Mark 14:32-72; Luke 22:39-71

At midnight, after the Lord had eaten the Last Supper with His disciples, He led them to a garden called Gethsemane. Jesus told the disciples to sit and wait for Him while He went into the garden to pray.

Jesus took Peter, James and John in with Him. When they were alone, He said to them, "My soul is deeply grieved, even to the point of death. Stay here and watch while I go a little farther into the garden to pray." Then He went a little way farther and threw Himself down on the ground. He cried out to His heavenly Father over and over again in agony, "My Father, if it is possible, let this cup pass from Me; yet let Your will be done, not Mine."

After He prayed, He went back to the three disciples and found them fast asleep. He said to Peter, "Couldn't you watch with Me just for one hour? You must keep watching and praying so that you do not fall into temptation. The spirit is willing, but the flesh is weak." Then He went away and prayed a second time, saying, "My Father, if this cup cannot pass away unless I drink it, Your will be done."

When He returned to the three disciples, they were asleep once again. He went back to pray a third time, using the same words. As He prayed His pain was so great that His sweat fell like big drops of blood.

When He went back to the three disciples this time, He said, "Go ahead and sleep. You need your rest. The time has come. The Son of Man is betrayed into the hands of sinners. Let's go. The one who will betray Me is nearby."

As He was speaking, Judas Iscariot came into the garden with some soldiers with swords and spears. They were sent by the chief priests and rulers of the people. Judas had arranged with these men that when they saw him greet someone with a

The disciples keep falling asleep while Jesus prays in the Garden of Gethsemane. (Matthew 26:40-43)

kiss, they should immediately take that man as their prisoner.

When he saw Jesus, Judas went to Him, saying, "Hello, Master," and he kissed Him.

Jesus looked at him, and said, "Friend, why have you come? Are you betraying the Son of Man with a kiss?" Then He said to the priests and soldiers who came with Judas, "Have you come to arrest Me as if you were catching a thief, using spears and swords? Didn't I teach in the Temple every day? You could have arrested Me then and you didn't touch Me. But this is your hour, and the hour of the prince of darkness. Take Me now, but let My disciples go in peace."

When the disciples saw what was happening, they ran away, leaving Jesus alone in the hands of His enemies.

The soldiers took Him to the high priest, Caiaphas, and his father-in-law, Annas. All the priests and rulers who hated Jesus were gathered in the court of Caiaphas.

The priests had done their best to find witnesses who would be willing to lie about Jesus so they could have Him sentenced to death. Finally, two men came forward, who said, "This Man said that He was able to destroy the Temple of God and build it again in three days."

Caiaphas asked Jesus what He had to say to that. But Jesus would not say a word. Caiaphas was angry and tried to make Jesus speak, but He would not. Then Caiaphas said, "Tell us, I demand in the name of God, whether You are the Christ, the Son of God."

Jesus answered, "You have said it yourself. But I tell you this. You will see the Son of Man sitting at the right hand of power and coming on the clouds of heaven."

Then the high priest tore his own robes and cried out, "He has blasphemed! We need no more witnesses. You have all heard what He said. What should we do with Him?"

Everyone shouted, "He should be put to death!" Then they

spat in His face, beat Him with their fists and slapped Him.

Now while this was all happening, Peter stood by the fires in the courtyard listening to what was being said. A servant girl came up to him and said, "You were with that Jesus of Galilee."

Peter was frightened and said in front of everyone, "I don't know what you're talking about!"

A little later another servant girl saw him as he stood on the porch. She also said, "This fellow was with Jesus of Nazareth!"

Peter angrily said, "I don't know the Man!" After a while some of the men came up to him and said, "Surely you are one of His followers. Your accent gives you away. You are a Galilean."

Then Peter cursed and said, "I do not know the Man." But just as he spoke, the rooster crowed. Peter remembered that Jesus had said the night before that before the rooster crowed, he would deny the Lord three times. And as Peter remembered this, Jesus turned and looked at him. Then Peter went out into the night, weeping bitterly.

Jesus went on a little farther and bowed with His face to the ground, praying, "My Father! If it is possible, let this cup of suffering be taken away from Me. Yet I want Your will to be done, not Mine."

Matthew 26:39

Crown of Thorns

Matthew 27:11–31; Luke 23:1–25

The Jewish leaders had Jesus arrested, but they didn't have the power to sentence any prisoner without the permission of the Roman governor. When Jesus' "trial" by Caiaphas was over, they dragged Him to the Roman governor, Pontius Pilate.

By then Judas had realized what a terrible thing he had done in betraying Jesus. He was very sorry so he went to the chief priests to give them back the money they had paid him. When he came to the Temple, he cried out to the priests, "I have done a wrong thing in betraying an innocent Man!"

They didn't care. They said, "What does that have to do with us? Take care of that yourself!" Judas tried to get them to take back the money they had paid him, but they refused. When they wouldn't take it, he threw the money down and went away and hanged himself. While this was happening, the priests went to the palace of Pontius Pilate with their prisoner, Jesus. When they told him why they were there, Pilate challenged them, "What's your charge against this Man?"

They answered, "If He hadn't done wrong, we wouldn't have brought Him to you!" That made Pilate angry so he said, "Judge Him according to your own law."

The Jews gave away the secret of what they were really trying to do when they said, "It is not legal for us to put any man to death."

Pilate went back into the judgment hall and called for Jesus to be brought to him privately. Pilate said to Him, "Are You the King of the Jews, as these people say You claim to be? You have heard their accusations. What do You have to say? What have You done?"

Jesus answered, "My kingdom is not of this world. If My kingdom were of this world, then My

Jesus appears before Pilate and the crowd insists that Pilate sentence Him to death. (Matthew 27:22-23)

disciples would have fought to save Me from My enemies. But My kingdom is of a different kind altogether."

Pilate asked again, "Tell me, though, are You really a King?" Jesus replied, "What you say is true. I am a King. I came into this world to make known the truth, and everyone who belongs to the truth listens to what I say and obeys Me."

"Truth!" said Pilate. "What is truth?" Then he walked out to the Jews and said to them, "I do not find any fault at all in your prisoner." He couldn't understand why they hated Jesus so much.

The priests angrily screamed, "He has been stirring up the people in Jerusalem and Galilee!"

That gave Pilate an idea. Jesus came from Galilee, and Galilee was under the control of Herod, who just happened to be in Jerusalem. Pilate decided to send the prisoner to Herod for the trial. This was the same Herod who had murdered John the Baptist.

Herod was very glad to see Jesus and he asked Him many questions. Jesus wouldn't say a word, even though the priests were accusing Him of all kinds of things. When he got no answers from Jesus, Herod allowed his guards to make fun of Jesus and beat Him. Then he sent Jesus back to Pilate.

So Jesus stood before Pilate again, tied up, beaten, exhausted and in pain. Before the governor started to question Him again, one of his servants brought a message from his wife: "Have nothing to do with that righteous Man. Last night I had a terrible dream because of Him." That frightened Pilate more than ever. He tried every way he could think of to get Jesus released.

It was the custom in those days that at the Passover season the governor would free one prisoner whom the people selected. At the time there was a well-known rebel called Barabbas in the prison. It seemed unlikely that the people would select him for release because he had committed many crimes, so Pilate had what he thought was a clever idea. He turned to the crowd and asked, "Whom do you want me to release for you? Barabbas, or Jesus who is called Christ?" He was horrified when he found that the priests and rulers had persuaded the crowd to demand the release of Barabbas. He tried to argue with them, but they kept on shouting for Barabbas. Then he said to them, "What shall I do then with Jesus?"

"Crucify Him! Crucify Him!" they screamed. He protested, "Why? What evil has He done?" But they only shouted all the more, "Let Him be crucified!"

Then Pilate stood in full view of the crowd and washed his hands, saying, "I am innocent of this Man's blood. Then he released Barabbas to them, and handed Jesus over to be crucified.

The Roman soldiers took Jesus, stripped His clothes from Him, and dressed Him in a scarlet robe. They made a crown of thorns and placed it on His head. In His right hand they put a reed. Then they kneeled before Him as if He were their king. They made fun of Him and insulted Him. "Hail, King of the Jews!" they cried and some even spat in His face. Then they took the reed and beat Him on the head so that the thorns pierced His brow and the blood ran down His face.

Pilate said to the people, "Look, here is your King!" "Away with Him," they yelled. "Away with Him! Crucify Him!"

John 19:14-15

The Darkest Day in History

Matthew 27:32-66; John 19:16-42

When the terrible and unfair trials were over, the soldiers of Pontius Pilate led Jesus Christ through the streets of Jerusalem to crucify Him. They planned to crucify Him on the hill named Calvary, or Golgotha, which means Place of the Skull.

The soldiers made Jesus carry His own cross. When the weight of it became too much for Him, He fell to the ground. The soldiers grabbed a man named Simon the Cyrenian and made him carry it the rest of the way.

The soldiers nailed Jesus to the cross by His hands and feet. Then they lifted it upright and dropped it into the ground so that His whole body hung from the nails. Alongside Him were crucified two robbers, one on His right side and one on His left. The one man cursed Him, but the other said to Jesus, "Lord, remember me when You come into Your kingdom."

Jesus answered, "Truly, I say to you, this very day you will be with Me in Paradise." But the other robber still cursed Him.

There was a small group of His followers at the foot of the cross, crying because of what had been done to their Lord. Jesus' mother, Mary, was with them. Mary's sister, the mother of Joseph and James, was also there. Mary Magdalene, for whom He had done so much and who loved Him very much, was there, too. The only one of His 12 disciples present was John.

Jesus had been hanging on the cross since nine o'clock in the morning. At about noon the sky became very dark. It stayed dark for three hours. Jesus didn't say anything that whole time.

Then suddenly He cried out in the darkness, "My God, My God, why have You forsaken Me?" These were the words that a prophet had said many years before that the Lord would say in His suffering.

Jesus is crucified. (Mark 15:25)

Then Jesus said, "I am thirsty." The soldiers nearby took a sponge soaked in sour wine and put it on the end of a stick and held it to His lips. When He tasted it, He said, "It is finished!" Then His head fell against His chest, and as He died, He said, "Father, into Your hands I give My spirit." At the moment He died a great earthquake shook the place. The great curtain in front of the Holy Place in the Temple tore in two, from the top to the bottom.

The next day was a special Sabbath day for the Jews. Their leaders asked the governor to take the bodies down from the crosses before the evening. When the soldiers came to the body of the Lord Jesus, they shoved a spear into His side to make sure He was dead. Blood and water came out of the wound.

Joseph of Arimathea, a secret disciple of the Lord Jesus, and Nicodemus, who had asked Jesus questions about the Gospel, took His body. They anointed it with oil, wrapped it in the best linen, and then laid it in a new rock tomb. The tomb was in a garden belonging to Joseph. They rolled a great rock against the mouth of the tomb to close it.

Although Jesus was dead, the chief priests were still worried. They went to Pilate and said, "Sir, Jesus said when He was alive that on the third day after He died, He would rise again. Please give orders that the tomb be sealed and guarded until the third day. If this is not done, His disciples will come and steal the body, and tell everybody that He has risen from the dead. Then things will be worse than when He was still alive."

Pilate said, "You have a Temple guard. Let your own men guard the tomb as well as you know how." So the Temple guards went to the tomb and sealed the rock door and kept watch until the three days were past.

Jesus said, "It is finished!" Then He bowed His head and released His spirit.

John 19:30

338

After Jesus died, Joseph and Nicodemus bury His body in a tomb. (John 19:38-42)

The Brightest Dawn in All History

Mark 16:1-14; Luke 24:1-49; John 20:1-23

The Sabbath was over and as dawn broke on the first day of the week, Mary Magdalene, Mary (the mother of James) and Salome took spices and ointments to anoint the body of Jesus. When they reached the tomb, they saw that it was open! An angel had come down from heaven and rolled back the rock from the door and was now sitting on it.

The men guarding the tomb were terrified. When the women saw the angel, they were afraid, too. But he said to them, "Do not be afraid. I know you are looking for Jesus, who was crucified. He is not here. He has risen from the dead, as He said He would. Come and see the place where His body was. Then go quickly and tell His disciples that He has risen from the dead and gone to Galilee. They will see Him there."

When the women told the disciples, Peter and John ran to the tomb. John reached the door first and bent down and looked in. He saw the strips of linen lying just where the body had been, but he didn't go inside. Then Peter came and went right in. He saw the linen cloths lying there. He also saw the cloth that had been around Jesus' head still folded as it had been, but lying in a different place. Then John went inside, too. Both of them believed that Jesus really had risen back to life.

Mary Magdalene stood by the tomb, crying. As she turned away, she saw a Man standing nearby. He said, "Woman, why are you crying? What are you looking for?"

Mary thought He must be the gardener and she said to Him, "Sir, if You have carried away His body, tell me where You have laid Him, and I will take Him away."

Then Jesus (that is who the man was) said to her, "Mary." When she heard her name, she

**Peter and John look inside the tomb and see that Jesus'
body is no longer there. (John 20:3-7)**

cried out, "Master!" She threw herself down and wanted to take hold of His feet and worship Him, but Jesus said, "Do not touch Me, for I have not yet ascended to My Father. Go to My brothers and tell them that I will ascend to My Father and yours, and to My God and yours."

Later, two of Jesus' followers were walking from Jerusalem to a village called Emmaus. As they walked, they talked about what had happened in the past few days. A stranger came up beside them and joined in their conversation. That stranger was really Jesus, although they were not able to recognize Him. He asked them why they were so sad and they told Him everything that had happened.

Then the stranger said, "O foolish people, you are so unwilling to believe what the prophets said would happen! Wasn't it necessary for the Christ to suffer these things and to enter into His glory?"

When they came close to Emmaus, the two said to the stranger, "Stay with us, for it is evening now and the day is nearly over." So He went inside with them. As they all sat at the table, He took bread and blessed it. Then, breaking the bread, He gave it to them. Suddenly their eyes were opened and they recognized Jesus, their beloved Lord. At that very moment He disappeared from their sight.

They rushed back to Jerusalem and found the disciples in a room together. Excitedly, they told them what had happened. Suddenly, while they were still telling the story, Jesus was standing there with them! He greeted them with the words, "Peace be with you!"

The disciples were frightened and thought for a moment that they had seen a ghost, but Jesus said to them, "Why are you afraid and disturbed? Look at My hands and My feet. You can see I am your Lord. And a spirit does not have flesh and bones as you see I have." They could hardly believe what had happened, because they were so full of joy.

He asked them, "Do you have anything here to eat?" They gave Him a piece of a broiled fish, and He ate it in front of them. Then He said, "When I was still with you I told you that everything must happen that was foretold of Me in the Law of Moses and the Prophets and the Psalms. Now you know that it has happened as I said."

Then He blessed them and vanished from their sight.

Then the angel spoke to the women. "Don't be afraid!" he said. "I know you are looking for Jesus, who was crucified. He isn't here! He is risen from the dead, just as He said would happen. Come, see where His body was lying."

Matthew 28:5-6

The Lord They Did Not Recognize

John 20:19-29; 21:1-14; Acts 1:1-11

Not all the disciples shared in the joy of knowing that Jesus was alive. Thomas was not with them that day. They told him that they had seen Jesus alive and well.

But Thomas was so heartbroken over Jesus' death that he wouldn't believe what they told him. "Unless I see in the scars in His hands, and put my finger into the wound in His side, I will not believe."

A whole week passed. On the first night of the new week the disciples were together again in the room in Jerusalem. This time Thomas was with them.

The doors were locked so that the disciples would be safe inside. Suddenly Jesus was right there in the middle of them and He greeted them with the lovely words, "Peace be with you!"

Then He turned to Thomas and said, "Thomas, put your finger into the holes in My hands, and place your hand in the wound in My side. Stop your doubting, and believe that I really am alive."

The only words Thomas could speak were, "My Lord and my God!"

Jesus said, "Since you have seen Me, you believe, but how blessed are those who do not see Me, but still believe!"

On His resurrection morning, Jesus and the angels sent the women with a message to the disciples to go into Galilee and they would see Jesus there.

One evening, while they waited for Him in Galilee, they decided to go fishing on the lake. They spent the whole night out on the lake, but they didn't catch a single fish. As the sun was coming up, their little boat was close to the shore.

They saw a Man standing on the shore, but they couldn't tell who it was. The Man called

**Jesus shows Thomas the nail marks in
His hands and the wound in His side. (John 20:27)**

out to them, "Have you caught anything?" They answered, "No, nothing at all."

Then He said, "Toss the net on the right side of the boat, and you will catch fish."

How surprised they were when the net filled up with so many fish that they couldn't pull it in! Then John realized who the Man was. He said to Peter, "It is the Lord!"

Peter was so excited that he jumped into the lake and swam to shore. The rest of the disciples rowed the boat to shore, dragging the net full of fish behind.

Jesus later appeared where the 11 disciples were eating a meal together. He gave them an important job to do in His name: "Go into all parts of the world and preach the Gospel to all people. Those that believe and are baptized will be saved, but those who do not believe will be damned."

Then He made a wonderful promise to them, "I am with you always, even to the end of the world."

The last time Jesus showed Himself to His people was when He told them goodbye before returning to heaven. He called them to the Mount of Olives and gave them His final message.

Then He told them to go back to Jerusalem and wait there quietly until the Holy Spirit came and filled them with power. He had promised to send the Holy Spirit to them.

The Holy Spirit would help them become witnesses for Jesus. They would preach the Gospel in Jerusalem and in all Judea, Samaria, and in every part of the world.

Jesus stretched out His arms and blessed them. Then, as they watched, He rose slowly into the sky until a cloud hid Him from their sight.

While they gazed up into the sky, two angels in white came to them and said, "Men of Galilee, why are you standing

Jesus tells His disciples to tell everyone in the world about Him. (Matthew 28:19)

here looking up into the sky? This same Jesus, who has been taken away from you into heaven, will come again in the same way you saw Him go."

"Go and make disciples of all the nations, baptizing them in the name of the Father and the Son and the Holy Spirit. Teach these new disciples to obey all the commands I have given you. And be sure of this: I am with you always, even to the end of the age."

Matthew 28:19-20

The Amazing Beginning of the Church

Acts 2

After the Lord Jesus went back to heaven, the disciples stayed together in Jerusalem, praying and worshiping and waiting for the coming of the Holy Spirit. It soon became clear that Peter would become one of their great leaders.

The 10th day after Jesus returned to heaven was the Jewish Festival of Pentecost. The name means "The 50th Day" because the festival was held on the 50th day after the Passover.

On that day, Jesus' followers were together in one place when there suddenly was a sound from heaven like the roaring of a strong wind. Then something that looked like tongues of fire settled on the heads of each person there, and they were all filled with the Holy Spirit.

The Spirit gave them the ability to speak in different languages. News of this amazing thing got out and crowds of people came to see what had happened.

Peter stepped up with the rest of the apostles and began to speak to the crowd. "Men of Judea, and all you who live in Jerusalem," he said, "This is what the prophet Joel was talking about when he said, 'It shall take place in the last days that I will pour out My

Jesus is taken up into heaven. (Acts 1:9)

Spirit on men of all flesh. Your sons and your daughters will prophesy, and your young men will see visions, and your old men will dream dreams. And everyone that calls on the name of the Lord will be saved.'"

Then Peter told them about Jesus. He reminded them of the miracles Jesus had done right in front of many of them, and how they had cruelly crucified Him, but God raised Him from the dead.

He explained to them how in the Old Testament it was foretold that the Christ, the Son of David, would rise again from the dead; and he told them that the disciples had seen the risen Lord. They knew He was the Christ; and now as the Lord Himself had promised, the Holy Spirit had been poured out on His chosen ones.

When they heard this, the people were worried and asked the disciples, "What should we do?"

Peter told them, "Repent of your sins and be baptized, every one of you, in the name of Jesus Christ, to receive forgiveness of your sins. Then you will also receive the gift of the Holy Spirit. The promise is to you and to your children, and to those that are far off, as many as the Lord shall call."

All the believers met together in one place and shared everything they had. They sold their property and possessions and shared the money with those in need. They worshiped together at the Temple each day, met in homes for the Lord's Supper, and shared their meals with great joy and generosity.

Acts 2:44-46

The Holy Spirit descends on the believers
like tongues of fire. (Acts 2:2-4)

Peter and John Help a Lame Man

Acts 3:1–4:22

God gave the apostles wonderful powers in the early days of the church. One afternoon at about three o'clock, Peter and John went to the Temple for the evening service. When they reached the Temple gate, called the Beautiful Gate, they saw a beggar sitting there who had been crippled his whole life.

As the apostles came near he asked them for money. Peter and John stopped and Peter said, "Look at us." The man thought they were going to give him some money. Instead, Peter said, "I have no silver or gold, but what I do have I will give to you. In the name of Jesus Christ of Nazareth, stand up and walk." Then Peter took him by the hand, and helped him up.

The man's feet and ankle bones were made strong at that very moment and he jumped up, and walked into the Temple with Peter and John, praising God the whole time.

All the people in the Temple saw the man and they were amazed, because they knew he was the man who couldn't walk and sat at the Temple gate. They crowded around to see him.

Then Peter spoke to the crowd. "Men of Israel," he said, "why are you amazed at this? And why do you look at us as if we have made this man well by our own power? He was healed by the God of Abraham, Isaac and Jacob; the God of our fathers has glorified His Son Jesus through this miracle. This is the same Jesus whom you delivered to the Gentiles and disowned in front of Pilate when the governor himself was willing to let Him go. You disowned the Holy and Righteous One and chose a murderer to be freed instead. You killed Him. But God raised Him from the dead and we are witnesses of that fact. We have seen Him alive! It is through faith in His name that this man has been healed."

Peter and John appear before the religious leaders. (Acts 4:5-6)

While Peter was speaking, the Sadducees and priests and the captain of the Temple guard came in. They were angry that the apostles were teaching there.

The Sadducees were especially angry because the apostles were teaching that through Jesus there would be a resurrection from the dead for all who believed.

The Sadducees did not believe in life after death. So they had Peter and John arrested and thrown into prison to keep them quiet.

The next day, Annas, the high priest, and Caiaphas came to Jerusalem to try the two apostles. When Peter and John were brought in, they asked them, "By what power or by what name have you done this thing?"

Peter was filled with the Holy Spirit and he answered, "If we are being questioned about the good deed done to the crippled man and are being asked how he was healed, we want all the people of Israel to know. This man stands before you healed by the name of Jesus Christ of Nazareth, whom you crucified, but whom God raised from the dead. This same Jesus is, as the psalmist said, the stone that was rejected by you, the builders. Now He has become the very cornerstone of the building. You will not find salvation anywhere else. There is no other name under heaven that has been spoken among men by which we must be saved."

The Temple leaders could find no reason for punishing the apostles. In fact, they were afraid of how the people would react if they did punish them. So they released Peter and John. But before they let them go, they threatened them with terrible punishment if they didn't stop speaking and teaching in Jesus' name.

Peter and John were filled with a power that the Temple rulers knew nothing about. It was the power of the Holy Spirit.

They went straight back to join the rest of the apostles in the Upper Room, which had been their meeting place since the Last Supper. They praised God and prayed for courage to keep on preaching the Gospel of salvation.

Let me clearly state to all of you and to all the people of Israel that he was healed by the powerful name of Jesus Christ the Nazarene, the Man you crucified but whom God raised from the dead. For Jesus is the One referred to in the Scriptures, where it says, "The stone that you builders rejected has now become the cornerstone."

Acts 4:10-11

Stephen Is Martyred

Acts 6:1–8:3

Many of the Christians who lived in Jerusalem were very poor. The richer Christians sold their possessions and gave the money to help the poor.

Some of the Christians were Hebrews and some were Greek Jews. Some jealousy grew between the two groups because the Greek Jews felt that their widows were not being cared for.

The apostles were worried so they called a meeting. At the meeting they told everyone that it was impossible for them to be in charge of all the work. The Lord had given them the job of preaching the Gospel, so other men needed to be in charge of caring for the poor and the sick.

The people agreed that this was a good idea and they chose Stephen, Philip and five other men to handle the care of those in need. The seven men came to the apostles, who laid their hands on their heads and prayed for them. From then on these men took care of the poor, but Stephen and Philip also became preachers of God's Word.

There was a special synagogue in Jerusalem where Jews from other places always worshiped together. Some of the men from this synagogue tried to argue against the things that Stephen taught, but he was guided by God's Spirit and was able to answer all their arguments.

When their arguments failed, the people lied about what Stephen was teaching. They said, "We have heard this Stephen say that Jesus of Nazareth will destroy this place and change all the customs that Moses gave to us." The high priest then questioned Stephen. "Is this true?" he asked.

Stephen answered in words that the Holy Spirit gave to him. He reminded them of how Moses had said many centuries before that God would one day give them a great prophet to speak to them in His name. God had given them that Prophet – His own Son. Stephen reminded them that, just as their fathers had been hardhearted when they persecuted God's messengers before, they had now murdered the Holy Son of God.

When they heard this accusation, the men were furious. But Stephen stood calmly in front of them. He looked up and saw heaven open in front of him, and the glory of God, and Jesus standing at God's right hand. Then he cried out, "Look, I see the heavens opened in front of me, and the Son of Man standing at the right hand of God."

But the men refused to listen. They grabbed him and dragged him out of the council room and outside the city walls. The men who had lied about Stephen took off their coats and gave them to a young man called Saul to hold. Then they began to throw stones at Stephen, while he cried out, "Lord Jesus, receive my spirit!" He fell to his knees under all the stones hitting him and he shouted, "Please, Lord, do not hold this sin against them." Then he fell down, dead.

The young man who held the coats watched and agreed with all that the liars did to Stephen. This began a terrible persecution against all the Christians in and around Jerusalem. Saul was at the head of it. He had Christian men and women dragged from their homes and thrown into prison. All those who could, except the apostles, ran to faraway parts of Judea and Samaria.

By the work of Saul and those who were with him, the church of Christ, where so many had lived in love and peace, was broken up. Its members were scattered far and wide. However, no harm came to the apostles in the city because they were kept hidden.

Stephen, full of the Holy Spirit, gazed steadily into heaven and saw the glory of God, and he saw Jesus standing in the place of honor at God's right hand.

Acts 7:55

Philip Shares the Good News
Acts 8:4–8, 26–40

The persecution that Saul and his followers subjected the Christians to did not stop them. Wherever they went, they preached about Jesus. After a while Philip went to Samaria and began to preach there.

God gave him the power to do many miracles and large crowds of people listened to him and believed in Jesus. He drove out evil spirits from many unhappy people and healed others who were paralyzed or crippled.

Then God's angel told Philip to go south on a desert road that led from Jerusalem to Gaza. As he walked down the road, Philip saw a chariot and an official of the royal court riding in it. The man believed in the God of Israel and he had been in Jerusalem to worship in the Temple. Now he was reading from the book of Isaiah as he returned home.

He was reading the verses in Isaiah 53 that say, "He was led like a lamb to the slaughter. And as a sheep is silent before the shearers, He did not open his mouth. Unjustly condemned, He was led away." Philip asked the man if he understood what he was reading. "How can I," he replied, "unless someone explains it to me? Who is the prophet talking about? Himself or someone else?" Then Philip used the verse he was reading to tell the man about the Lord Jesus Christ. Philip told him the good news about Jesus. When he heard what Philip said, the man believed! They were just passing by a stream. So, right then and there the official asked Philip to baptize him.

When the baptism was over, the Spirit of God took Philip away miraculously so that he disappeared from the man's sight. But the man continued home, praising God for what had happened.

As they rode along, they came to some water, and the eunuch said, "Look! There's some water! Why can't I be baptized?" He ordered the carriage to stop, and they went down into the water, and Philip baptized him.

Acts 8:36-38

A Changed Man
Acts 9:1–31; 22:1–23; Galatians 1:1–10

Saul disliked the Christians. He wanted to cause them trouble, not only in Jerusalem but also in all the places where the Christians lived. He went to the high priest and asked for letters of authority so that he could go to Damascus to the synagogues there, arrest Christians and bring them back to Jerusalem as prisoners.

The high priest gave Saul the letters and Saul found some men to go with him to Damascus. It was a long walk that took quite a few days.

As Saul got close to Damascus, a light that was brighter than the sun shone from heaven all around Saul. He fell to the ground and as he lay there he heard a voice saying, "Saul,

On his way to Damascus, a bright light shines on Saul and Jesus speaks to him. (Acts 9:3-5)

Saul, why do you persecute Me?"

Saul answered, "Who are You, Lord?" Then the voice spoke again: "I am Jesus, whom you are persecuting. It is hard for you to fight against Me. Go into Damascus; when you get there you will be told what you must do."

The men who were traveling with Saul were speechless. They had heard a voice speaking, but didn't see anyone. They helped Saul get up from the ground. His eyes were open, but he couldn't see anything. They had to lead him by the hand until they came to the city of Damascus. For three days Saul was blind, and did not eat or drink anything.

A disciple of Jesus named Ananias lived in Damascus. He had a vision where the Lord said to him, "Ananias, go to the street called Straight, to the house of a man named Judas. Saul of Tarsus is staying there. Ask for him when you get there. He is praying, and in a vision he has seen a man named Ananias come and lay his hands on him so that he may be able to see again."

Ananias answered, "But, Lord, I've heard many people speak about the harm this man has done to the believers in Jerusalem. And now he has authority from the high priest to persecute Christians in Damascus as well." But the Lord said, "Ananias, go to him as I have told you because he is My chosen servant to be a witness for Me to the Gentiles and even before kings, as well as to the children of Israel. I will show him how much he will have to suffer for My name's sake."

So Ananias went to the house of Judas. He found Saul there as the Lord had told him. He laid his hands on the blind man and said, "Brother Saul, the Lord Jesus, who appeared to you while you were coming to Damascus, has sent me to you so that you may be given your sight again and receive the Holy Spirit." In that very moment something that looked like scales fell from Saul's eyes and he could see again! Then he got up, was baptized and became a follower of the Lord

Jesus Christ. For three days he hadn't eaten anything. Now he feasted with Ananias and Judas as a Christian believer.

Saul stayed for several days with the disciples in Damascus. Every day he went into the synagogues and preached the Gospel of Jesus Christ. He told the people that Jesus is the Son of God.

Those who heard him were amazed because they knew how Saul had hated and hurt the Christians. Each day his words were firmer and clearer. No one could argue against him when he proved that Jesus is the Christ.

At first, many of the Christians wouldn't have anything to do with Saul. They still remembered his terrible persecution of the believers and were afraid. But one man, Barnabas, became his close friend. Barnabas told all the Christians how the Lord Jesus had met with Saul. He told them how Saul had preached fearlessly in Damascus. Soon Saul was accepted in all the congregations, and preached the Gospel in all parts of Jerusalem.

The Lord said to me, "Go, for I will send you far away to the Gentiles!"

Acts 22:21

The Gospel Is for All Nations
Acts 9:43; 10:1–11:18

There was a Roman officer stationed in Caesarea named Cornelius. He was a believer in the God of Israel, a godly man who was kind to the Jews and spent a lot of time in prayer. One afternoon while he was praying, he saw in a vision an angel coming toward him, who said, "Cornelius, your prayers and your gifts to the poor have been noticed by God in heaven. Send some men to Joppa, to the house of Simon the tanner. There they will find another man named Simon Peter. They must bring him to you in Caesarea."

Cornelius sent three men to Joppa at once.

At noon the next day, while these men were on their way from Caesarea, Peter went to pray on the roof of the house where he was staying.

While he was praying, he saw a vision from God. He saw heaven opened up and an object like a great sheet lowered down by its four corners to the ground. In this sheet were all kinds of animals and birds. A voice said to Peter, "Get up, Peter, kill the animals and eat."

But Peter said, "No, Lord. I have never eaten anything that according to the law is unholy or unclean."

The voice answered, "What God has made clean, you must not call unholy." This happened three times. Then, in the vision, the sheet was pulled back into heaven. Peter was confused about the meaning of what he had seen.

At the same time the men from Cornelius arrived and asked for Simon Peter. The Holy Spirit said to Peter, "Three men are looking for you. Go down to them. I have sent them to you Myself."

The next day Peter departed with the men for Caesarea. Cornelius was waiting and he explained about the angel who had told him to send for Peter. Now everyone gathered to hear what the Lord had commanded Peter to say.

This is what Peter said: "Through all that has happened, I know now that God is not partial to the people of one nation only. In every nation those who fear God and keep His commandments are His blessed children. The wonderful message about Jesus Christ, whom God has sent, is not only for the Jews, but for people of all nations. You know about the life of Jesus Christ, how God anointed Him with power and how He went about doing good and healing those who were sick or tormented by the devil. You know, too, how He was crucified; but God raised Him on the third day. Many of His disciples saw Him after His

The wonderful message about Jesus is for everyone in the world and not just for the Jews. (Acts 11:18)

resurrection and even ate and drank with Him. Now He has told us to go and preach to all people that He is the One who will one day judge the living and the dead. He is the Messiah the prophets told us about. All who trust in Him will receive forgiveness for their sins."

While they were still listening to what Peter said, the Holy Spirit came into their hearts, and many believed in Jesus Christ.

All who believed were baptized in Jesus' name, and from then on the Gospel was preached to both Jews and Gentiles.

When the others heard this, they stopped objecting and began praising God. They said, "We can see that God has also given the Gentiles the privilege of repenting of their sins and receiving eternal life."

Acts 11:18

The First Missionaries

Acts 11:19–30; 13; 14:8–10

The Gospel of the Lord Jesus Christ was first preached in Jerusalem. But when the persecution began in that city, the Christians fled to other parts of the land. They took the Gospel with them and told others about the Lord. Some Christians went to Phoenicia, some to Cyprus, and some to Antioch. At first they only spoke to other Jews. But there were some Christians who came to Antioch and they began to tell not only the Jews, but Gentiles, too, about the wonderful truth about salvation through the Lord Jesus. Many of the Gentiles they spoke with put their trust in the Lord. The news about this soon reached the believers in Jerusalem. They sent Barnabas to Antioch to see what was happening and to see if any further help was needed.

Barnabas decided that more workers were needed, so he went to Tarsus to find

Saul. When he found him, he brought him to Antioch and the two of them spent a whole year teaching there. It was in Antioch that believers in the Lord Jesus were called Christians for the first time.

There were now a number of strong leaders in the church in Antioch. There was Saul and Barnabas, and Simeon and Lucius, and Manaen, a young man who had been brought up with Herod the king. One day they were fasting and praying together when the Holy Spirit brought them a special message. He told them they must set apart Barnabas and Saul for the special work of carrying the Gospel to places where its message had not yet been heard. Antioch was becoming the headquarters for missionary work in the young Christian church.

After fasting and prayer, the leaders in the church laid hands on Barnabas and Saul and sent them out as the first missionaries. The two men traveled from town to town, preaching the Gospel everywhere.

When they reached the town of Paphos, they found a Jewish magician who was a false prophet named Bar-Jesus. He was sometimes called Elymas. He was with a man named Sergius Paulus, the governor. Now Sergius Paulus was a wise man and he wanted very much to hear the Word of God so he sent for Barnabas and Saul. After they listened to what the two missionaries said, Elymas started arguing with them and tried to turn Sergius Paulus against the faith.

Saul, who was now called Paul, looked Elymas straight in the eyes and said, "You are full of deceit and fraud, you are the enemy of good and you are the son of the devil. When will you stop twisting the truths of God? The hand of the Lord is upon you and you will be blind for a while." Immediately everything turned misty and dark to Elymas. He had to beg others to lead him by the hand because he couldn't see where he was going. When he saw what happened to Elymas, Sergius Paulus became a Christian.

After they had finished their work, Paul and Barnabas left by ship for Perga in Pamphylia, which is part of the country now called Turkey. Paul and Barnabas went inland to Antioch. This was not the Syrian city they had just come from, but another town of the same name. On the Sabbath, they went to the synagogue for the service. After a reading from the Old Testament, the synagogue officials invited them to speak if they had any message for the congregation.

Paul got up and told them about the Lord Jesus Christ. He told how the prophets had promised that Jesus would come to be the Savior, and how He died and rose again. He told them that through faith in the Lord Jesus they could be forgiven for their sins and become children of God. Many of the listeners were impressed by what Paul said, and followed him and Barnabas out of the synagogue to hear more of their teaching.

The next week, a very big crowd came to the synagogue to listen, but when the Jews saw this they began to argue with Paul and Barnabas and to say things against the Lord.

Then the two men took a brave stand and said, "It was necessary for the Gospel to be preached to you first, as Jews, but since you have rejected it, and decided you are unworthy of eternal life, we will turn now to the Gentiles. This is the instruction given to us by the Lord, who said, 'I have set you to be a light for the Gentiles, so that you may bring the word of salvation to the farthest parts of the earth.'"

From there the apostles went to Iconium. Once again they went into the synagogue to preach the Gospel. They spoke with such power that a great number of Jews and Gentiles became Christians.

Once again, though, unbelieving Jews stirred up the Gentiles and turned them against the apostles. Eventually there was great complaint against the new teaching, so to avoid being stoned Paul and Barnabas left the city and went to the cities of Lystra and Derbe.

The first missionaries set out to spread the wonderful message about Jesus. (Acts 11:27)

In Lystra they met a man who had crippled feet and had never been able to walk. One day he was brought to listen to Paul preach. When Paul looked at him and saw that he believed, he said to the man, "Stand up!" The man jumped to his feet and began to walk!

When the crowd saw what Paul had done, they began to shout that the gods had become like men and had come down to earth. They called Paul and Barnabas by the names of Hermes and Zeus, the names of their heathen gods. The priest of the temple of Zeus, which was just outside the city, brought garlands to hang around their necks. He even brought oxen to sacrifice to them!

Paul and Barnabas went into the crowd and shouted, "Men, why are you doing this? We are human beings just like you. We have come to preach the Gospel to you so that you may worship the living God who made the heaven and the earth and the sea, and all that is in them."

However, before long, Jews came from other cities and stirred up the people against Paul and Barnabas. The people stoned Paul until they thought he was dead and dragged his body out of the city. But while the Christians stood around him, mourning, Paul got up and went back into the city. The next day he and Barnabas left and traveled to various towns, stopping in each place to teach the believers and to encourage them in the faith.

"I have made you a light to the Gentiles, to bring salvation to the farthest corners of the earth."

Acts 13:47

Paul preaches to the people. (Acts 17:10-12)

Paul Preaches in the Synagogues

Acts 17–18

After Paul and Silas left Philippi, they went to the city of Thessalonica, where there was a Jewish synagogue. As usual, Paul went to the synagogue. For three Sabbath days he taught the Jews from the Scriptures, explaining that Christ had to suffer and die, and rise again from the dead. Then he told them that Jesus was the promised Christ. Some of the listeners believed and joined Paul and Silas. Some of the God-fearing Greeks believed, too.

The Jewish leaders did their best to stop Paul's preaching and after trouble with the authorities, Paul and Silas left the city and went to Berea.

In Berea, Paul began teaching as usual in the synagogue. The people listened to Paul with eagerness and carefully studied their Bibles to see whether his teaching was correct. Because of this, many of them believed, and a number of the leading Greeks did as well.

When the Jews of Thessalonica heard of this, they sent men to Berea to cause problems. To avoid trouble, Paul left for the coast and went by ship south to Athens. Silas and Timothy remained in Berea for the time being, encouraging the believers there. They joined Paul later.

While Paul waited in Athens, he was horrified to see all the idol worship that was taking place everywhere in that great city. In the synagogue he talked with the Jews and the Greek believers. Every day he preached in the market place to all who would listen.

Because there was such interest, the people asked him to explain the new teaching he had been sharing. They said, "We are hearing strange things about your doctrine."

Paul stood up and said to them, "Men of Athens, I notice that you are a very religious people. I see you have even built an altar 'To an Unknown God,' so you are sure not to leave out any of the gods that you feel ought to be worshiped.

"Now the God unknown to you, the real God, is the One I am telling you about. He is the God of heaven and earth, who made the world and all things in it. He does not live in man-made temples, and doesn't need our gifts, because He is the Giver of life and breath to all. It is He who has made one family of all the nations that live on earth, and has decided when they should rise and fall. Therefore all should seek God to serve Him and worship Him, though He is not far from any of us. As our own poets have said, 'In Him we live and move and have our being.'

"If we are then His creation, we ought not to think that He is like gold or silver or stone, nor like an image made by the art and thought of man. God has overlooked men's ignorance in the past, but now He is calling on everyone in the whole world to repent. He has set a day for the judgment of the world in righteousness. And the Judge will be the Man whose appointment He has sealed by raising Him from the dead."

When they heard Paul mention the resurrection of the dead, some of them sneered and said, "We'll talk more about this later."

So Paul left them, but a few who had heard him believed and became Christians.

He is the God who made the world and everything in it. Since He is Lord of heaven and earth, He doesn't live in man-made temples, and human hands can't serve His needs – for He has no needs. He Himself gives life and breath to everything, and He satisfies every need.

Acts 17:24-25

Paul Goes to Corinth

Acts 18:1-23

When he left Athens, Paul went to another great Greek city, Corinth. There he came across a Jew named Aquila, who had recently come from Italy with his wife, Priscilla.

The Emperor Claudius had driven all the Jews out of Rome and Aquila and Priscilla had come to Greece for safety. Paul stayed with them because they were tentmakers by trade. Paul was also a tentmaker and they could work together.

Each Sabbath, Paul taught in the synagogue and told both Jews and Greeks the truth of the Gospel.

When Silas and Timothy arrived, Paul left his tentmaking and spent all his time preaching and trying to show the Jews that Jesus was the Christ. But they wouldn't listen to him. They cursed him for what he taught, so he left them, saying, "Your blood be on your own heads. From now on I shall go to the Gentiles."

In a vision, God encouraged Paul and told him, "Don't be afraid. Go on speaking. I am with you, and no one will hurt you or attack you, for I have many people in this city."

For 18 months Paul preached the Gospel without being disturbed at all. Then, when Gallio became ruler in Achaia, the Jews planned to hurt Paul and had him brought before Gallio.

"This man," they said, "persuades people to worship God in a way that is against our law."

Just as Paul was about to defend himself, Gallio interrupted. "If this were a serious crime," he said, "I should deal with it. But if you wish to argue here about words and religious laws, I will have nothing to do with you."

For a while longer Paul remained in Corinth. Then he began his missionary journeys again. This time Priscilla and Aquila went with him.

First they went to Cenchrea, and then to Ephesus, where he left his traveling companions. Before he went on, though, he first taught for a short while in the synagogue. The people asked him to stay, but he decided not to, though he promised to come back later if it was the will of God.

Taking a ship from Ephesus, Paul returned to Caesarea near Jerusalem. After a short stay he went to Jerusalem to greet the church there. Then he traveled to Antioch, to the church that had originally sent him out as a missionary.

One night the Lord spoke to Paul in a vision and told him, "Don't be afraid! Speak out! Don't be silent! For I am with you, and no one will attack and harm you, for many people in this city belong to Me."

Acts 18:9-10

Riots in Ephesus

Acts 18:24–20:1

Paul spent some time preaching in Antioch, but he also rested and got ready for a new missionary trip. Then he left for the provinces of Galatia and Phrygia, where he visited all the new churches and taught the disciples. He especially encouraged the leaders who had faced a lot of opposition from unbelievers.

After this Paul went to the synagogue, where he taught regularly for a period of three months. At first the people listened with interest, but then some of them argued against him and caused disturbances when he was teaching so Paul left the synagogue.

Paul took those who trusted in the Lord Jesus with him. He taught in the hall of a philosopher called Tyrannus. For two years he taught there, so that any who lived in the province of Asia, both Jews and Greeks, were able to hear the Lord's Word. God gave Paul wonderful powers at this time so that even handkerchiefs or aprons that he had touched were brought to the sick and they were healed and evil spirits expelled!

Paul's power was so amazing that some false teachers in the area tried to copy what he was doing. Men who claimed to be able to drive out evil spirits tried to use the name of the Lord Jesus over demon-possessed people by saying, "We charge you to come out, in the name of Jesus whom Paul preaches." The seven sons of Sceva, a Jewish priest, were doing this, but they were horrified one day when one of the evil spirits turned on them.

As they spoke to it, the evil spirit cried out, "Jesus I know, and Paul I know, but who are you?" Then the demon-possessed man attacked them and hurt them. They escaped from the house with their clothes torn off and cuts and bruises on their bodies.

This news soon spread around Ephesus and all who practiced magic became afraid of what might happen to them.

Many came to Paul and told him what they had been doing. They brought their books of magic and piled them up and set them on fire. The value of those books amounted to millions.

Many people put their trust in the Lord Jesus Christ because of what had happened to the magicians of Ephesus.

It was Paul's plan to go into Macedonia and Achaia, and then on to Jerusalem. After that he would go to Rome.

Before he left, however, he sent two of his helpers, Timothy and Erastus, to Macedonia to get the churches ready for his coming.

Soon after they had left, the situation in Ephesus took an unpleasant turn. Many of the magicians had given up their work because the people had begun to see how worthless the works of the magicians were. Much of their magic had been connected with the worship of a goddess named Diana, or Artemis in Greek.

The silversmiths of the city had done big business making small silver idols of the goddess. But now their business was falling off badly.

One of them, named Demetrius, called together the rest of the silversmiths to discuss their position. "Men, you know that our prosperity and the prosperity of the city depends on this trade of ours.

"Now this Paul has come here and persuaded many of the people, not only in Ephesus, but in much of the province of Asia, that gods made with hands are not gods at all. There is danger now that our business will completely fail, and that even the temple of the goddess Diana will be dishonored."

When they heard this, the silversmiths were very angry and shouted, "Great is Diana of the Ephesians!" Then they rushed into the streets, stirring up the people of the town against the Christians.

In the square there was a great deal of pushing and shouting and confusion. Not all the people knew what the fuss was about, but for two hours they continued shouting, "Great is Diana of the Ephesians!"

Eventually the city mayor managed to quiet them down and speak to them.

This is what he said: "Men of Ephesus, is there any person, after all, who does not know that the city of Ephesus is the guardian of the temple of Diana, and of the image that fell down from Jupiter? So what's the need for this commotion?

"If Demetrius and his companions have a complaint against anyone, there are courts and magistrates they can be brought to. And if you want anything more to be done, there is the city assembly. But this riotous behavior must not continue, or else the provincial authorities will call us to account for it."

After this the mayor sent the crowd away. When the uproar

had settled down, Paul said goodbye to the disciples and left for Macedonia as he had planned to do before the trouble began.

Then Paul went to the synagogue and preached boldly for the next three months, arguing persuasively about the Kingdom of God.

Acts 19:8

Paul's Last Journey

Acts 20:2–21:14

After the trouble in Ephesus, Paul left the province of Asia and went by ship across to Macedonia. He visited many of the churches and towns, preaching and encouraging the Christians.

Then he went to Greece, where he spent about three months. Paul planned to go back to the church that had sent him out as a missionary, but he had to change his plans because he discovered that the Jews were once more waiting to cause trouble for him.

Back through Macedonia he went. This time a number of Macedonian Christians went with him from town to town as he preached.

In Troas, Paul and his disciples gathered for the breaking of the bread (communion). Paul preached to them that night and he spoke until midnight.

Now they were all together in the upstairs room of a house. Some of the listeners sat on the window ledges because the room was so crowded.

One young man named Eutychus sat on a window sill. During the sermon he fell asleep and fell out of the window. Some of Paul's listeners rushed to him, but he was already dead.

Paul quickly went down and took him in his arms and said, "Do not be distressed. Life is still in him." Then the young man came back to life and all the people were greatly comforted. Paul went back to his meeting and preached until morning.

Paul then started off on the first stage of his journey to Jerusalem. He wanted to be there for the Festival of Pentecost. He met the rest of his party and boarded a ship with them. After a few days of sailing, they arrived at Miletus, where they stayed for a few days.

Paul sent for the elders of the church in Ephesus. When they came, he gave them a very serious message. "You know how," he said, "since the first day I set foot in Asia, I have served the Lord in all humility, even with tears and suffering because of what the Jews have done to me. I have not kept back from you any of the teaching God sent me to give. I have preached both publicly and privately, from house to house, telling both Jews and Greeks to repent and believe in our Lord Jesus Christ. Now the Holy Spirit has made it clear to me that

I must go to Jerusalem. I do not know what will happen to me there, but the Holy Spirit keeps telling me that prison and all kinds of sufferings are ahead of me. I do not look upon my life as a thing to be held on to. What matters most is the faithful performance of the ministry to which the Lord has called me, to proclaim the Gospel of the grace of God.

"I warn you to take care of yourselves and of the whole church over which the Holy Spirit has made you shepherds, because after I leave, fierce wolves will get in among you to destroy the flock. False teachers will appear in your own ranks and will draw disciples away from the truth. So keep on the alert always and remember that for three years I did not stop advising and teaching you, even through my tears.

"Now I commend you to God's keeping. I have wanted none of your possessions. You know that my own hands ministered to my needs and the needs of all my party. By my example, I have shown you that by working hard you must help the weak, and always remember that the Lord Jesus Himself said, 'It is more blessed to give than to receive.'"

Paul and his party were warned by the Holy Spirit that Paul was going into great danger. They begged him not to continue his journey to Jerusalem, but he wouldn't listen.

From Tyre, they sailed on to Caesarea, where they left the ship to continue their journey overland to Jerusalem. At Caesarea, Paul and his party stayed in the house of Philip the evangelist. He was one of the seven chosen to care for the needs of widows and the poor and sick in the church at Jerusalem.

While they were there, a prophet named Agabus came to see Paul. Walking up to Paul's party, he took Paul's belt and used it to tie his own feet and hands. Then he said, "This is what the Holy Spirit says, 'In the same way as I have bound my hands and feet, the Jews in Jerusalem will bind the man that owns this belt, and hand him over to the Romans.'"

Now when they heard that, Paul's friends and all the Christians who had gathered at Philip's house were very upset and begged Paul not to go to Jerusalem.

But he said to them, "What are you trying to do, crying and breaking my heart? I am ready not only to be bound, but even to die in Jerusalem for the sake of the Lord Jesus Christ."

When they saw that they couldn't make him change his mind, they said, "The Lord's will be done."

Paul said, "Why all this weeping? You are breaking my heart! I am ready not only to be jailed at Jerusalem but even to die for the sake of the Lord Jesus."

Acts 21:13

Paul Explains His Ministry

Acts 21:26–22:29

After Paul arrived in Jerusalem, some of the Jews who had caused so much trouble saw him. He went to the Temple every day to worship and the troublemakers stirred up the people against Paul.

They grabbed him and shouted, "Men of Israel, help! This is the man who is turning everyone against the Law of Moses and against the worship that is carried on here. He has even brought Gentiles into the Temple and defiled it!" (They had seen him in the street with an Ephesian named Trophimus, and thought that Paul had brought him into the Temple.)

The Jews who had accused Paul dragged him out of the Temple, beating him as they went. The news reached the captain of the Roman guard that there was a riot starting. He called together his officers and soldiers and ran down to put a stop to the trouble. As soon as the Jews saw the Roman soldiers, they stopped hitting Paul and the Romans took him prisoner instead.

Just as Paul was being taken through the doorway of the prison, he spoke to the captain of the guard and asked for permission to speak to the crowd before he was locked up.

"Brothers," he called out, "hear my defense. I am a Jew, brought up in Tarsus in the province of Cilicia, it is true, but as strictly a Jew as any man could be." Then he told them how he had persecuted Christians and how God had spoken to him on the road to Damascus. He told them of his blindness and how through God's power Ananias had healed him again.

"Soon after my sight was restored I came back to Jerusalem. One day while I was in the Temple praying, I heard the Lord warning me to leave Jerusalem quickly because the people would not listen to what I taught about Him. The Lord said, 'Go! I am sending you far away to the Gentiles.'" The crowd had been quiet up to this point, but when they heard Paul speak of going to the Gentiles, they became angry again. "Away with him!" they shouted. "He ought not to be allowed to live!"

The captain of the guard felt that Paul should be taken to a safer place, so he ordered him to be brought inside the barracks. But the barracks was not really so much safer! The soldiers stretched out Paul's arms and legs and fastened them down with leather strips so that they could beat him.

When Paul realized what they were doing, he said to the centurion in charge, "Is it lawful for you to beat a man who is a Roman citizen and has not been found guilty of any crime?"

The centurion went at once to the captain of the guard and said, "What are you doing? This man is a Roman!" The captain quickly went to Paul and asked him if this was true. When Paul said it was, the captain was afraid.

The captain decided that Paul must be released at once and a proper hearing must be held of all the complaints against him.

However, for Paul's own safety he was to remain in the barracks until the time was set for the hearing.

The Lord said to me, "Go, for I will send you far away to the Gentiles!" The crowd listened until Paul said that word. Then they all began to shout, "Away with such a fellow! He isn't fit to live!" They yelled, threw off their coats, and tossed handfuls of dust into the air.

Acts 22:21-23

Serving the Savior in Prison

Acts 22:30; 23:12–35; 24

Forty Jews met together and worked out a plan to kill Paul. But the captain heard of their plot and he wanted to see that Paul had a fair trial. He sent Paul under guard to the Roman governor Felix.

Felix asked which province Paul came from in order to make sure that he had the right to deal with the case. Then he ordered that Paul should be imprisoned in Herod's palace until his accusers arrived.

Five days later, Ananias, the high priest, arrived with some of the elders and a lawyer called Tertullus. They stated their evidence against Paul.

Tertullus made a long speech to the governor in which he spoke of Paul as a perfect pest, a man who had caused trouble among the Jews in all parts of the empire, and a ringleader in the sect of the Nazarenes. He even accused Paul of trying to defile the Temple by bringing heathen men into it. The elders all gave strong agreement with what Tertullus said.

Then the governor gave Paul a chance to speak. Paul said, "You will be able to understand the defense I put forward. It is only 12 days since I went to Jerusalem. In that time I have caused no trouble, either in the Temple or elsewhere in the city, and I have not argued with anyone. I confess to you that I do worship God as a Christian, a way which these men call false, but I still place the fullest confidence in the Law of Moses and in the writings of the prophets."

"I believe exactly as these men do that there is to be a resurrection both of the righteous and of the wicked. These men found me worshiping in the Temple. But there were other men there from the province of Asia, who stirred up trouble against me. Those men are the ones who ought to be here today as my accusers, if they have anything to say against me. But those who are here, let them say of what crime they found me guilty when I appeared before the council in Jerusalem! Unless, of course, it was because I said I believed in the resurrection of the dead!"

Felix was unwilling to carry on with the case. He understood a little about the Christian faith. He put the Jewish leaders off by saying that he would examine the case more fully when Lysias, the captain of the guard, came to Caesarea from Jerusalem. Then he told one of the centurions to take care of Paul, giving him some freedom and allowing his friends to visit him and take care of him.

A few days later, Felix and his wife, Drusilla, who was a Jewess, sent for Paul to listen to what he had to say about the Lord Jesus Christ. However, Felix was a dishonest man and was hoping that Paul would pay him a bribe to let him go free.

Felix sent often for Paul and talked to him about the Christian faith, but he was not really interested in anything except the money he thought Paul might give him.

After two years, Porcius Festus was appointed governor in the place of Felix. Because Felix wanted to leave a good impression in the minds of the Jews, he kept Paul as a prisoner for Festus to deal with.

I admit that I follow the Way, which they call a cult. I worship the God of our ancestors, and I firmly believe the Jewish law and everything written in the prophets. I have the same hope in God that these men have, that He will raise both the righteous and the unrighteous. Because of this, I always try to maintain a clear conscience before God and all people.

Acts 24:14-16

The King Who Heard but Didn't Act

Acts 25–26

Soon after Festus arrived in Caesarea, he decided to go to Jerusalem to meet the Jewish leaders. One of the first things those leaders wanted to discuss with him was what should happen to Paul.

They asked for him to be brought to Jerusalem to be put on trial there. They still had a plan to ambush the guards and kill Paul. Festus said he would soon be returning to Caesarea. The Jews were to send their leaders with Paul, and if he had done anything wrong, they could bring their evidence against him there.

About 10 days later, the case began in Caesarea. The Jews who came from Jerusalem brought many serious charges against Paul, but they couldn't prove any of them.

Then Paul stood up and said, "I have done nothing wrong against the Jewish law, nor against Caesar."

Festus asked him if he was willing to go to Jerusalem and stand trial before him there, but Paul said, "I am standing before the Roman tribunal now, and that is where I ought to be tried. I have done no wrong to the Jews, as you know already.

"If I have done anything that deserves the death penalty, I am willing to die. But if none of the charges that these men bring against me are true, no one can hand me over to them. As a Roman citizen, I appeal to Caesar."

Festus discussed the matter with his advisers and then gave his verdict: "You have appealed to Caesar; to Caesar you shall go."

A little while after this, Herod Agrippa, the king of Judea, and his sister, Bernice, arrived in Caesarea to welcome Festus, the new Roman governor. Festus told them about Paul.

Paul appears before Festus. (Acts 26:24)

Agrippa was curious about the whole matter. "I should like to hear the man myself," he said. The meeting was arranged for the next day. In the morning, Agrippa and Bernice went into the audience hall and took their seats on the royal thrones with great pomp and ceremony.

Festus then sent for Paul to be brought in. "The Jewish rulers have demanded that this man be put to death, but I have not found him to be guilty of any serious crime," Festus said.

"Now he has appealed to Caesar Augustus, and I must send him to Rome. But I do not know what to write in my report that must go to Caesar. For this reason I have brought him in front of you. You may examine him so that I may have something to put in writing."

Then King Agrippa told Paul to explain his position. This is what Paul said: "King Agrippa, I feel fortunate in being asked to explain my views to you, because I know how well you understand the Jewish customs and laws that I am accused of breaking. The Jews know of my background. They know that from my childhood I have kept the law, and lived as a Pharisee, a member of the strictest party in our Jewish faith. And now I stand trial because of what I believe in connection with the promise God made to our forefathers, of One He would send to be our Savior.

"It is the fulfillment of this promise that our 12 tribes long for. They worship fervently day after day. Because of this I am accused by the Jews and made to seem like a criminal! Why is it thought unbelievable by any of you that God should raise the dead?"

Then Paul continued and told of how he persecuted the Christians and how he was stricken down on the road to Damascus.

Agrippa said, "Paul, do you think you can persuade me to become a Christian so quickly?" Paul answered, "I wish to God that not only you, but all who listen to me here might become Christians, but not in chains like me!"

Then the king and queen the Roman governor, and the people sitting with them got up to leave the hall.

Privately they talked about the matter and agreed that Paul had done nothing that deserved death or imprisonment.

Agrippa said to Festus, "We could have set this man free if he had not appealed to Caesar."

If they would admit it, they know that I have been a member of the Pharisees, the strictest sect of our religion. Now I am on trial because of my hope in the fulfillment of God's promise made to our ancestors.

Acts 26:5-6

A Storm at Sea

Acts 27

Paul was in prison for two years without his case being heard. Then it was decided that he and some other prisoners should be taken to Rome.

Under the guard of a centurion called Julius, they were taken on board a ship that was about to sail by the seaports of the province of Asia.

From Caesarea they sailed north up the coast to Sidon. There Julius the centurion very kindly allowed Paul to

visit his Christian friends and be cared for by them.

After leaving Sidon, they sailed across the Phoenician Sea. Then they skirted the coast of the island of Cyprus to have shelter from heavy winds.

Passing the north end of Cyprus, they came to the port of Myra in Lycia. There they transferred to a ship from Alexandria that was going to Italy.

At first they made slow progress. Then the winds were

**Paul and the sailors swim safely to shore as the ship
is torn to pieces by the storm. (Acts 27:41, 43-44)**

difficult and they had trouble keeping to their course. It was decided to sail around the southern side of Crete so they would be sheltered from the fierce winds, which could make sailing dangerous at that time of year.

With great difficulty they reached a place called Fair Havens. Here Paul warned them that if they went on at that time of year, it would be very dangerous. But the centurion chose instead to take the advice of the captain and the ship's owner.

Because the harbor was not a good place to spend the winter, they decided to try to reach the harbor of Phoenix near the western end of Crete. Here there would be enough protection, where they would be able to spend the worst part of the winter.

When the wind picked up, they felt the time had come to set sail for Phoenix for the winter. They kept close to shore for safety's sake.

But then a violent wind burst upon them from the direction of the island. It was so powerful that they could not turn back toward the island, but simply had to let the ship drift with the wind.

For days they didn't see the sun or stars, as the storm raged. Finally, they gave up all hope of ever safely reaching land. They had very little food left. If they didn't die by drowning it seemed they might starve to death!

Paul spoke to the captain and said, "The ship will be lost, but there will not be any loss of life. An angel of the God I serve appeared to me this very night and said, 'Do not be afraid, Paul. You must appear before Caesar, and all the men who are with you will be safe as well.' So I'm telling you, keep up your courage, because I trust God that it will turn out exactly as I have been told. But we will run aground on a certain island."

The storm raged on for 14 nights. Their ship was being driven all around in the sea. One night, at about midnight, the sailors reported that they were approaching land. Taking some measurements, they found that they were driving rapidly toward the land. Fearing that they might end up on the rocks, the sailors threw out four anchors.

The sailors wished that the night would end so that they could better see what was going on.

Just before dawn, Paul encouraged them all to take a little food, because they hadn't eaten much and because of what was ahead for them.

"Do not be afraid," Paul said. "Not a hair on your heads will be harmed." Then he took bread himself, and gave thanks to God in front of them all and began to eat. The rest of them followed his example.

When morning came, they saw a safe-looking beach and decided to try to direct the ship to it if they could. However, the ship struck a reef where two currents met and the vessel ran aground. It was stuck in the rocks and the waves began to break up the ship.

The sailors thought they should kill all of the prisoners in case they swam ashore and escaped, but the centurion told those who could swim to jump overboard first and get to land. The rest of the sailors and prisoners were to follow on planks or anything else that could float. Everyone arrived safely on the shore.

Last night an angel of the God to whom I belong and whom I serve stood beside me, and he said, "Don't be afraid, Paul, for you will surely stand trial before Caesar! What's more, God in His goodness has granted safety to everyone sailing with you." So take courage! For I believe God. It will be just as He said.

Acts 27:23-25

The Good News Reaches Rome

Acts 28

When they were able to look around, they found that they were on the island of Malta. The people there were very kind to Paul and all the others who had been shipwrecked.

Publius, the most important man on the island, entertained them for three days. His father was very sick with fever and stomach trouble.

Paul went to see him and after Paul had laid his hands on the old man and prayed for him, he was healed.

When news of this got around, many other people who suffered from one illness or another were brought to Paul. Every one of them was cured.

When the group finally arrived in Rome, the centurion handed over the prisoners to the captain of the guard. Paul was allowed to live in a house of his own with only one soldier to guard him.

For two years, Paul remained in that house, and though he was a prisoner, he lived in safety. Through Paul, the Word of God was taught in Rome.

For the next two years, Paul lived in Rome at his own expense. He welcomed all who visited him, boldly proclaiming the Kingdom of God and teaching about the Lord Jesus Christ. And no one tried to stop him.

Acts 28:30-31

Paul teaches the people in Rome about God's Word. (Acts 28:23-24)

The Throne of God

The last of the apostles was John, the son of Zebedee. When he was an old man, the Roman emperor made him move to the lonely island of Patmos in the Aegean Sea, about 25 miles off the coast of Asia. He lived there all alone.

One day while John was worshiping God, he was held by the power of God's Spirit. Suddenly he heard behind him a great voice speaking like the sound of a war trumpet.

The voice said, "I am the Alpha and the Omega, the First and the Last." It was the Lord speaking! He went on to say, "You must write down quickly what you see in this vision and send the writing to the seven churches in Asia."

John turned to see who was speaking to him and he saw seven golden lampstands. In the middle of the lampstands stood One whom John knew was the Lord Jesus Christ, the Son of Man. But He looked more glorious than John had seen Him before. In His right hand, He held seven stars.

When John saw Jesus, he fell down in fear and adoration. The Lord laid His right hand on John and said, "Do not be afraid! Write down the things you see and all about what is happening and what will still happen. The seven stars in My right hand are the leaders of the seven churches. The seven golden lampstands are the churches themselves."

Then the Lord gave John a special message for each of the seven churches. John had to write the messages in the form of letters, but the words in them were all from the Lord Himself.

The seven churches were in Ephesus, Smyrna, Pergamum, Thyatira, Sardis, Philadelphia and Laodicea.

After this John saw a door open into heaven. A great voice like

**John sees the seven golden lampstands and Jesus
in the middle of them. (Revelation 1:12-13)**

a trumpet called him to come and said he would be told some of the things that would happen in the future.

Immediately John was in the power of the Holy Spirit and was able to see some of the glories of heaven. In front of him stood a throne. On the throne sat a Being so full of glory that John could not look directly at Him.

Around the throne was a great ring like a rainbow, colored green like an emerald. Arranged around the throne were 24 other thrones. On each of them sat an elder, clothed in white, with a golden crown on their head.

From the great throne came flashes of lightning, and rumblings like thunder and the sound of many voices. In front of the throne were seven blazing torches and the floor was a sea of transparent glass shining like crystal. Around the throne, at the center of each side of the throne, stood four living creatures, full of eyes in front and behind. One looked like a lion, one like an ox, one like a man, and one like an eagle. Each of them had three pairs of wings.

They kept saying, without stopping, "Holy, holy, holy, Lord God Almighty, who was and is and is to come."

Then John saw between the throne and the four living creatures a Lamb standing, as if it had been killed. He knew that the Lamb was the Lord Jesus Christ.

The Lamb came and took the scroll out of the hand of the One that sat on the throne. As He stepped forward again, the four living creatures and the 24 elders worshiped before Him.

Blessing and honor and glory and power belong to the One sitting on the throne and to the Lamb forever and ever.

Revelation 5:13

The City of God

Revelation 7; 21–22

John's vision on the island of Patmos was a long one. The Lord Jesus told him many things about what was going to happen in the future.

One part of the vision was of all God's people gathered together in glory. He saw a great crowd of people; so many that no one could count them, gathered from all the nations on earth. They stood in front of the throne of God and in front of the Lamb.

Clothed in white robes, and with palm branches in their hands, they cried out in a loud voice, "Salvation belongs to our God who is seated on the throne, and to the Lamb!"

As they shouted out this mighty shout, all the angels and the elders and the living creatures threw themselves down around the throne in worship.

Then one of the elders asked John a question: "Who are these people clothed in white robes? And where do they come from?"

John replied, "Sir, you know."

Then the elder said, "These are people who have come out of great tribulation, and I have washed their robes and made them white in the blood of the Lamb. That is why they stand here in the presence of God and serve Him day and night in His Temple.

"He will protect them and spread His tent over them forever. They will never again be hungry or thirsty. The sun will not scorch them. The Lamb in the center of the heavenly throne will be their Shepherd. He will guide them to fountains of living water. God will wipe away all the tears from their eyes."

A while later, John saw the city of God, where all those who love the Lamb will live. A great voice cried out to him, and said, "Look! The dwelling place of

God is with men. They shall be His people, and He will live in the midst of them. They will no longer know the meaning of sorrow, nor pain, nor death. All these things have passed away."

Then God spoke from the throne, "See, I make all things new. To those who are thirsty, I will give from the fountain of the Water of Life. Those who win the victory over sin and Satan will inherit all things. I will be their God, and they will be My children."

Then an angel of God came and carried John away in the spirit to a high mountain. The angel showed John the city of God, the New Jerusalem, which came down out of heaven.

After this, John saw the crystal-clear river of the Water of Life, flowing from the throne of God and the Lamb, and passing through the city of God. Beside the river grew the Tree of Life.

The Tree of Life bore 12 different kinds of fruit, one for each month of the year. The leaves of that tree were meant for the healing of the nations. In that city was no darkness at all. No light of any kind was needed, because the Lord God Himself would give light to all His people there forever.

When John saw and heard these glorious things, he fell down at the feet of the angel who had shown these things to him.

The angel said to him, "You must not do that! I am a servant of God like you are, and like the prophets, and like all who obey the teaching of this Book. Worship God and Him only!"

Then the angel said, "Do not hide away the teaching of this Book, but tell it to all believers. The time for its fulfillment is near."

After this, the Lord Jesus Himself ended John's vision by saying to him, "I, Jesus, have sent My angel to tell you about these things so that My people in the churches may hear about them.

"I am the Root and Offspring of David. I am the Bright Morning Star. The Spirit and the Bride say, 'Come!' Let everyone who is thirsty in soul come and take freely from the Water of Life. He who tells you of the certainty of these things, says, 'Look! I will come swiftly. Amen.'"

"I am the Alpha and the Omega, the First and the Last, the Beginning and the End."

Revelation 22:13

In his vision, John sees the city of God in all its glory. (Revelation 21:2)

Old Testament Books

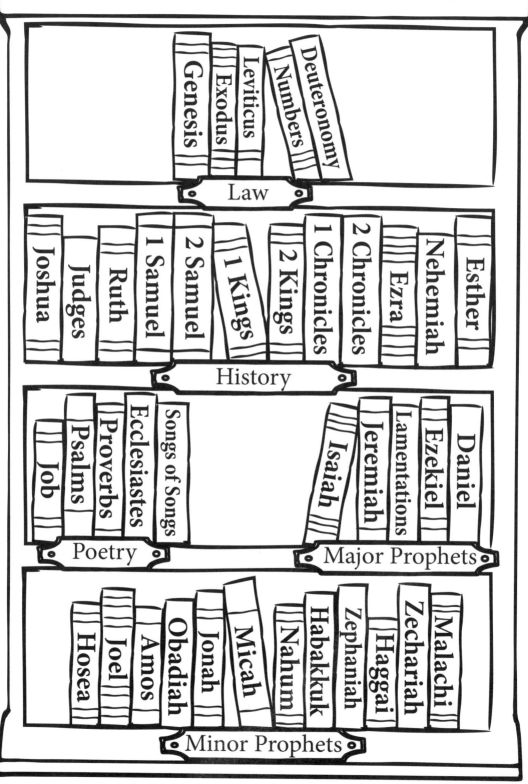

Law
Genesis · Exodus · Leviticus · Numbers · Deuteronomy

History
Joshua · Judges · Ruth · 1 Samuel · 2 Samuel · 1 Kings · 2 Kings · 1 Chronicles · 2 Chronicles · Ezra · Nehemiah · Esther

Poetry
Job · Psalms · Proverbs · Ecclesiastes · Songs of Songs

Major Prophets
Isaiah · Jeremiah · Lamentations · Ezekiel · Daniel

Minor Prophets
Hosea · Joel · Amos · Obadiah · Jonah · Micah · Nahum · Habakkuk · Zephaniah · Haggai · Zechariah · Malachi

These bookshelves contain all 66 books of the Bible.

New Testament Books

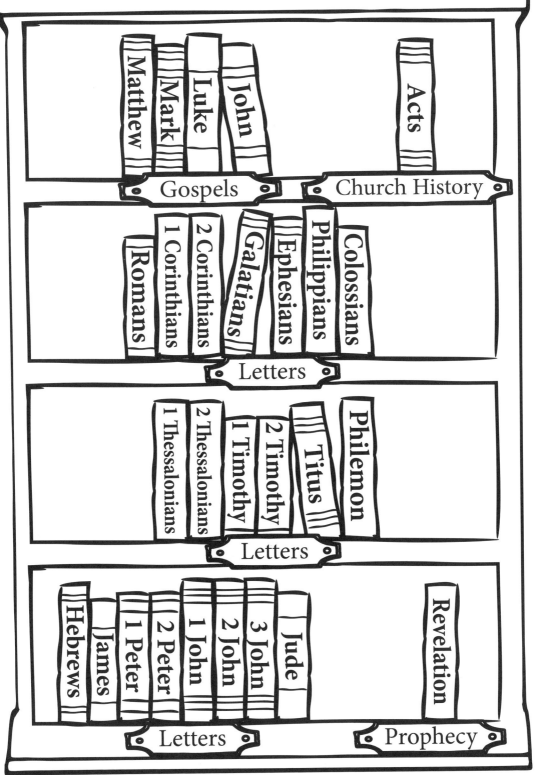

Matthew Mark Luke John

Gospels

Acts

Church History

Romans 1 Corinthians 2 Corinthians Galatians Ephesians Philippians Colossians

Letters

1 Thessalonians 2 Thessalonians 1 Timothy 2 Timothy Titus Philemon

Letters

Hebrews James 1 Peter 2 Peter 1 John 2 John 3 John Jude

Revelation

Letters

Prophecy

Color them in and memorize them as you go along from Genesis to Revelation.

The Armor of God

Read Ephesians 6:10-17 and color in the parts of God's armor.

THE 10 COMMANDMENTS

Find the 10 Commandments on page 64 and fill them in here

1

2

3

4

5

6

7

8

9

10

MY PRAYER OF PRAISE
AND THANKS TO GOD:

MY FAVORITE
SCRIPTURE VERSES:

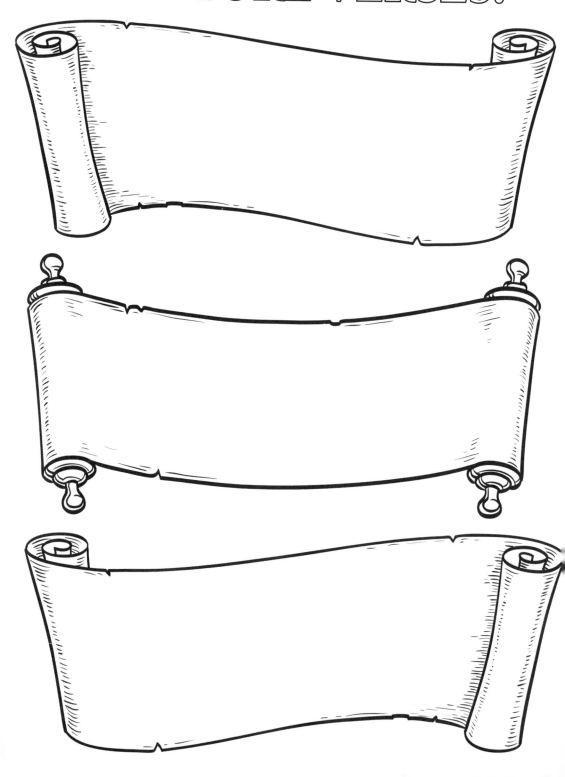

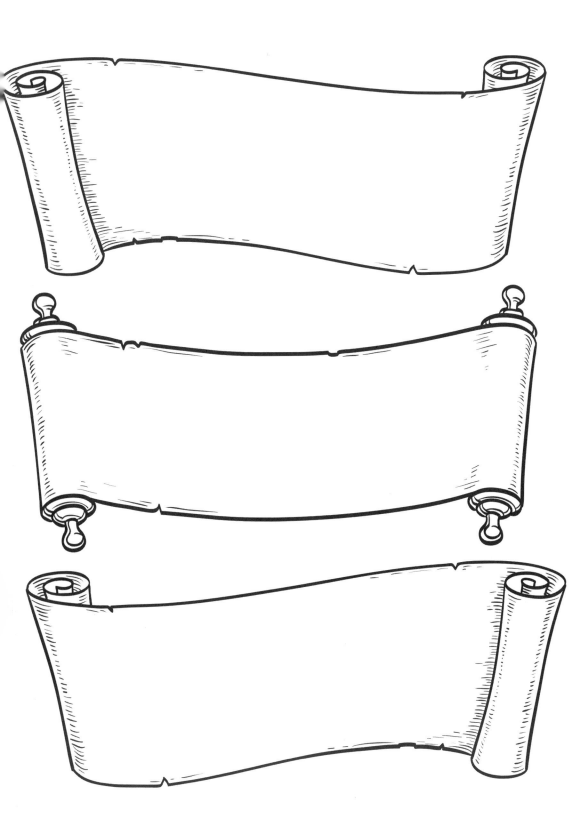

Notes